INTRODUCTION
TO
ISLAM

Dr. Muhammad Hamidullah

KiTAB BHAVAN
New Delhi-110002

KITAB BHAVAN

Publishers, Distributors, Exporters & Importers

1784, Kalan Mahal, Darya Ganj,

New Delhi - 1100 02 (India)

Phones	:	(91-11) 23277392/93, 23274686, 32906494
Fax	:	(91-11) 23263383
Website	:	www.kitabbhavan.com
Email	:	nasri@vsnl.com
	:	nusrat@bol.net.in

First Published in India ... 1999
2nd Edition 2009

ISBN : 81-7151-263-1
Book Code No. : I00344

Printed & Published in India by :
Nusrat Ali Nasri for KITAB BHAVAN
1784, Kalan Mahal, Darya Ganj,
New Delhi - 1100 02 [India]

CONTENTS

INTRODUCTION

Bismillah !

(With the Name of God)

INTRODUCTION

It is encouraging to note that this humble effort of the *Centre Culturel Islamique*, Paris, is attracting more and more attention. Not only three large English editions, published so far by us—and as large four to five unauthorized editions in three different countries, that have come to our knowledge,— are exhausted, but also translations are undertaken in ever-increasing number of languages. Several of these have come out, others are either waiting financial means or are still in more or less advanced stage of completion. All praise to God,

It is an honour to us to see that the work is prescribed as text book, in several countries. Opportunity of a new edition is taken to revise the text and make a few additions or corrections.

We welcome criticism and suggestions for ameliorating and correcting. God will reward the readers who would contribute in this respect.

For the Editorial Board,
Centre Culturel Islamique,
59, rue Claude Bernard,
F. 75005—Paris, France,

Paris 1393 H./1973.   **Muhammad Hamidullah.**

From the 3rd Edition :

Opportunity is taken to revise the text and add chapters and paragraphs, to make the work as complete as its dimensions permit. References are also added in considerable instances, to satisfy the curiosity of some and the scepticism of others.

Printing is done away from here. Proof reading is done by the diligent and painstaking assistance of Mr. Muhammad Habibullah, to whom go our best thanks.

From us the effort, from God the enabling power. Praise be to Him, first and last.

Paris, 1388 H. (1968)   M. H.

From the 2nd Edition :

The first edition was exhausted in a few months. Opportunity is taken of the second edition to improve the text and carry out several amelioration, which, it is hoped, will be appreciated. It is a pleasant duty to acknowledge with thanks numerous friendly suggestions received from various quarters.

Paris, Rajab 1378 H. (1959)   M. H.

From the 1st Edition :

There has been a wide demand for a correspondence course on Islam. In response to this, a modest effort has been made with the help of several collaborators, particularly of Prof. M. Rahimuddin and the present series of fifteen monographs has been prepared under the joint auspices of the *Centre Culturel Islamique* and *the Mosque*, in Paris. This will, it is hoped, give a general idea of Islam, its history and culture and its handling of the diverse aspects and problems of life. Each subject is a monograph in itself and self-contained, hence a certain repetition has been unavoidable, the more so because life is a variegated affair and the fields of human activities are closely related to one another and often overlap.

For further inquiries, suggestions or useful criticism the "Centre Culturel Islamique, c/o The Mosque, Place Puits de l'Ermite, Paris v., France," may be referred to.

for the Editorial Board,

MUHAMMAD HAMIDULLAH.

Paris, Sha'ban 1376 H, (1957)

BISMILLAH !

CHAPTER I

The Prophet of Islam—
His Biography

In the annals of men, individuals have not been lacking who conspicuously devoted their lives to the socio-religious reform of their connected peoples. We find them in every epoch and in all lands. In India, there lived those who transmitted to the world the Vedas, and there was also the great Gautama Buddha; China had its Confucius; the Avesta was produced in Iran. Babylonia gave to the world one of the greatest reformers, the Prophet Abraham (not to speak of such of his ancestors as Enoch and Noah about whom we have very scanty information). The Jewish people may rightly be proud of a long series of reformers: Moses, Samuel, David, Solomon, and Jesus among others.

2. Two points are to note: Firstly these reformers claimed in general to be the bearers each of a Divine mission, and they left behind them sacred books incorporating codes of life for the guidance of their peoples. Secondly there followed fratricidal wars, and massacres and genocides became the order of the day, causing more or less a complete loss of these Divine messages. As to the books of Abraham, we know them only by the name; and as for the books of Moses, records tell us how they were repeatedly destroyed and only partly restored.

CONCEPT OF GOD

3. If one should judge from the relics of the past already

brought to light of the *homo sapiens*, one finds that man has always been conscious of the existence of a Supreme Being, the Master and Creator of all. Methods and approaches may have differed, but the people of every epoch have left proofs of their attempts to obey God. Communication with the Omnipresent yet invisible God has also been recognised as possible in connection with a small fraction of men with noble and exalted spirits. Whether this communication assumed the nature of an incarnation of the Divinity or simply resolved itself into a medium of reception of Divine messages (through inspiration or revelation), the purpose in each case was the guidance of the people. It was but natural that the interpretations and explanations of certain systems should have proved more vital and convincing than others.

3/a. Every system of metaphysical thought develops its own terminology. In the course of time terms acquire a significance hardly contained in the word and translations fall short of their purpose. Yet there is no other method to make people of one group understand the thoughts of another. Non-Muslim readers in particular are requested to bear in mind this aspect which is a real yet unavoidable handicap.

4 By the end of the 6th century, after the birth of Jesus Christ, men had already made great progress in diverse walks of life. At that time there were some religions which openly proclaimed that they were reserved for definite races and groups of men only, of course they bore no remedy for the ills of humanity at large. There were also a few which claimed universality, but declared that the salvation of man lay in the renunciation of the world. These were the religions for the elite, and catered for an extremely limited number of men. We need not speak of regions where there existed no religion at all, where atheism and materialism reigned supreme, where the thought was solely of occupying one self with one's own

pleasures, without any regard or consideration for the rights of others.

ARABIA

5. A perusal of the map of the major hemisphere (from the point of view of the proportion of land to sea), shows the Arabian Peninsula lying at the confluence of the three great continents of Asia, Africa and Europe. At the time in question, this extensive Arabian sub-continent composed mostly of desert areas was inhabited by people of settled habitations as well as nomads. Often it was found that members of the same tribe were divided into these two groups, and that they preserved a relationship although following different modes of life. The means of subsistence in Arabia were meagre. The desert had its handicaps, and trade caravans were features of greater importance than either agriculture or industry. This entailed much travel, and men had to proceed beyond the peninsula to Syria, Egypt, Abyssinia, Iraq, Sind, India and other lands.

6. We do not know much about the Lihyanites of Central Arabia, but Yemen was rightly called *Arabia Felix*. Having once been the seat of the flourishing civilizations of Sheba and Ma'in even before the foundation of the city of Rome had been laid, and having later snatched from the Byzantians and Persians several provinces, greater Yemen which had passed through the hey-day of its existence, was however at this time broken up into innumerable principalities, and even occupied in part by foreign invaders. The Sassanians of Iran, who had penetrated into Yemen had already obtained possession of Eastern Arabia. There was politico-social chaos at the capital (Mada'in = Ctesiphon), and this found reflection in all her territories. Northern Arabia had succumbed to Byzantine influences, and was faced with its own particular problems. Only Central Arabia remained immune from the demoralising effects of foreign occupation.

4

7. In this limited area of Central Arabia, the existence of the triangle of Mecca-Ta'if-Madinah seemed something providential. Mecca, desertic, deprived of water and the amenities of agriculture in physical features represented Africa and the burning Sahara. Scarcely fifty miles from there, Ta'if presented a picture of Europe and its frost. Madinah in the North was not less fertile than even the most temperate of Asiatic countries like Syria. If climate has any influence on human character, this triangle standing in the middle of the major hemisphere was, more than any other region of the earth, a miniature reproduction of the entire world. And here was born a descendant of the Babylonian Abraham, and the Egyptian Hagar, Muhammad the Prophet of Islam, a Meccan by origin and yet with stock related, both to Madinah and Ta'if.

RELIGION

8. From the point of view of religion, Arabia was idolatrous; only a few individuals had embraced religions like Christianism, Mazdaism, etc. The Meccans did possess the notion of the One God, but they believed also that idols had the power to intercede with Him. Curiously enough, they did not believe in the Resurrection and After-life. They had preserved the rite of the pilgrimage to the House of the One God, the Ka'bah, an institution set up under divine inspiration by their ancestor Abraham, yet the two thousand years that separated them from Abraham had caused to degenerate this pilgrimage into the spectacle of a commercial fair and an occasion of senseless idolatry which far from producing any good, only served to ruin their individual behaviour, both social and spiritual.

SOCIETY

9. In spite of the comparative poverty in natural resources, Mecca was the most developed of the three points

of the triangle. Of the three, Mecca alone had a city-state, governed by a council of ten hereditary chiefs who enjoyed a clear division of powers. (There was a minister of foreign relations, a minister guardian of the temple, a minister of oracles, a minister guardian of offerings to the temple, one to determine the torts and the damages payable, another in charge of the municipal council or parliament to enforce the decisions of the ministries. There were also ministers in charge of military affairs like custodianship of the flag, leadership of the cavalry etc.). As well reputed caravan-leaders, the Meccans were able to obtain permission from neighbouring empires like Iran, Byzantium and Abyssinia—and to enter into agreements with the tribes that lined the routes traversed by the caravans—to visit their countries and transact import and export business. They also provided escorts to foreigners when they passed through their country as well as the territory of allied tribes in Arabia (cf Ibn Habib, *Muhabbar*). Although not interested much in the preservation of ideas and records in writing, they passionately cultivated arts and letters like poetry, oratory discourses and folk tales. Women were generally well treated, they enjoyed the privilege of possessing property in their own right, they gave their consent to marriage contracts, in which they could even add the condition of reserving their right to divorce their husbands. They could remarry when widowed or divorced. Burying girls alive did exist in certain classes, but that was rare.

BIRTH OF THE PROPHET

10. It was in the midst of such conditions and environments, that Muhammad was born in 569 - 570 and 571 are both wrong and untenable — after Christ. His father, 'Abdullah had died some weeks earlier, and it was his grandfather who took him in charge. According to the prevailing custom, the child was entrusted to a Bedouin foster-mother, with whom he

passed several years in the desert. All biographers state that the infant prophet sucked only one breast of his foster-mother, leaving the other for the sustenance of his foster-brother. When the child was brought back home, his mother, Aminah, took him to his maternal uncles at Madinah to visit the tomb of 'Abdullah. During the return journey, he lost his mother who died a sudden death. At Mecca, another bereavement awaited him, in the death of his affectionate grandfather. Subjected to such privations, he was at the age of eight, consigned at last to the care of his uncle, Abu–Talib, a man who was generous of nature but always short of resources and hardly able to provide for his family.

11. Young Muhammad had therefore to start immediately to earn his livelihood; he served as a shepherd boy to some neighbours. At the age of ten he accompanied his uncle to Syria when he was leading a caravan there. No other travels of Abu-Talib are mentioned, but there are references to his having set up a shop in Mecca. (Ibn Qutaibah, *Ma'arif*). It is possible that Muhammad helped him in this enterprise also.

12. By the time he was twenty-five, Muhammad had become well known in the city for the integrity of his disposition and the honesty of his character. A rich widow, Khadijah, took him in her employ and consigned to him her goods to be taken for sale to Syria. Delighted with the unusual profits she obtained as also by the personal charms of her agent, she offered him her hand. According to divergent reports, she was either 28 or 40 years of age at that time, (medical reasons prefer the age of 28 since she gave birth to seven more children). The union proved happy. Later, we see him sometimes in the fair of Hubashah (Yemen), and at least once in the country of the 'Abd al-Qais (Bahrain-Oman), as mentioned by Ibn Hanbal. There is every reason to believe that this refers to

the great fair of Daba (Oman), where, according to Ibn al-Kalbi (cf. Ibn Habib, *Muhabbar*), the traders of China, of Hind and Sind (India, Pakistan), of Persia, of the East and the West assembled every year, travelling both by land and sea. There is also mention of a commercial partner of Muhammad at Mecca. This person, Sa'ib by name, reports: "We relayed each other; if Muhammad led the caravan, he did not enter this house on his return to Mecca without clearing accounts with me; and if I led the caravan, he would on my return enquire about my welfare and speak nothing about his own capital entrusted to me".

AN ORDER OF CHIVALRY

13. Foreign traders often brought their goods to Mecca for sale. One day a certain Yemenite (of the tribe of Zubaid) improvised a satirical poem against some Meccans who had refused to pay him the price of what he had sold, and others who had not supported his claim or had failed to come to his help when he was victimised. Zubair, uncle and chief of the tribe of the Prophet, felt great remorse on hearing this just satire. He called for a meeting of certain chieftains in the city and organized an order of chivalry, called *Hilf al-fudul*, with the aim and object of aiding the oppressed in Mecca, irrespective of their being dwellers of the city or aliens. Young Muhammad became an enthusiastic member of the organisation. Later in life he used to say: "I have participated in it, and I am not prepared to give up that privilege even against a herd of camels; if somebody should appeal to me even today, by virtue of that pledge, I shall hurry to his help".

BEGINNING OF RELIGIOUS CONSCIOUSNESS

14. Not much is known about the religious practices of Muhammad until he was thirty-five years old, except that he had never worshipped idols. This is substantiated by all his

biographers. It may be stated that there were a few others in Mecca, who had like-wise revolted against the senseless practice of paganism, although conserving their fidelity to the Ka'bah as the house dedicated to the One God by its builder Abraham.

15. About the year 605 of the Christian era, the draperies on the outer wall of the Ka'bah took fire. The building was affected and could not bear the brunt of the torrential rains that followed. The reconstruction of the Ka'bah was thereupon undertaken. Each citizen contributed according to his means and only the gifts of honest gains were accepted. Everybody participated in the work of construction, and Muhammad's shoulders were injured in the course of transporting stones. To identify the place whence the ritual of circumambulation began, there had been set a black stone in the wall of the Ka'bah, dating probably from the time of Abraham himself. There was rivalry among the citizens for obtaining the honour of transposing this Stone in its place. When there was a danger of blood being shed, somebody suggested leaving the matter to Providence, and accepting the arbitration of him who should happen to arrive there first. It chanced that Muhammad just then turned up there for work as usual. He was popularly known by the appellation of *al-Amin* (the honest), and everyone accepted his arbitration without hesitation. Muhammad placed a sheet of cloth on the ground, put the stone on it and asked the chiefs of all the tribes, in the city to lift together the cloth. Then he himself placed the Stone in its proper place, in one of the angles of the building, and everybody was satisfied.

16. It is from this moment that we find Muhammad becoming more and more absorbed in spiritual meditations. Like his grandfather, he used to retire during the whole month of Ramadan to a cave in Jabal-an-Nur (mountain of light).

The cave is called 'Ghar-i-Hira' or the cave of research. There he prayed, meditated, and shared his meagre provisions with the travellers who happened to pass by.

REVELATION

17. He was forty years old, and it was the fifth consecutive year since his annual retreats, when one night towards the end of the month of Ramadan, an angel came to visit him, and announced that God had chosen him as His messenger to all mankind. The angel taught him the mode of ablutions, the way of worshipping God and the conduct of prayer. He communicated to him the following Divine message :

With the name of God, the Most Merciful, the All-Merciful.
Read : with the name of thy Lord Who created,
Created man from a clot.
Read : and thy Lord is the Most Bounteous,
Who taught by the pen,
Taught man what he knew not.   (Quran 96/1-5)[1] .

18. Deeply affected, he returned home and related to his wife what had happened, expressing his fears that it might have been something diabolic or the action of evil spirits. She consoled him, saying that he had always been a man of charity and generosity, helping the poor, the orphans, the widows and the needy, and assured him that God would protect him against all evil.

19. Then came a pause in revelation, extending over three years. The Prophet must have felt at first a shock, then a calm, an ardent desire, and after a period of waiting, a growing impatience or nostalgia. The news of the first vision

---

1. *For the references of the Holy Quran, we follow the Islamic numbering of chapters and verses, and not the European one, which both differ from each other occasionally by a few verses.*

had spread and at the pause the sceptics in the city had begun
to mock at him and cut bitter jokes. They went so far as to
say that God had forsaken him.

20. During these three years of waiting, the Prophet had
given himself up more and more to prayers and to spiritual
practices. The revelations were then resumed, and God assured
him that He had not at all forsaken him; on the contrary it was
He Who had guided him to the right path; therefore he should
take care of the orphans and the destitute, and proclaim the
bounty of God on him (cf. Q. 93/3-11). This was in reality an
order to preach. Another revelation directed him to warn
people against evil practices, to exhort them to worship none
but the One God, and to abandon everything that would
displease God (Q. 74/2-7). Yet another revelation commanded
him to warn his own near relatives (Q. 26/214); and: "Proclaim
openly that which thou art commanded, and withdraw from the
Associators (idolaters). Lo! We defend thee from the scoffers"
(15/94-5). According to Ibn Ishaq, the first revelation (§ 17)
had come to the Prophet during his sleep, evidently to reduce
the shock. Later revelations came in full wakefulness

THE MISSION

21. The Prophet began by preaching his mission secretly
first among his intimate friends, then among the members of
his own tribe, and thereafter publicly in the city and suburbs. He
insisted on the belief in One Transcendent God, in Resurrection
and the Last Judgement. He invited men to charity and beneficence. He took necessary steps to preserve through writing
the revelations he was receiving, and ordered his adherents
also to learn them by heart This continued all through his
life, since the Quran was not revealed all at once, but in fragments as occasions arose.

22 The number of his adherents increased gradually; but
with the denunciation of paganism, the opposition also grew
more intense on the part of those who were firmly attached to

their ancestral beliefs. This opposition degenerated in the course of time into physical torture of the Prophet and of those who had embraced his religion. These were stretched on burning sands, cauterized with red hot iron and imprisoned with chains on their feet. Some of them died of the effects of torture but none would renounce his religion. In despair the Prophet Muhammad advised his companions to leave their native town and take refuge abroad, in Abyssinia, "where governs a just ruler, in whose realm nobody is oppressed" (Ibn Hisham). Dozens of Muslims profited by his advice, though not all. These secret flights led to further persecution of those who remained behind.

23. The Prophet Muhammad called his religion "Islam,'' i,e , submission to the will of God. Its distinctive features are two: (1) a hormonious equilibrium between the temporal and the spiritual (the body and the soul), permitting a full enjoyment of all the good that God has created, (Quran 7/32), enjoining at the same time on everybody duties towards God, such as worship, fasting, charity, etc. Islam was to be the religios of the masses and not merely of the elect. (2) A universality of the call—all the believers becoming brothers and equals without any distinction of class or race or tongue. The only superiority which it recognizes is a personal one, based on the greater fear of God and greater piety (Quran 49/13).

SOCIAL BOYCOTT

24. When a large number of the Meccan Muslims migrated to Abyssinia, the leaders of paganism sent an ultimatum to the tribe of the Prophet, demanding that he should be excommunicated and outlawed and delivered to the pagans for being put to death. Every member of the tribe, Muslim and non-Muslim rejected the demand. (cf. Ibn Hisham). Thereupon the city decided on a complete boycott of the tribe: Nobody was to talk to them or have commercial or matrimonial relations with them. The group of Arab tribes, called Ahabish, inhabiting the

suburbs, who were allies of the Meccans, also joined in the boycott, causing stark misery among the innocent victims consisting of children, men and women, the old and the sick and the feeble. Some of them succumbed, yet nobody would hand over the Prophet to his persecutors. An uncle of the Prophet, Abu Lahab, however left his tribesmen and participated in the boycott along with the pagans. After three dire years, during which the victims were obliged to devore even crushed hides, four or five non-Muslims, more humane than the rest and belonging to different clans, proclaimed publicly their denunciation of the unjust boycott. At the same time, the document promulgating the pact of boycott which had been hung in the temple (Ka'bah),was found, as Muhammad had predicted, eaten by white ants, that spared nothing but the words God and Muhammad. The boycott was lifted, yet owing to the privations that were undergone the wife and Abu Talib, the chief of the tribe and uncle of the Prophet died soon after. Another uncle of the Prophet, Abu Lahab, who was an inveterate enemy of Islam, now succeeded to the headship of the tribe. (cf. Ibn Hisham, *Sirah*).

THE ASCENSION

25. It was at this time that the Prophet Muhammad was granted the *mi'raj* (ascension): He saw in a vision that he was received on heaven by God, and was witness of the marvels of the celestial regions. Returning, he brought for his community, as a Divine gift, Islamic worship, which constitutes a sort of communion between man and God. It may be recalled that in the last part of the Islamic service of worship the faithful employ as a symbol of their being in the very presence of God, not concrete objects as others do at the time of communion, but the very words of greeting exchanged between the Prophet Muhammad and God on the occasion of the former's *mi'raj*: "The blessed and pure greetings for God!—Peace be with thee, O Prophet, as well as the mercy and blessing of God!—Peace be with us and with all the well-behaving servants of God!"

The Christian term "communion" implies participation in the Divinity. Finding it pretentious, Muslims use the term "ascension" towards God and reception in His presence, God remaining God and man remaining man and no confusion between the twain.

26. The news of this celestial meeting led to an increase in the hostility of the pagans of Mecca; and the Prophet was obliged to quit his native town in search of an asylum elsewhere. He went to his maternal uncles in Ta'if, but returned immediately to Mecca, as the wicked people of that town chased the Prophet out of their city by pelting stones on him and wounding him.

MIGRATION TO MADINAH

27. The annual pilgrimage of the Ka'bah brought to Mecca people from all parts of Arabia. The Prophet Muhammad tried to persuade one tribe after another to afford him shelter and allow him to carry on his mission of reform. The contingents of fifteen tribes, whom he approached in succession, refused to do so more or less brutally, but he did not despair. Finally he met half a dozen inhabitants of Madinah who being neighbour of the Jews and the Christians, had some notion of prophets and Divine messages. They knew also that these "people of the Books" were awaiting the arrival of a prophet— a last comforter. So these Madinans decided not to lose the opportunity of obtaining an advance over others, and forthwith embraced Islam, promising further to provide additional adherents and necessary help from Madinah. The following year a dozen new Madinans took the oath of allegiance to him and requested him to provide with a missionary teacher. The work of the missionary, Mus'ab, proved very successful and he led a contingent of seventy-three new converts to Mecca, at the time of the pilgrimage. These invited the Prophet and his Meccan companions to migrate to their town, and promised to shelter the Prophet and to treat him and his companions as their own kith and kin. Secretly and in small groups, the greater part of

the Muslims emigrated to Madinah. Upon this the pagans of Mecca not only confiscated the property of the evacuees, but devised a plot to assassinate the Prophet. It now became impossible for him to remain at home. It is worthy of mention, that in spite of their hostility to his mission, the pagans had unbounded confidence in his probity, so much so that many of them used to deposit their savings with him. The Prophet Muhammad now entrusted all these deposits to 'Ali, a cousin of his, with instructions to return them in due course to the rightful owners. He then left the town secretly in the company of his faithful friend, Abu-Bakr. After several incidents, they succeeded in reaching Madinah in safety. This happened in 622, whence starts the Hijrah calendar.

REORGANIZATION OF THE COMMUNITY

28. For the better rehabilitation of the displaced immigrants, the Prophet created a fraternization between them and an equal number of well to-do Madinans. The families of each pair of the contractual brothers worked together to earn their livelihood, and aided one another in the business of life.

29. Further he thought that the development of the man as a whole would be better achieved if he co-ordinated religion and politics as two constituent parts of one whole. To this end he invited the representatives of the Muslims as well as the non-Muslim inhabitants of the region: Arabs, Jews, Christians and others, and suggested the establishment of a City-State in Madinah. With their assent, he endowed the city with a written constitution—the first of its kind in the world—in which he defined the duties and rights both of the citizens and the head of the State—the Prophet Muhammad was unanimously hailed as such—and abolished the customary private justice. The administration of justice became henceforward the concern of the central organisation of the community of the citizens. The document laid down principles of defence and foreign policy; it organized a system of social insurance, called ma'aqil, in cases of too heavy obligations. It recognized that the

Prophet Muhammad would have the final word in all differences, and that there was no limit to his power of legislation. It recognized also explicitly liberty of religion, particularly for the Jews, to whom the constitutional act afforded equality with Muslims in all that concerned life in this world (cf. infra § 303).

30. Muhammad journeyed several times with a view to win the neighbouring tribes and to conclude with them treaties of alliance and mutual help With their help, he decided to bring to bear economic pressure on the Meccan pagans, who had confiscated the property of the Muslim evacuees and also caused innumerable damage. Obstruction in the way of the Meccan caravans and their passage through the Madinan region exasperated the pagans, and a bloody struggle ensued.

31. In the concern for the material interests of the community, the spiritual aspect was never neglected. Hardly a year had passed after the migration to Madinah, when the most rigorous of spiritual disciplines, the fasting for the whole month of Ramadan every year, was imposed on every adult Muslim, man and woman

STRUGGLE AGAINST INTOLERANCE AND UNBELIEF

32. Not content with the expulsion of the Muslim compatriots, the Meccans sent an ultimatum to the Madinans, demanding the surrender or at least the expulsion of Muhammad and his companions but evidently all such efforts proved in vain. A few months later, in the year 2 H., they sent a powerful army against the Prophet, who opposed them at Badr; and the pagans thrice as numerous as the Muslims, were routed. After a year of preparation, the Meccans again invaded Madinah to avenge the defeat of Badr They were now four times as numerous as the Muslims. After a bloody encounter at Uhud, the enemy retired, the issue being indecisive. The mercenaries in the Meccan army did not want to take too much risk, or endanger their safety.

33. In the meanwhile the Jewish citizens of Madinah began to foment trouble. About the time of the victory of Badr, one of their leaders, Ka'b ibn al-Ashraf, proceeded to Mecca to give assurance of his alliance with the pagans, and to incite them to a war of revenge. After the battle of Uhud, the tribe of the same chieftain plotted to assassinate the Prophet. They invited him to come to their village along with two or three persons only, pretexting that they were ready to embrace Islam all of them if the Prophet convinced their rabbis in the discussion of religious questions. (An Arab lady, married to a Jew of this tribe sent secretly word and so averted the execution of the plot, as Samhudi has mentioned on the authority of old sources, and has reason to say that this version is preferable to that of Ibn Is'haq). In spite of all this, the only demand the Prophet made of the men of this tribe was to leave the Madinan region, taking with them all their properties, after selling their immovables and recovering their debts from the Muslims. The clemency thus extended had an effect contrary to what was hoped. The exiled not only contacted the Meccans, but also the tribes of the North, South and East of Madinah, mobilized military aid, and planned from Khaibar an invasion of Madinah, with forces four times more numerous than those employed at Uhud The Muslims prepared for a siege, and dug a ditch, to defend themselves against this hardest of all trials Although the defection of the Jews still remaining inside Madinah at a later stage upset all strategy, yet with a sagacious diplomacy, the Prophet succeeded in breaking up the alliance, and the different enemy groups retired one after the other.

34. Alcoholic drinks, gambling and games of chance were at this time declared forbidden for the Muslims.

THE RECONCILIATION

35. The Prophet attempted reconciliation once more with the Meccans and proceeded to Mecca. The barring of the route of their Northern caravans had ruined their economy. The

Prophet promised them transit security, extradition of their fugitives and the fulfilment of every condition they desired, agreeing even to return to Madinah without accomplishing the pilgrimage of the Ka'bah. Thereupon the two contracting parties promised at Hudaibiyah in the suburbs of Mecca, not only the maintenance of peace, but also the observance of neutrality in their conflicts with third parties.

36. Profiting by the peace, the Prophet launched an intensive programme for the propagation of his religion. He addressed missionary letters to the foreign rulers of Byzantium, Persia (Iran), Abyssinia and other lands. The Byzantine autocrat priest—Dughatur of the Arabs—embraced Islam, but for this, was lynched by the Christian mob; the prefect of Ma'an (Palestine) suffered the same fate, and was decapitated and crucified by order of the emperor. A Muslim ambassador was assassinated in Syria–Palestine; and instead of punishing the culprit, the emperor Heraclius rushed with his armies to protect him against the punitive expedition sent by the Prophet (battle of Mu'tah).

37. The pagans of Mecca hoping to profit by the Muslim difficulties, violated the terms of their treaty. Upon this, the Prophet himself led an army, ten thousand strong, and surprised Mecca which he occupied in a bloodless manner. As a benevolent conqueror, he caused the vanquished people to assemble, reminded them of their ill deeds, their religious persecution, unjust confiscation of the evacuee property, ceaseless invasions and senseless hostilities for twenty years continuously. He asked them : "Now what do you expect of me?" When everybody lowered his head with shame, the Prophet proclaimed : "May God pardon you; go in peace; there shall be no responsibility on you today; you are free!" He even renounced the claim for the Muslim property confiscated by the pagans. This produced a great psychological change of heart instantaneously. When a Meccan chief advanced with a fullsome heart towards the Prophet, after hearing this general amnesty, in order to declare his acceptance of Islam, the Prophet told him : "And

in my turn, I appoint you the governor of Mecca! " Without leaving a single soldier in the conquered city, the Prophet retired to Madinah. The Islamization of Mecca, which was accomplished in a few hours, was complete.

38. Immediately after the occupation of Mecca, the city of Ta'if mobilized to fight against the Prophet. With some difficulty the enemy was dispersed in the valley of Hunain, but the Muslims preferred to raise the siege of nearby Ta'if and use pacific means to break the resistance of this region. Less than a year later, a delegation from Ta'if came to Madinah offering submission. But it requested exemption from prayer, taxes and military service, and the continuance of the liberty to adultery and fornication and alcoholic drinks. It demanded even the conservation of the temple of the idol al-Lat at Ta'if. But Islam was not a materialist immoral movement; and soon the delegation itself felt ashamed of its demands regarding prayer, adultery and wine. The Prophet consented to concede exemption from payment of taxes and rendering of military service; and added : You need not demolish the temple with your own hands : we shall send agents from here to do the job, and if there should be any consequences, which you are afraid of on account of your superstitions, it will be they who would suffer. This act of the Prophet shows what concessions could be given to new converts. The conversion of the Ta'ifites was so whole-hearted that in a short while, they themselves renounced the contracted exemptions, and we find the Prophet nominating a tax collector in their locality as in other Islamic regions.

39. In all these "wars", extending over a period of ten years, the non-Muslims lost on the battlefield only about 250 persons killed, and the Muslim losses were even less. With these few incisions, the whole continent of Arabia, with its million and more of square miles, was cured of the abscess of anarchy and immorality. During these ten years of disinterested struggle, all the peoples of the Arabian Peninsula and the southern regions of Iraq and Palestine had voluntarily embraced

Islam. Some Christian, Jewish and Parsi groups remained attached to their creeds, and they were granted liberty of conscience as well as judicial and juridical autonomy.

40. In the year 10 H., when the Prophet went to Mecca for *Hajj* (pilgrimage), he met 140,000 Muslims there, who had come from different parts of Arabia to fulfil their religious obligation. He addressed to them his celebrated sermon, in which he gave a resume of his teachings : "Belief in One God without images or symbols, equality of all the Believers without distinction of race or class, the superiority of individuals being based solely on piety; sanctity of life, property and honour; abolition of interest, and of vendettas and private justice; better treatment of women; obligatory inheritance and distribution of the property of deceased persons among near relatives of both sexes, and removal of the possibility of the cumulation of wealth in the hands of the few. The Quran and the conduct of the Prophet were to serve as the bases of law and a healthy criterion in every aspect of human life.

41. On his return to Madinah, he fell ill; and a few weeks later, when he breathed his last, he had the satisfaction that he had well accomplished the task which had been entrusted to him—to preach to the world the Divine message.

42. He bequeathed to posterity, a religion of pure mono-theism; he created a well-disciplined State out of the existent chaos and gave peace in place of the war of everybody against everybody else; he established a harmonious equilibrium bet-ween the spiritual and the temporal, between the mosque and the citadel; he left a new system of law, which dispensed impartial justice, in which even the head of the State was as much a subject to it as any commoner, and in which religious tolerance was so great that non-Muslim inhabitants of Muslim countries equally enjoyed complete juridical, judicial and cultural autonomy. In the matter of the revenues of the State, the Quran fixed the principles of budgeting, and paid more thought to the poor than to anybody else. The revenues were

declared to be in no way the private property of the head of the State. Above all, the Prophet Muhammad set a noble example[1] and fully practised all that he taught to others.

---

(1) Consequently we do not propose to speak at length of miracles. Miracles or extraordinary happenings are facts. Muslims have to believe in them, since the Quran speaks of them. But if they look to us as extraordinary, to the Almighty Creator of causes and effects they are His prearranged events, and they happen when we do not expect them.

If they take place at the prayers of a prophet, they are called mu'jizah *(that which puts others in the incapacity); at the hands of the saints, they are* karamah *(honour, i.e. God honours them therewith); and at the insolence of the diabolical persons, they are* istidraj *(test, i.e. God tests the faith of a believer thereby). It is not easy for the ordinary man to distinguish which is what. Again, the life of the Prophet Muhammad has been predestined by God to be the "perfect model to imitate"* (uswah hasanah) *for each and every Muslim; and naturally a Muslim of the commonalty cannot get miracles at command. For these and other imperative reasons we have not described here the miracles of the Prophet of Islam, which are greater and more numerous than those of any other former prophet, and even of all of them combined. Twice dead persons came to life at the call of Muhammad, the moon split into two, small quantity of food or water sufficed for a large number of persons, water gushed from under his fingers; he said: bring a small* surat *of three verses like that of the Quran, and call all the men and jinns to collaborate therein (and the challenge has remained unanswered since the last fourteen hundred years). And so on and so forth; and they have filled entire volumes. But the Quran himself has told us to take heed of the teaching and the practice of the Prophet, and not of the miracles (cf. 29/50-51). A good Muslim like Abu Bakr did not require to see miracles, and a perverted person like Abu Jahl and Abu Lahab did not believe even on seeing most extraordinary miracles of the Prophet. They are intended only for the intellectually under-developed.*

In the most orthodox book of Muslim dogmas, Sharh Mawaqif *there is this thought-provoking phrase: The miracles of a prophet are intended for the members of his community to try to realise the same thing by ordinary technical means of causes and effects.*

CHAPTER II

Preservations of the Original Teachings of Islam

THERE could be nothing in common between the true and the false and no two things in the world could be as opposed to each other as these. In the commonplace material things of daily life, the evils of falsehood are obvious and acknowledged by all. Of course in matters of eternal salvation, of beliefs, and of the original teachings of a religion, the evil that falsehood does transcends all other evils.

44. An honest and reasonable man would experience no difficulty in judging whether a certain teaching is just and acceptable, or not. In matters of dogmas however what often happens is that one judges first the person of the teacher prior to his precepts. If he is found trustworthy, one is the more easily persuaded to acknowledge one's own defects of understanding part of his teachings rather than reject totally his words. In such cases, the fact of the authenticity of his words and of his teachings, particularly when the teacher has died, becomes all the more imperative.

45. All the important religions of the world are based on certain sacred books, which are often attributed to Divine revelations. It will be pathetic if, by some misfortune, one were to lose the original text of the revelation; the substitute could never be in entire conformity with what is lost. The Brahmanists, Buddhists, Jews, Parsis, and Christians may compare the method employed for the preservation of the basic teachings of their respective religions with that of the Muslims. Who wrote their books? Who transmitted them from generation

to generation? Has the transmission been of the original texts or only their translations? Have not fratricidal wars caused damage to the copies of the texts? Are there no internal contradictions or lacunae to which references are found elsewhere? These are some of the questions that every honest seeker of truth must pose and demand satisfactory replies.

MEANS OF PRESERVATION

46. By the time there emerged what we call the great religions, men had not only relied on their memory, but had also invented the art of writing for preserving their thoughts, writing being more lasting than the individual memories of human beings who after all have a limited span of life.

47. But neither of these two means is infallible when taken separately. It is a matter of daily experience that when one writes something and then revises it, one finds more or less inadvertent mistakes, omission of letters or even of words, repetition of statements, use of words other than those intended, grammatical mistakes, etc., not to speak of changes of opinion of the writer, who also corrects his style, his thoughts, his arguments, and sometimes, rewrites the entire document. The same is true of the faculty of memory. Those who have the obligation or habitude to learn by heart some text and to recite it later, especially when it involves long passages, know that sometimes their memory fails during the recitation: they jump over passages, mix up one with the other, or do not remember at all the sequence; sometimes the correct text remains subconscious and is recalled either at some later moment or at the refreshing of the memory by the indication of someone else or after consulting the text in a written document.

48. The Prophet of Islam, Muhammad of blessed memory, employed both the methods simultaneously, each helping the other and strengthening the integrity of the text and diminishing to the minimum the possibilities of error.

23

ISLAMIC TEACHINGS

49. The teachings of Islam are based primarily on the
Quran and the Hadith, and as we shall presently see, both are
based on Divine inspiration (cf Quran 53/3-4). As to the Quran,
Prophet Muhammad himself dictated it fragmentarily over a
period of 23 years, and said: This is the Word of God, revealed
to me through the archangel Gabriel. Hadith is the record of
what the Prophet said yet did not order to incorporate in the
Quran, and also what he did. The noting of his words and the
describing of his acts were undertaken by his companions on
their private initiative and according to their capacities. If at a
given time no Divine inspiration came to him, he consulted his
companions. So one has to distinguish between Muhammad
the human being and Muhammad the Message-bearer of God.

HISTORY OF THE QURAN

50. Quran literally means reading or recitation. While
dictating this to his disciples, the Prophet assured them that it
was the Divine revelation that had come to him. He did not
dictate the whole at one stretch: the revelations came to him in
fragments, from time to time. As soon as he received one, he
used to communicate it to his disciples and ask them not only
to learn it by heart—in order to recite it during the service of
worship—but also to write it down and to multiply the copies.
On each such occasion, he indicated the precise place of the
new revelation in the text of till-then-revealed Quran; this was
not a chronological compilation. Whenever a passage of the
Quran was revealed to him, he not only dictated it to one of
his amanuenses, but also ordered him at the end to read out
what he had taken down, in order to be able to correct if a
mistake was committed by the scribe. One cannot admire too
much, this precaution and care taken for accuracy, when one
takes into consideration the standard of the culture of the Arabs
of the time.

51. It is reasonable to believe that the earliest revelations received by the Prophet were not committed to writing immediately, for the simple reason that there were then no disciples or adherents. These early portions were neither long nor numerous. There was no risk that the Prophet would forget them, since he recited them often in his prayers and proselytising talks.

52. Some facts of history give us an idea of what happened. 'Umar is considered to be the fortieth person to embrace Islam. This refers to the year 5 of the Mission (8 before the Hijrah). Even at such an early date there existed written copies of certain chapters of the Quran, and as Ibn Hisham reports, it was due to the profound effects produced by the perusal of such a document that 'Umar embraced Islam. We do not know precisely the time since when the practice of writing down the Quran began, yet there is little doubt that during the remaining eighteen years of the life of the Prophet, the number of Muslims as also that of the copies of the sacred text went on increasing day by day. The Prophet received the revelations in fragments, it is but natural that the revealed text should have referred to the problems of the day. It may be that one of his companions died; the revelation would be to promulgate the law of inheritance; it could not be that the penal law regarding theft, murder, or wine-drinking for instance, should have been revealed at that moment. The revelations continued during the whole missionary life of Muhammad, thirteen years at Mecca and ten at Madinah. A revelation consisted sometimes of a whole chapter, short or long, and sometimes of only a few verses.

53. The nature of the revelations necessitated that the Prophet should recite them constantly to his Companions and check continually that the sequence and the contents of the fragments were correct. It is authoritatively known that the Prophet recited every year in the month of Ramadan, in the presence of the angel Gabriel, the portion of the Quran till then

revealed, and that in the last year of his life, Gabriel asked him to recite the whole of it twice. The Prophet concluded thereupon that he was soon going to depart his life. Whatever the spiritual meaning of his angelic aid to the Prophet, his Companions attended these public recitations (called 'ardah, and the celebrated last presentation: the 'ardah akheerah) and corrected their private copies of the Quran. Thus the Prophet used to recite in the fasting month verses and chapters and put them in their proper sequence. This was necessary, because of the continuity of new revelations. Sometimes a whole chapter was revealed at a stretch, at others fragments of the same chapter came continually, and this posed no problems. The same was not the case if several chapters began simultaneously to be revealed in fragments (suwar dhawat al-'adad of the historians). In this last case one had perforce to note them provisionally and separately on handy materials, such as shoulder blades, palm leaves, slate-like stones, pieces of hides etc., and as soon as a chapter was entirely revealed, the secretaries classified these notes (nu'allif al-Quran) under the personal supervision of the Prophet and made a fair copy (cf. Tirmidhi, Ibn Hanbal, Ibn Kathir etc.). It is also known, that the Prophet was in the habit of celebrating an additional service of worship during the fasting month, every night, sometimes even in congregation, in which he recited the Quran from the beginning to the end, the task being completed in the course of the month. This service of Tarawih continues to be observed with great devotion to this our day.

54. When the Prophet breathed his last, a rebellion was afoot in certain parts of the country. In quelling it, several people fell who knew the whole of the Quran by heart. The caliph Abu-Bakr felt the urgency of codifying the Quran and the task was accomplished a few months after the death of the Prophet.

55. During the last years of his life, the Prophet used to employ Zaid Ibn Thabit as his chief amanuensis for taking the

dictation of the newly received revelations. Abu-Bakr charged this same gentleman with the task of preparing a fair copy of the entire text in the form of a book. There were then in Madinah several *hafizes* (those who knew the whole Quran by heart) and Zaid was one. He had also attended the *'ardah akheerah* referred to above. The caliph directed him to obtain two written copies of each portion of the text from among those which had been collated with the recitation of the Prophet himself, prior to its inclusion in the corpus. At the direction of the caliph, the people of Madinah brought to Zaid copies of the various fragments of the Quran which they possessed. The sources declare authoritatively that only two verses were such as had a single documentary evidence and that the rest were supported by the production of numerous copies.

56. The fair copy thus prepared was called the *Mus'haf* (bound leaves). It was kept in his own custody by the caliph Abu-Bakr, and after him by his successor 'Umar. In the meanwhile the study of the Quran was encouraged everywhere in the Muslim empire. Caliph 'Umar felt the need of sending authentic copies of the text to the provincial centres, to avoid deviations; but it was left to his successor, 'Uthman, to bring the task to a head. One of his lieutenants having returned from far off Armenia, reported that he had found conflicting copies of the Quran, and that there were some times even quarrels among the different teachers of the Book on this account. 'Uthman caused immediately the copy prepared for Abu-Bakr to be entrusted to a commission, presided over by the above-mentioned Zaid ibn Thabit, for preparing seven copies; he authorized them to revise the old spelling if necessary. When the task was completed the caliph caused a public reading of the new "edition" before the experts present in the capital, from among the companions of the Prophet, and then sent these copies to different centres of the vast Islamic world, ordering that thenceforward all copies should be based only on the authentic edition. He ordered the destruction of copies

which in any way deviated from the text thus officially established.

57. It is conceivable that the great military conquests of the early Muslims persuaded some hypocritical spirits to proclaim their outward conversion to Islam, for material motives, and to try to do it harm in a clandestine manner. They could have fabricated versions of the Quran with interpolations. The crocodile tears shed at the order of the caliph 'Uthman, regarding the destruction of unauthenticated copies of the Quran, could have been only by such hypocrites.

58. It is reported that sometimes a passage of the Quran was revealed to the Prophet which changed or replaced a passage which had been revealed and communicated to the people previously. There were Companions, who had learnt the first version, but were not aware of the later modifications, either because of death or of residence outside Madinah. These persons might have left copies to their posterity, which although authentic were yet outdated. Again, some Muslims had the habit of asking the Prophet to explain certain terms employed in the holy text, and noting these explanations on the margins of their copies of the Quran, in order not to forget them. The copies made later, on the basis of these annotated texts could sometimes have caused confusion in the matter of the text and the gloss. In spite of the order of the caliph 'Uthman to destroy the inexact texts, there existed in the 3rd and 4th centuries of the Hijrah enough matter of compiling voluminous works on the "Variants in the Quran." These have come down to us, and a close study shows that these "variants" were due either to glosses or mistakes of deciphering the old Arabic writing which neither possessed vowel signs nor distinguished between letters of close resemblance by means of points, as is done now. Moreover, there existed different dialects in different regions, and the Prophet had allowed the Muslims of such regions to recite in accordance with their

dialects, and even to replace the words which were beyond their ken by synonyms which they knew better. This was just an emergent measure of grace and clemency. By the time of the caliph 'Uthman, however public instruction had advanced enough and it was felt desirable that concessions should no more be tolerated lest the Divine text be affected and variants of reading take root.

59. The copies of the Quran sent by 'Uthman to provincial centres gradually disappeared, in the succeeding centuries; one of them is at present in the Topkapi Museum of Istanbul; another incomplete one is now in Tashkent. The Czarist Government of Russia had published this latter with a facsimile reproduction; and we see that there is complete identity between these copies and the text otherwise in use. The same is true of other extant MSS. of the Quran, both complete and fragmentary, dating from the first century cf the Hijrah onwards.

60. The habit of learning by heart the text of the entire Quran dates from the time of the Prophet himself. The caliphs and other heads of Muslim States have always encouraged this habit. A happy coincidence has further reinforced the integrity of the text. In fact from the very beginning, Muslims have been accustomed to read a work in the presence of its author or one of his authorised pupils, and obtain his permission of further transmission of the text established and corrected at the time of study and collation. Those who recited the Quran by heart or simply read the written text, also acted in the same manner. The habit has continued down to our own day, with this remarkable feature that every master indicates in detail in the certificate given by him not only the fact that the rendering of his pupil was correct, but also that it was in conformity with that which this master had learned from his own master, and that this last had affirmed that he in his turn had learnt it from his master, the chain mounting up to the Prophet. The writer of these lines studied the Quran at Madinah with Shaikh al-Qurra, Hasan ash-Sha'ir, and the certificate he obtained

notes, among other things, the chain of masters and masters of masters, and in the final act how the master had studied simultaneously from ʾUthman, ʾAli,. Ibn Masʾud, Ubaiy ibn Kaʾb and Zaid ibn Thabit (all companions of the Prophet) and that all had taught exactly the same text. The number of *hafizes* is now counted in the world by hundreds of thousands, and millions of copies of the text are found in all parts of the globe. And what deserves to be noted is that there is absolutely no difference between the memories of the hafizes and the texts employed.

61. The original of the Quran was in Arabic, and the same text is still in use. Translations have been made in all the important languages of the world, more or less serviceable to those who do not know Arabic. It is to be remembered however that it is in the original Arabic language that the text has come down to us, and there has been no need of retranslating into Arabic from some later translation.

61/a. Languages have the tendency of changing gradually and becoming in course of time incomprehensible to the people. The English of Chaucer (d. 1400) is understood today in England by nobody except the specialized students of the old English. Same is true of all languages of the world, old or new: Greek, Latin, French, German, Russian and all else. The only exception is the Arabic, which since at least 1500 years has changed neither in vocabulary, nor grammar, nor spelling, nor even pronunciation; and if there is change, it means that if formerly there were two practices, now one has prevailed and the other has fallen in desuetude. Is it not providential that for a lasting message of God only such a stable language was selected by the Almighty.

62. A text in the original language, a codification under the auspices of the Prophet himself, a continued preservation by the simultaneous double control of memory and writing, in addition to studying under qualified teachers, and this by a large

number of individuals in every generation, and the absence of any variants in the text—these are some of the remarkable features of the Quran, the holy book of the Muslims.

CONTENTS OF THE QURAN

63. As stated previously, the Muslims believe that the Quran is the Word of God, revealed to His messenger Muhammad. This messenger is only an intermediary for the reception and communication of the revelations; his role is neither of an author nor of compiler.

64. God is transcendent and beyond all physical perception of man, and it is through the medium of a celestial messenger, an angel, that God causes His will and His command to be revealed to His human messenger, for the sake of mankind. God is above all bounds of language. We may in explanation employ the metaphor, that the prophets are bulbs, and the revelation the electric current; with the contact of the current, the bulb gives a light according to its voltage and colour. The mother-tongue of a prophet is the colour of the bulb. The power of the bulb, the current and other things are determined by God Himself; the human factor is just an instrument of transmission, only an intermediary.

64/a. The Quran is, according to Islam, the Word of God; and the Quran itself repeats again and again, that the believer must recite it day and night, whenever one can. The mystics have well explained that it is a travelling of man towards God by means and through the word of God, the word of God being the high road, even as the electric current is the road for light, which joins the lamp with the power house. This is not an empty verbosity. In fact the Prophet Muhammad has strongly recommended that one should read the whole of the Quran once a week. This has led to its division into seven parts called *manzils*. Further the Quran has 114 chapters, called *surats*, each of which has a number of verses, called *aayats*. In Arabic *manzil* means a station after the day's journey; *surat* means a walled enclosure, a room; and the root *awa*, from which the word *aayat* is derived, means to go to bed. Station, room, bed, these are the three elements of the journey of the traveller, spiritual or temporal. The traveller undertaking a long spiritual journey has to halt in a station after the day's journey, requires a room and a bed to take rest before the further march the next day in this eternal journey towards the Eternal and Limitless!

65. The Quran is addressed to all humanity, without distinction of race, region or time. Further, it seeks to guide man in all walks of life: spiritual, temporal, individual and collective. It contains directions for the conduct of the head of a State, as well as a simple commoner, of the rich as well as of the poor, for peace as well as for war, for spiritual culture as for commerce and material well-being. The Quran seeks primarily to develop the personality of the individual; every being will be personally responsible to his Creator. For this purpose, the Quran not only gives commands, but also tries to convince. It appeals to the reason of man, and it relates stories, parables and metaphors. It describes the attributes of God, Who is one, Creator of all, Knower, Powerful, capable of resuscitating us after death and taking account of our worldly behaviour, Just. Merciful, etc. It contains also the mode of praising God, of pointing out which are the best prayers, what the duties of man are with regard to God, to his fellow-beings and to his own self; this last because we do not belong to ourselves but to God, who has deposited our self with us. The Quran speaks of the best rules relating to social life, commerce, marriage, inheritance, penal law, international law, and so on. But the Quran is not a book in the ordinary sense; it is a collection of the Words of God, revealed from time to time, during twenty-three years, to His messenger sent among human beings. The Quran employs graphically the word "king" for God, and "slave" for man; when the king desires to communicate a message to His slave He sends a messenger, and gives His instructions to his envoy; therefore there are certain things understood and implied; there are repetitions, and even changes

of the forms of expression. . Thus God speaks sometimes in the first person and sometimes in the third. He says "I" as well as "We" and "He", but never "They". It is a collection of revelations sent occasion by occasion — and this fact must be recalled to the beginner—and one should therefore read it again and again in order to better grasp the meaning. It has directions for everybody, every place and for all time.

66. The diction and style of the Quran are magnificent and appropriate to its Divine quality. Its recitation moves the spirit of even those who just listen to it, without understanding it. In passing, the Quran (cf. 17/88, 11/13, 2/23, 10/38) has by virtue of its claim of a Divine origin, challenged men and jinn to produce unitedly even a few verses equal to those of the Quran. The challenge has remained unanswered to this day.

THE HADITH

67. The narrations on Muhammad, the Prophet of Islam, are called *Hadith*, whether they concern what he said or did or even simply tolerated among his disciples if they said or did something in his presence. This tacit approval implies the permissibility of the conduct in question of the public.

68. The Quran has reminded dozens of times the juridical importance of the Hadith: ".........obey God and obey the messenger........." (4/59), "......what the messenger giveth you, take it; and whatever he forbiddeth, abstain from it........." (59/7), "nor doth he speak of his own desire: it is naught save a revelation that is revealed" (53/3-4), 'And verily in the messenger of God ye have a good example for him who looketh unto God and the Last Day and remembereth God much" (33/21). Thus whatever the Holy Messenger commanded, it was, in the eyes of the community, the will of his Divine sender. There have been cases when the Prophet, not having received a revelation, had made a personal effort to formulate opinion through common sense. If God did not approve that,

a revelation came to correct him. This internal process of the formation of the Hadith came only *post evetum* to the knowledge of the community, and had no practical consequences. But the Hadith has another importance as under:

69. The Quran is often succinct; it is in the practice of the Prophet that one must look for the method of application, the details and necessary explanations. An illustration in point is: The Quran has said only: "Establish the service of worship", without giving the details of the manner in which it should be celebrated. The Prophet also could not describe everything merely by words. That is why one day he told the faithful: "Look at me, see how I worship, and follow me."

70. The importance of the Hadith is increased for the Muslims by the fact that the Prophet Muhammad not only taught, but also took the opportunity of putting his teachings into practice in all the important affairs of life. He lived for twenty-three years after his appointment as the messenger of God. He endowed his community with a religion, which he scrupulously practised himself. He founded a State, which he administered as supreme head, maintaining internal peace and order, heading armies for external defence, judging and deciding the litigations of his subjects, punishing the criminals, and legislating in all walks of life. He married, and left a model of family life. Another important fact is that he did not declare himself to be above the ordinary law which he imposed on others. His practice was therefore not mere private conduct, but a detailed interpretation and application of his teachings.

71. Muhammad, as a man, was careful in his actions and modest. As a messenger of God, he took all necessary and possible steps for the communication, as well as the preservation of the Divine message, the Quran. Had he taken the same steps for the preservation of his own sayings, he would have been considered by some as an egoist. For this reason, the story of the Hadith is quite different from that of the Quran.

OFFICIAL DOCUMENTS

72. There is a part of the Hadith, the very nature of which required that it should be written down, namely the official documents of the Prophet.

73. From a passage of the *Ta'rikh* of at-Tabari it appears that, when the Muslims of Mecca, persecuted by their compatriots, went to Abyssinia for refuge, the Prophet gave them a letter of recommendation addressed to the Negus. There are some other documents likewise written by him before the Hijrah, but when he left his native town to settle in Madinah and found invested in himself the State authority, the number and the subject-matter of his letters increased from day to day.

74. Shortly after his arrival in Madinah, he succeeded in establishing there a city-state, composed both of the Muslim and non-Muslim inhabitants; and he endowed that State with a written constitution, in which he mentioned in a precise manner the rights and duties of the head of the State and the subjects, and laid down provisions regarding the functioning of this organisation. This document has come down to us. The Prophet also delimited in writing the frontiers of this city-state. About the same time, he ordered a written census of the entire Muslim population, and al-Bukhari says, the returns showed 1,500 individual registries.

75. Moreover there were treaties of alliance and of peace, concluded with many Arabian tribes. Sometimes two copies of the treaty were prepared and each party kept one. Letters-patent were awarded extending protection to the submitting chieftains, and confirming their previous proprietary rights on land, water sources, etc. With the extension of the Islamic State, there was naturally a certain amount of correspondence with provincial governors for communicating new laws and other administrative dispositions, for revising certain judicial or

administrative decisions emanating from the private initiative of officials, for replying to questions set by these officials to the central government, and regarding taxes, etc.

76. There were also missionary letters sent to different sovereigns inviting them to embrace Islam, such as those despatched to the tribal chieftains in Arabia, emperors of Byzantium and Iran, Negus of Abyssinia and others.

77. For every military expedition, volunteers were raised, and written lists were maintained. Captured booty was listed in detail to enable an equitable distribution among the members of the expeditionary force.

78. The liberation as well as purchase and sale of slaves also seems to have been made by written documents. At least three such documents, emanating from the Prophet himself, have come down to us.

79. An interesting incident may here be mentioned. On the day of the capture of Mecca in the year 8 H., the Prophet had made an important pronouncement which included certain legal provisions. At the demand of a Yemenite, the Prophet ordered that a written copy of his pronouncement should be prepared and handed over to the person, Abu-Shah.

80. We may also mention a case of the translation of the Quran. The Prophet had prescribed that every Muslim should celebrate his worship in Arabic. Certain Persians embraced Islam; and they did not want to put off prayer till the time they should have committed to memory the Arabic texts or chapters of the Quran. With the approval of the Prophet, Salman al-Farsi, a Muslim of Persian origin knowing Arabic, translated into Persian the first chapter of the Quran for the immediate above mentioned requirements of the Persian converts. They employed it till they learned the Arabic text by heart. (Cf. *Mabsut* of Sarakhsi, 1,37; *Nihayah Hashiyat al-Hidayah* by Taj ash-Shari'ah ch. salaat).

81. Works incorporating these kinds of documents of the time of the Prophet cover several hundreds of pages.

82. It may be observed that the Prophet was particularly interested in public instruction, and he used to say: "God has sent me as a teacher (*Mu'allim*)." On his arrival in Madinah, his first act was the construction of a mosque, where a part was reserved for school purposes. This was the famous *Ṣuffah* which served as dormitory during the night and as lecture hall during the day for all those who wanted to profit by this facility. In the year 2 H., when the pagan army of Meccans was routed at Badr and a number of prisoners captured, the Prophet ordered that all those prisoners who knew reading and writing could pay their ransom by giving instruction to ten Muslim boys each (cf. Ibn Hanbal and Ibn Sa'd). The Quran (11/282) also ordained that commercial credit transactions could only be executed by written documents attested by two witnesses. These and other arrangements contributed to the rapid increase of literacy among the Muslims. It is not surprising that the companions of the Prophet grew ever more interested in the preservation by writing of the pronouncements of their supreme guide. Like every new and sincere convert, their devotion and enthusiasm were great. A typical example is the following: 'Umar reports that on his arrival at Madinah, he became contractual brother of a local Muslim— at the time of the famous Fraternisation ordered by the Prophet rehabilitating the Meccan refugees — and both of them worked alternately in a farm of date palms. When 'Umar worked, his companion visited the Prophet and reported to 'Umar in the evening all that he had seen or heard in the presence of the Prophet; and when his turn came 'Umar did the same. Thus both of them were abreast of what was passing around the Prophet, e.g., the promulgation of new laws, learning the questions of politics and defence, and so on. As to the written compilation of the Hadith, during the lifetime of the Prophet, the following incidents will speak for themselves :

COMPILATIONS OF THE TIME OF THE PROPHET

83. At-Tirmidhi reports: One day an Ansarite (Madinan Muslim) complained to the Prophet that he had a weak memory and that he forgot quickly the Prophet's instructive discourses. The Prophet replied : Take the aid of thy right hand (i.e., write down).

84. A large number of sources (at-Tirmidhi, Abu Dawud, etc.) narrate that 'Abdallah ibn 'Amar ibn al-'As, a young Meccan, had the habit of writing all that the Prophet used to say. One day his comrades rebuked him, saying that the Prophet was a human being, he could sometimes be happy and satisfied, at other times annoyed or angry, and that it was not desirable that one should note indiscriminately all that he uttered. 'Abdallah went to the Prophet, and asked him if one could note all that he said. He replied: "Yes". To be surer, 'Abdallah persisted : Even when thou art happy and satisfied, even when thou art angry! The Prophet said: "Of course; by God! Nothing that comes out of this mouth is ever a lie." 'Abdallah gave his compilation, the name of "Sahifa Sadiqah" (the book of truth). For several generations it was taught and transmitted as an independent work; it was later incorporated into the larger collections of the Hadith compiled by Ibn Hanbal and others. Ad-Darimi and Ibn 'Abd al-Hakam report: Once this same 'Abdallah had his pupils around him and somebody asked : "Which of the two cities will be captured by Muslims first, Rome or Constantinople? 'Abdallah caused an old box to be brought to him, took a book out of it. and having turned its pages awhile, read as follows: "One day when we were sitting around the Prophet to write down what he was saying, someone asked him : Which of the two cities will be captured first, Rome or Constantinople? He replied: The city of the descendants of Heraclius." This narration definitely proves that the companions of the Prophet were interested even during his lifetime in writing down his very words.

85. More important is the case of Anas. One of the rare Madinans who could read and write when only ten years old, he was presented by his devoted parents to the Prophet as his personal attendant. Anas did not quit the company of the Prophet till he died. Remaining night and day in his house, Anas had the opportunity of seeing the Prophet and hearing from him that which was not practicable for others. It is Anas who reports the saying of the Prophet: "Capture the science by means of writing." In later times, one of the pupils of Anas reports: If we insisted — another version: if we were numerous — Anas used to unroll his sheets of documents and say: These are the sayings of the Prophet, which I have *noted and then also read out to him* to correct any mistake." — This important statement speaks not only of the compilation during the lifetime of the Prophet, but also of its collation and verification by the Prophet. The case is cited by numerous classical authorities, such as ar-Ramhurmuzi (d. about 360 H.), al-Hakim (d. 405), al-Khatib al-Baghdadi (d. 463) and these great traditionists cite earlier sources.

COMPILATIONS OF THE TIME OF THE COMPANIONS OF THE PROPHET

86. It was natural that the interest in the biography of the Prophet should have increased after his death. His Companions left for the benefit of their children and relatives, accounts of what they knew of the Prophet. The new converts had a thirst for the sources of their religion. Death was diminishing daily the number of those who knew Hadith at first hand ; and this was an added incentive to those who survived, to pay closer attention to the preservation of their memoirs. A large number of works were thus compiled on the sayings and doings of the Prophet, based on the narration of his Companions, after the death of the Master. Of course that refers to the first hand knowledge.

87. When the Prophet nominated 'Amr ibn Hazm as governor of Yemen, he gave him written instructions regarding

the administrative duties he had to perform. 'Amr preserved this document, and also procured copies of twenty-one other documents emanating from the Prophet, addressed to the tribes of Juhainah, Judham, Taiy, Thaqif, etc., and compiled them in the form of a collection of official documents. This work has come down to us. (See appendix in Ibn Tulun's *I'lam as-Sa'ilin*).

88. In the *Sahih* of Muslim, we read that Jabir ibn Abdallah compiled an opuscule on the pilgrimage of Mecca, in which he gave an account of the last pilgrimage of the Prophet and.included his celebrated farewell address pronounced on the occasion. Several sources mention also a *Sahifah* of Jabir, which his pupils used to learn by heart. Probably it dealt with the general sayings and doings of the Prophet.

89. Two other companions of the Prophet, Samurah ibn Jundab and Sa'd ibn 'Ubadah are also reported to have compiled their memoirs, for the benefit of their children. Ibn Hajar, speaking of them, adds that the work of Samurah was big and voluminous. Ibn 'Abbas, who was very young at the death of the Prophet, learnt many things from his elder comrades, and compiled with this material numerous works. The chroniclers state : When he died, he left a camel-load of writings. Ibn Mas'ud, one of the greatest jurists among the Companions, had also compiled a book on Hadith, and later his son 'Abd ar-Rahman used to show that to his friends (Cf. al-Hakim, *al-Mustadrak*, ch. Ibn Mas'ud).

90. Al-Bukhari narrates, that 'Abdallah ibn Abi Awfa, Abu Bakrah, and al-Mughirah ibn Shu'bah taught Hadith by correspondence : If anyone desired information about the Prophet, they replied in writing. They even took the initiative of communicating, to officials and friends for instance, decisions of the Prophet bearing on the problems of the hour.

91. More instructive is the following report, preserved by numerous sources (such as Ibn 'Abd al-Barr's *Jami' Bayan al-'Ilm*): One day a pupil of Abu-Hurairah told him: Thou hadst told me such and such a thing. Abu-Hurairah, who was apparently in his old age, with enfeebled memory refused to believe the Hadith, yet when his pupil insisted that it was from him that he had learnt it, Abu-Hurairah replied: If thou hadst learnt it from me, it must be in my writings. He took him by his hand, and conducted him to his house, showed him "many books on the Hadith of the Prophet," and at last he found the narration in question. Thereupon he exclaimed: I had told thee, that if thou hadst learnt it from me, it must be found in my writings.—It is to be noted that the story employs the expression: "many books". Abu-Harairah died in the year 59 H. To one of his pupils, Hammam ibn Munabbih, he dictated (or gave in writing) an opuscule of 138 traditions about the Prophet. This work, which dates from the first half of the first century of the Hijrah, has been preserved. It enables us to make a comparison with later compilations of the Hadith and to confirm the fact that the memoirs of the ancients on the Hadith have been preserved with great care for the benefit of posterity.

92. Adh-Dhahabi (*Tadhkirat al-Huffaz*) reports: The caliph Abu-Bakr compiled a work, in which there were 500 traditions of the Prophet, and handed it over to his daughter 'Aishah. The next morning, he took it back from her and destroyed it, saying: "I wrote what I understood; it is possible however that there should be certain things in it which did not correspond textually with what the Prophet had uttered." As to 'Umar, we learn on the authority of Ma'mar ibn Rashid, that during his caliphate, 'Umar once consulted the companions of the Prophet on the subject of codifying the Hadith. Everybody seconded the idea. Yet 'Umar continued to hesitate and pray to God for a whole month for guidance and enlightenment. Ultimately he decided not to undertake the task, and said: "Former peoples neglected the Divine Books and concentrated only on the conduct of the prophets; I do not want to set up

the possibility of confusion between the Divine Quran and the Prophet's Hadith.'' Latest research shows that formal reports testifying to the writing down of the Hadith concern not less than fifty Companions of the Prophet. Details would be too long here.

INTERDICTION ON THE WRITING DOWN OF HADITH

93. The last two narrations, regarding Abu-Bakr and 'Umar, are important in as much as they explain the real implication of the tradition which says that the Prophet had forbidden to write down his sayings. If there was really a general interdiction these two foremost Companions of the Prophet would not have dared to even think of the compiling of the Hadith; and when they renounced the idea of recording the Hadith, they would not have invoked a reason other than the interdiction of the Prophet, to silence those who remained in favour of the idea. As far as we know, the only narrators who are reported to have said that the Prophet had ordered not to write down anything other than the Quran, are Abu-Sa'id al-Khudri, Zaid ibn Thabit, and Abu-Hurairah. Neither the context nor the occasion of this direction is known. One should note that Abu-Sa'id al-Khudri and Zaid ibn Thabit were among the young companions of the Prophet: in the year 5 H., they were scarcely 15 years old. However intelligent they might have been, it is comprehensible that the Prophet prohibited them in the early years after the Hijrah from noting down his talks. As to Abu-Hurairah, we have just seen that he had himself compiled "many books on the Hadith." He is known in history as a very pious man, puritan and rigid; and it is unthinkable that a man of his character should have violated an express prohibition of the Prophet, if he had not heard later from the Prophet himself of the lifting of the prohibition Abu-Hurairah came from Yemen in the year 7 H., to embrace Islam. It is possible that in the first days after his conversion, the Prophet ordered him to write down nothing but the Quran; and later when he had mastered the Quran and was able to

distinguish between the Divine Book and the Hadith, the reason of the interdiction ceased to exist. An important fact is that Ibn 'Abbas is also reported to have said, as his personal opinion, without reference to the Prophet, that the Hadith should not be compiled in writing. Nevertheless, as we have seen above, by his prolificity he surpassed those companions of the Prophet who had consigned the Hadith in writing. The contradiction between the word and the deed of those who are nevertheless known for their piety and scrupulous observance of the directions of the Prophet confirms our supposition that the injunction against writing down of the Hadith had a certain context which has not been preserved to us in the narrations, and that it had a limited scope. Of the three reports attributing the interdiction to the Prophet himself, the narrations of Abu Hurairah and Zaid ibn Thabit under discussions are to reject from the point of view the methodology of the Hadith, since one or more intermediary narrators are considered to be weak; the report of Abu Sa'id alone has found place in the *Sahih* of Muslim. Yet even this last one was not acceptable to the great specialist Bukhari, who considered (cf. Ibn Hajar, *Fat'h al-Bari*, I, 218) that this was the personal opinion of Abu Sa'id, and not really order of the Prophet. But if one were nevertheless to disregard this technical aspect and were to suppose that the Prophet had in fact once ordered that his sayings should not be written down, one will have to seek to reconcile between the two contradictory orders of the Prophet rather than reject them both.

94. Three possible explanations come to our mind : (1) The interdiction might have been individual, and concerned those who had recently learnt the art of writing, or those who had recently embraced Islam and were hardly able to distinguish between the Quran and the Hadith. The interdiction was waived in case of the proficiency later acquired. (Abu-Hurairah, for instance, came from Yemen, and it is probable that he mastered the *Musnad* or Himyarite script and not the so-called

Arabic script prevalent in Mecca and from thence introduced in Madinah). (2) It might have aimed only at forbidding writing of the Hadith on the same sheets of paper which contained chapters of the Quran, in order to avoid all possible confusion between the text and the commentary. Abu-Sa'id al-Khudri alludes to it; and we possess the formal injunction of the caliph 'Umar against this particular way of writing Hadith. (3) It might have concerned some particular discourses of the Prophet, for instance, the occasion when he made prophecies regarding the future of Islam and its great spiritual and political conquests; the injunction being motivated by the desire that the belief in predestination may not lead certain people to abandon the spirit of endeavour.

95. Other explanations may be adduced, but these would for the present suffice.

IN LATER CENTURIES

96. In the beginning the compilations of the Hadith were short and individual, every Companion noting down his own recollections. In the second generation, when students attended lectures of more than one master, it became possible to collect several memoirs in larger volumes noting carefully the difference of the sources. A few generations later all the memoirs of the Companions of the Prophet were collected, and later still an attempt was made to classify these traditions according to subject matter, and deduce juridical rules, and other scientific usages. As in the case of the Quran, it was required to learn by heart every Hadith; and to aid the memory, one utilized the written texts. Learning from qualified and authorized teachers was also a condition *sine qua non*. This triple method of preservation and security was rigorously observed by some, and less so by others. Hence the relative importance of the different masters and their trustworthiness.

97. Not long after the Prophet, the reporters of the *Hadith* adopted the habit of mentioning not only the name of the

Prophet as the ultimate source of the knowledge in question, but also the means one after another of obtaining that information. Al-Bukhari, for instance, would say: "My master Ibn Hanbal has said: I have heard my master 'Abd-ar-Razzaq saying: My master Ma'mar Ibn Rashid told me. I heard my master Hammam ibn Munabbih told me: My master Abu-Hurairah told me: I heard the Prophet saying" such and such a thing. For every single report of a few words upon the Prophet, there is such an exhaustive chain of references relating to successive authorities. In a single chain of the narrators, which we have just cited, we find reference made not only to the *Sahih* of al-Bukhari, but also the *Musnad* of Ibn Hanbal, the *Musannaf* of 'Abd ar-Razzaq, the *Jami'* of Ma'mar, and the *Sahifah* of Hammam dictated to him by Abu-Hurairah, the companion of the Prophet. We find the reports of this chain in all these works — which luckily have all come down to us — in exactly the same words. In the presence of a succession of such authoritative sources, it would be a foolish presumption and rank calumny to suggest, for instance, that al-Bukhari had invented the narration and attributed it to the Prophet or fabricated himself the chain of the narrators, or simply collected the folklore, the hearsay of his epoch and attributed it to the Prophet.

CONCLUSION

98. It is by this triple method of safeguard, viz., committing to memory and preserving at the same time by writing and studying the same under qualified teachers—in which each method helps the other and makes the integrity of the reports triply sure—that the religious teachings of Islam have been preserved from the beginning down to our day. This is true as much of the Quran as of the *Hadith* which consists of the memoirs of the companions of the Prophet, concerning the sayings, doings and tacit approval by him of the conduct of his companions. It may be remembered that as a founder of religion too, the Prophet Muhammad had had an immense success.

In fact in the year 10 H., he was able to address at 'Arafat (Mecca), a gathering of Muslims numbering about 140,000 Muslims who had come for pilgrimage (without counting many others who had not come to Mecca that year) The biographers of the companions of the Prophet affirm that the number of the companions of the Prophet Muhammad who have reported at least one incident of the life of the Prophet exceeds a hundred thousand. There are bound to be repetitions, but the very multiplicity of the sources recounting one and the same event does but add to the trustworthiness of the report. We possess in all about ten thousand reports (eliminating the repetitions) of the *Hadith*, on the life of the Prophet of Islam, and these concern all aspects of his life including directions given by him to his disciples in spiritual as well as temporal matters.

CHAPTER III

The Islamic Conception of Life

THE vitality of a society, a people or a civilization depends in a large measure on the philosophy of life conceived and practised. In his natural state, man scarcely thinks of anything but his own individual interest, and only later of his close relatives. There have however been human groups, in every epoch, which have particularly distinguished themselves. When we study the features and characteristics of the past score of civilizations,—and possibly we are now at the dawn of another one—we find that even though one group may become distinguished as the torch-bearer of a civilization in a particular epoch, that does not necessarily mean that all other contemporary groups would be living in a state of savagery. There is rather a relative pre-eminence of one over the others, in the ladder of graded civilizations. When the Phoenicians, for instance, appeared on the scene and developed a brilliant civilization, several other contemporary peoples were perhaps almost as civilized, although lacking the occasion and a suitable field of their activity. At the Arabo-Islamic epoch, the Greeks, the Romans, the Chinese, the Indians and others possessed all the characteristics of civilized peoples; nonetheless they did not rise to the heights of the standard-bearers of the civilization of their epoch. In our own time, if the people of the U.S.A. and Russia form the vanguard with their nuclear might, and other claims, the British, the Chinese, the Frenchmen and the Germans follow close behind. Notwithstanding this progress of some, there are, at the same time, even in this second half of the 20th century, in certain parts of the globe, groups still in savagery if not actual cannibalism.

100. The question arises as to why the evolution of some is rapid, and of others slow? In an epoch when the Greeks enjoyed a glorious civilization why was it that Western Europe was barbarian? Why did barbarism prevail in Russia when the Arabs had risen to the height of splendour? The same question may be posed in respect of several countries in several epochs. Is it purely and simply a question of chance and circumstance, or is it due to the fact that some individuals of lofty note and noble personality were born in one human group to the exclusion of other groups? There are perhaps other possible explanations also, more complex and depending upon a variety of co-existing causes, governing the accomplishments of some, and the frustration or even extinction of the other.

101. There is still another question. After a momentary state of splendour, why do people fall anew into relative obscurity if not into a semi-barbarous state?

102. We propose to investigate these questions, in relation to contemporary Islam, and discuss, if possible, the chances it has of survival.

103. If one were to believe Ibn Khaldun, the biological factor is the essential cause. At the end of a single generation, the race exhausts its vitality, and for purposes of rejuvenation there must be a change at least in the family of men at the helm of affairs. This racial theory, even if it be considered as a learned exaggeration, can affect ethnic civilizations and such religions as do not admit conversion. Islam luckily escapes this cycle of decadence; for its followers are found among all races, and it continues to achieve greater or smaller progress everywhere in the world. Moreover it is unanimously recognized that Islam has almost completely effaced, inside its community, racial prejudices, a feature which permits it to accept without hesitation, men of any race to be its leaders and standard-bearers. The systematic emancipation of slaves, which was ordered by the Quran, presents another glorious example. As

a matter of fact there have been several dynasties of Muslim rulers in history, drawn solely from slaves who had been freshly liberated.

104.   The life and death of a civilization depend in an equal measure on the quality of its basic teaching. If it invites its adherents to renounce the world, spirituality will certainly make great progress, yet the other constituent parts of man, his body, his intellectual faculties, etc., will not be allowed to perform their natural duties and will die even before their season of bloom. If, on the other hand, a civilization lays emphasis only on the material aspects of life man will make great progress in those aspects at the expense of others; and such a civilization may even become a sort of boomerang causing its own death. For materialism often engenders egoism and lack of respect for the rights of others, creating enemies, who await their chance for reprisals. The result is mutual killing. The story of the two brigands is well known. They had captured some booty. One of them went to the town to buy provisions, and the other had to collect wood to prepare the meal. However each one resolved secretly in his heart to get rid of the other and monopolize the illicit gain. So the one who had gone shopping, poisoned the provisions; while his comrade awaited him in ambush, and killed him on his return from the town; but when he tasted the food, he too joined his companion in the other world.

105.   There may be another defect inherent in a civilization, when its teachings do not contain an innate capacity for development and adaptation to circumstances. However nice its teaching may be for one epoch or one environment, it may not prove so for another; to be captivated by such a teaching will evidently be fatal to those who come later. An ordinary example will illustrate the point. At a time, when there was no electric lighting and when the centres of cults had no stable revenues, it was certainly an act of piety to light a candle in some place of religious interest, frequented during the night.

Nothing may be said against a belief that an act of piety, on the part of a repentant, constitutes an expiation and an efface- ment of the crime committed against God, or against man which otherwise was hard to repair. But can the continuation of lighting a candle in a place which is already brilliantly lit with electric lamps be anything more than a wastage? Let us study Islam in the light of these circumstances.

ISLAMIC IDEOLOGY

106. It is well known that the motto of Islam is summed up in the expression of the Quran (2/101), "well-being in this world and well-being in the Hereafter". Islam will certainly not satisfy the extremists of either school, the ultra-spiritualists (who want to renounce all worldly things and mortify them- selves as a duty) and the ultramaterialists (who do not believe in the rights of others), yet it can be practised by an overwhel- ming majority of mankind, which follows an intermediate path, and seeks to develop simultaneously the body and the soul, creating a harmonious equilibrium in man as a whole. Islam has insisted on the importance of both these constituents of man, and on their inseparability, so that one should not be sacrificed for the benefit of the other. If Islam prescribes spiritual duties and practices, these contain also material advantages; similarly if it authorizes an act of temporal utility, it shows how this act can also be a source of spiritual satis- faction. The following examples will illustrate the argument

107. One will agree that the aim of spiritual practices is to get closer to the Necessary Being (*dhat wajib al-wujud*), our Creator and Lord, and to obtain His pleasure. Therefore, man tries to "dye himself with the colour of God," as the Quran (2/138) enjoins, in order to see with His eyes, to speak with His tongue, to desire with His will, — as a Hadith says, in short to behave entirely according to His will, seeking even to imitate Him according to one's humble human capacities. A believer must fast at the moment prescribed by the Quran, because that is the order of God. To obey the order of the

Lord is in itself piety, but in addition to that, the fast weakens the body, which fortifies the soul by diminishing material desires. One feels a spiritual uplift, thinks of God and of all that He does for us, and enjoys other spiritual benefits But the fast also does material good. The acidities which secrete from the glands, when one is hungry and thirsty, kill many a microbe in the stomach. One develops also the capacity to bear privation at moments of a crisis and still carry on one's normal duties undistrubed. If one fasts for material ends, it has no spiritual value ; yet if one fasts for gaining the good will of God, the material advantages are never lost. Without entering into a detailed discussion, it may be observed that all other spiritual acts or practices of Islam have also the same double effect, spiritual and temporal. So is it in worship, individual or congregational, and so is it in the abnegation of the self at the moment of the pilgrimage to the House of God, in charities to the poor, and in other religious and spiritual practices apart from the obligatory minimum. If one does something solely for the sake of God, it has a double merit: spiritual advantage without the least loss of material benefits, On the contrary, if one does the same thing with only a material aim, one may obtain this object but the spiritual advantage would be completely lost. Let us recall the celebrated saying of the Prophet Muhammad : "Verily actions are solely according to motives and intentions." (cf. Bukhari. Muslim, etc.)

108. Speaking of a strictly temporal act, such as a tax or a war, one pays taxes to the government. It should not be astonishing, that Islam considers this act as one of the five basic elements of the Faith, as important as belief, worship,

---

1. *In the Quranic terminology, zakat does not mean charity It is a tax on agricultural product, on mineral extractions, on commerce, on herds and all these taxes are called zakat. The expenditure is mentioned in the Quran 9/60, for details see infra chapter 10.*

fasting and pilgrimage! The significance is deep: One unites the spiritual and the temporal in a single whole, and one pays the tax not as a corvee or even as a social duty, but solely for the sake of God. When this duty of paying the taxes becomes fixed in the mind as something sacred, a duty unto God from Whom nothing can be concealed and Who is, moreover, capable of resuscitating us and demanding our account, one can easily understand with what care and scruple a believer will pay his dues in the performance of this obligation. Similarly, war is forbidden in Islam except in the way of God; and it is not difficult to understand that such a soldier is more apt to be humane and will not seek any earthly gain in the course of risking his life. By spiritualizing the temporal duties, Islam has had no other motive but strengthening the spiritual side of man, who, in this manner, far from seeking the material advantage of the material thing, aspires thereby to obtain only the pleasure of God. The Prophet has said: Ostentation is a sort of polytheism (*shirk*); and the reason as explained by al-Ghazali, is that when he said: If somebody worships or fasts for ostentation, it is *shirk* (polytheism), a worship of one's self, not of God Almighty; on the contrary, if one even cohabits with one's own wife — not for the carnal pleasure, but for performing the duty imposed by God — that is an act of piety and devotion, meriting the pleasure of and reward from God, as the Prophet has observed (cf. Ibn Hanbal, V 154, 167, 187 etc.)

109. A corollary perhaps of the same all-embracing conception of life, is the fact that the Quran uses very often the double formula "believe and do good deeds", the mere profession of faith, without application or practice, has not much value. Islam insists as much on the one as on the other. The doing of good deeds without the belief in God is certainly preferable, in the interests of society, to the practice of evil deeds; yet from the spiritual standpoint, a good deed without faith cannot bring salvation in the Hereafter.

110. But how to distinguish the good from the evil? In the first instance, it is the revealed law which alone can be the criterion, but in the last resort, it is one's conscience which can be one's arbiter, When a problem is posed, one can refer to the text of the Islamic law, personally if one can, and with the help of the learned and the experts if necessary. Yet a jurisconsult can only reply on the basis of facts which have been brought to his notice. If certain material facts should have been concealed from him, whether intentionally or otherwise, the consequent injustice cannot be imputed to law. We may recall a charming little discourse of the Prophet, who said one day: "People! in the complaints which come to me, I decide only on the basis of facts brought to my knowledge; if, by lack of full information, I decide in favour of someone who has no right, let him know that I accord him a part of the Hell-fire". (cf. Bukhari, Muslim, etc.). An Islamic judicial maxim stresses the same when it says: "Consult thy conscience even if, the jurisconsults provide justification to thee." (contained in a Hadith reported by Ibn Hanbal and al-Darimi).

111. Never to think of others, but of one's own self, is not human but beastly. To think of others after having satisfied one's own needs is normal and permitted. Yet the Quran praises those "who prefer others above themselves though poverty become their lot." (59:9). Evidently this is only a recommendation, and not an obligatory duty laid on the average man; if one does not observe it, one will not be considered a criminal or a sinner. We can cite the famous saying of the Prophet, in the same vein of recommendation: "The best of men is the one who does good to others."

112. The Quranic direction may be considered as a characteristic trait of Islam, to wit: "and of the bounty of thy Lord (on thee) by thy discourse" (93:11). A saying of the Prophet (cited by Tirmidhi) explains it in an impressive manner: "God likes to see the traces of His bounty on His

creature." It had so happened, that one of his companions came to see him with a miserable attire, even though he was a well-to-do person. When the Prophet asked him the reason, he replied that he preferred to have a wretched look, not for miserliness but for piety, as he preferred the needy to his own self. The Prophet did not approve it, and put a limit to self-sacrifice and ordered (cf. Abu Dawud): "When God has given you means, the traces of His bounty should be visible on you." The Quran (28:77) further enjoins "......and neglect not thy portion of this world." Islam does not admit that man should cease to work and become a parasite; on the contrary one must use all one's gifts and talents for profiting by God's creations, and acquire as much as possible; what exceeds one's requirements may go to the aid of those who lack the necessaries. The Prophet has unequivocally said: "It is better that you leave behind you your relatives well-off, rather than obliged to beg alms of others." (Bukhari). Notwithstanding the imposition of heavy daily practices, Islam does not demand mortification or voluntary misery; on the contrary the Quran reproaches those who would develop such an attitude:

"Say: Who hath forbidden the adornment of God which He hath brought forth for His servants, and the delicious things of nourishment? Say: they are, in the life of this world, for those who believe, being exclusively for them on the Day of Resurrection. Thus do We detail Our commands for people who have knowledge." (7/32).

There are things permitted by the Divine 'law: to deny voluntarily for one's self is not necessarily an act of piety, as would be the case of abstaining from things forbidden by the same law.

BELIEF IN GOD

113. Man seems to have always sought to know his Creator for the sake of obeying Him. The best religious leaders of every epoch and civilization have established certain rules of

54

conduct for this purpose. The primitive people worshipped the manifestations of the power and beneficence of God, hoping thus to please Him. Some others believed in two separate gods, one of the good and the other of the evil; yet they overlooked the logical consequences of such a distinction which implies a civil war between gods. Yet others have enshrouded God with mysteries which mystify sometimes the person of God. And some others have felt the need of such symbols, formulas or gestures, which hardly distinguish their theological conceptions from idolatry or Polytheism.

114. In this field, Islam has its particularity. It believes in the absolute Oneness of God, and prescribes a form of worship and prayer which admits neither images nor symbols (considering them to be the remnants of primitivism and idolatry). In Islam, God is not only transcendent and non-material, beyond any physical perception, (cf. Quran 6/103: "Sights comprehend Him not"), but He is also Immanent, Omnipresent and Omnipotent (cf. Quran 50/16, 56, 85, 58/7). The relations between man and his Creator are direct and personal, without requiring any intermediary. Even the saintliest of the saints, such as prophets, are only guides and messengers; and it is left to the individual man to make his choice and be directly responsible to God.

115. It will thus be seen that Islam seeks to develop the personality of the individual. It admits that man has his weaknesses, as he is constituted simultaneously of the capacities both of good and evil; yet it does not admit that there is original sin in him, as this would be an injustice. If Adam had committed a sin, this should create no responsibility on his posterity, each individual human being remaining responsible for his personal account only.

116. In his weakness, the individual may commit offences against God or against fellow creatures. Each offence has in principle a proportionate liability (punishment), yet Islam

recognizes the possibility of pardon, the elements of which are repentance and reparations. As to offences against man, they should be amended, as far as possible; so that the victim may pardon either gratuitously; or at the restitution of the object taken away from him or by having it replaced, or in any similar way. As regards offences against God, man may receive either a suitable punishment or a gracious pardon from the Lord. Islam does not admit that God needs to punish first some innocent person in order to accord His pardon to other repentant sinners; for this vicarious punishment would be unjust on the part of God.

SOCIETY

117. Even as Islam seeks to develop individuality in man, it seeks also social collectivity. This could be seen in all its prescriptions, be they religious or temporal. Thus the service of worship is collective in principle, (if in case of need there is some exemption regarding the five daily prayers, there is none regarding the weekly or annual prayer services); pilgrimage is an even more manifest example, since the believers assemble in the same place, coming from all points of the globe; the collective aspect of fasting manifests itself in the fact that it takes place in the same month for the faithful all over the world; the requirement of having a caliph, the obligation of paying the zakat-tax intended for the needs of the collectivity, etc. — all these things testify to the same objective. It goes without saying that in collectivity, or society, there is a force which persons do not possess individually.

118. For reasons best known to Him, God has endowed different individuals with different talents. Two children of the same couple, two pupils of the same class do not always have the same qualities or capacities. All lands are not equally ertile; climates differ; two trees ef the same species do not produce the same quantity or quality. Every being, every part of a being has its own peculiarities. On the basis of this natural phenomenon, Islam affirms, on the one hand, the original equality of all, and on the other, the superiority cf

individuals one over the other : All are creatures of the same Lord, and it is not material superiority which counts for obtaining the greater appreciation of God. Piety alone is the criterion of the greatness of the individual. After all, life in this world is but ephemeral, and there must be a difference between the behaviour of a man and a beast.

NATIONALITY

119. It is in this sense, that Islam rejects the narrow basis of birth and common blood as the element of solidarity. The attachment to parentage or to the soil on which one is born, is no doubt natural; yet the very interest of the human race demands a certain tolerance towards other similar groups The distribution of the natural wealth in different parts of the world in varying quantities renders the world interdependent. Inevitably one is forced to "live and let live"; otherwise an interminable succession of vendettas will destroy all Nationality on the basis of language, race, colour, or birthplace is too primitive; therein is a fatality, an impasse — something in which man has no choice. The Islamic notion is progressive, and is based solely on the choice of the individual. For it proposes the unity of all those who believe in the same ideology, without distinction of race, tongue, or place of abode. Since extermination or subjugation of others is excluded, the only valid possibility is assimilation. And which means can serve better such assimilation, if not belief in the same ideology? It may be repeated that Islamic ideology is a synthesis of the requirements both of the body and the soul; moreover it inculcates a tolerance. Islam has proclaimed that God has always sent His messengers, at different epochs among different peoples. Islam itself claims nothing more than the function of renewing and reviving the eternal message of God, so often repeated at the hands of prophets. It prohibits all compulsion in the matter of religious beliefs; and however unbelievable it may sound, Islam is under the self-imposed religious dogmatic duty of giving autonomy to non-Muslims

residing on the soil of the Islamic State. The Quran, the Hadith
and the practice of all time demand that non-Muslims should
have their own laws, administrated in their own tribunals by
their own judges, without any interference on the part of the
Muslim authorities, whether it be in religious matters or social
(cf. *infra* ch. 12 § 406 ff).

ECONOMIC OUTLOOK

120. The social importance of economic questions is too
evident to require emphasis. The Quran does not exaggerate
when it declares (4 : 5) that the material goods constitute the
very, means of the subsistence of humanity. If everyone were
to think of none but his single self, society would be more and
more in danger, for the simple reason that there are always a
very few rich and a very many poor; and at a moment of
struggle for existence, the vast majority of the famishing will in
the long run exterminate the small minority of the rich. One
can bear many privations, but not of ailments. The Islamic
conception on this subject is well known. It envisages the
constant redistribution and circulation of the national wealth.
Thus, the poor are exempt from taxation, whereas the rich are
taxed to provide for the needy. Again, there are laws, which
require the obligatory distribution of the heritage, those which
forbid the accumulation of wealth in the hands of the few, by
banning interest on loans, and prohibiting bequest to the
detriment of the near relatives, etc., and those which prescribe
rules for the expenditure of the State revenue, aiming at the
beneficial redistribution of the income among the beneficiaries
among which the poor top the list. If this principle is kept in
view, it tolerates differences in the means and methods according to regions, epochs and circumstances, provided the goal is
achieved. The competition of free enterprises may be tolerated
if this does not degenerate into the cut throat exploitation and
ruin of those who are economically weak. The planning of the
whole may equally be tolerated if that appears necessary, due
to circumstances or economico-demographical evolution. In

any case, wastage of goods as well as of energy is to be avoided, and such means adopted which are better adapted to the needs of the moment.

FREE WILL AND PREDESTINATION

121. This leads us to the philosophic question of the free will. This eternal dilemma can never be resolved by logic alone. For, if man enjoys free will with respect to all his acts, the omnipotence of God suffers thereby. Similarly, if God predestines, why should man be held responsible for his acts? The Prophet Muhammad has emphatically recommended his adherents not to engage in discussions on this topic, "which has led astray those peoples who preceded you", (as Ibn Hanbal, Tirmidhi and others report); and he has separated the two questions, viz., the omnipotence of God and the responsibility of man. In fact there is no logic in love, and the Muslim loves his Creator: he cannot admit that God should have defective attributes; God is not only wise and powerful, but also just and merciful in the highest degree. Islam separates celestial affairs, which are the attributes of God, from human temporal matters, and insists on the faithful to act; and since the Divine will rests concealed from man, it is man's duty never to despair after a preliminary failure, but to try again and again until the object is either realized or becomes impossible of attainment. The Islamic concept of predestination comes in this latter case to console man: that was the will of God, and the success or failure in this world has no importance in connection with eternal salvation, in which matter God judges according to intention and effort and not according to the measure of realization and success.

122. According to the Quran (53/36-42, among other passages) such is the truth always revealed by God to His successive messengers:

"Or hath he not news of what is in the leaves (Books) of Moses and of Abraham who paid his debt: That no laden one shall bear another's load, and that man hath only that for which he maketh effort, and that his effort will be seen, and afterwards he will be repaid for it with the fullest payment; and that thy Lord. He is the goal......?"

We are rewarded only because we have accepted also to be punished for acts which are predestined. This seems to be the Divine Deposit with which we have been entrusted, when the Quran (33/72) reports: "We did indeed offer the Trust to the heavens and the earth and the mountains; but they refused to undertake it being afraid thereof; but Man undertook it; — he was indeed unjust and ignorant." God said : I shall predestine your acts, and want to reward or punish you according to whether they are good or evil. Other created beings said: How? Thou willt create, and we have to be responsible for the same? They got afraid. Man believed in the limitless mercy of the Lord, and said: Yes Lord, I accept to take this responsibility and this Depost of Thine. This pleased the Lord so much that He ordered even the angels to prostrate before Man. To sum up, since Islam separates completely the two questions, it is not difficult for it to admit simultaneously the requirements of man (effort, sense of responsibility) and the rights of God with all His attributes, including the power to predetermine.

123. Predetermination in Islam has another significance, not less important, namely, it is God Who alone attributes to a human act the quality of good or evil; it is God Who is the source of all law. It is the Divine prescriptions which are to be observed in all our behaviour; and which He communicates to us through His chosen messengers. Muhammad being the last of these, also the one whose teaching has been the better preserved. We do not possess originals of the ancient messages which have suffered damages in the unhappy fracticidal wars of the human society. The Quran is not only an exception to

the rule, but also constitutes the latest Divine message. It is commonplace that, a law later in date abrogates the former dispositions of the same legislator.

124. Let us, in conclusion, refer to another trait of Islamic life: It is the duty of a Muslim not only to follow the Divine law in his daily behaviour in his life as an individual as well as a part of the collectivity, in matters, temporal as well as spiritual. He is also to contribute according to his capacities and possibilities, to the propagation of this ideology, which is based on Divine revelation and intended for the well-being of all.

125. It will be seen that such a composite creed covers the entire life of man, not only material but also spiritual; and that one lives in this world in preparation for the Hereafter.

CHAPTER IV

Faith and Belief

MEN believe in very many sorts of things: in truth, with all the relativity which this concept has; in superstitions, and sometimes even in what is based on misapprehensions. The beliefs may change with age and experience, among other factors. But certain beliefs are shared by a whole group in common. In this context, the most important aspect is the idea of man regarding his own existence: whence has he come? where does he go? who has created him? what is the object of his existence? and so on and so forth. Metaphysics tries to answer these questions of mental anguish, but that is only a part of religion which is more comprehensive and answers to all the allied questions. The science which treats this is religion. Beliefs are purely personal affairs. Nevertheless, the history of the human species has known in this connection many an act of fratricidal violence and horror, of which even the beasts would be ashamed. The basic principle of Islam in this matter is the following verse of the Quran (2:256):

"There is no compulsion in religion; the right direction is henceforth distinct from error; and he who rejecteth the Devil and believeth in God hath grasped a firm hand-hold which will never break; God is Hearer, Knower."

It is charity, and even a sacrifice, to guide others and to struggle for dispelling the ignorance of fellow-beings without compelling anybody to any belief whatsoever—such is the attitude of Islam.

127. The knowledge and intelligence of man are in a process of continuous evolution. The medical or mathematical knowledge of a Galen, or of an Euclid scarcely suffices today

even for the matriculation examination; the university students require much more knowledge than that. In the field of religious dogmas, primitive man was perhaps even incapable of the abstract notion of a transcendental God, Whose worship would require neither symbols nor material representations. Even his language was incapable of translating sublime ideas without being forced to use terms which would not be very appropriate for abstract notions.

128. Islam lays very strong emphasis on the fact that man is composed simultaneously of two elements: his body and his soul; and that he should not neglect any one of these for the sole profit of the other. To devote oneself exclusively to spiritual needs would be to aspire to become an angel (whereas God has created angels other than us); to dedicate oneself to purely material needs would be to be degraded to the condition of a beast, a plant, if not a devil, (God has created for this purpose objects other than men). The aim of the creation of man with a dual capacity would remain unfulfilled if he does not maintain a harmonious equilibrium between the requirements of the body and those of the soul simultaneously.

129. Muslims owe their religious faith to Muhammad, the messenger of God. One day the Prophet Muhammad himself replied to a question as to what is Faith and said: "Thou shalt believe in the One God, in His angelic messengers, in His revealed books, in His human messengers, in the Last Day (of Resurrection and final judgement) and in the determination of good and evil by God". On the same occasion, he explained as to what signifies submission to God in practice, and what is the best method of obedience, points which shall be treated in the next two chapters.

GOD

130. Muslims have nothing in common with atheists, polytheists, and those who associate others with the One God. The Arabic word for One God is *Allah*, Lord and Creator of the universe.

131. Even the simplest, the most primitive and uncultured man knows well that one cannot be the creator of one's own self: there ought to be a Creator of us all, of the entire universe, Atheism and materialism does not respond to this logical need.

132. To believe in polytheism will entail the difficulty of the division of powers between the several gods, if not a civil war among them. One can easily see that all that is in the universe is interdependent. Man, for instance, requires the aid of plants, metals, animals and stars, even as each one of these objects needs another's help in some way or other. The division of Divine powers thus becomes impracticable.

133. In their praiseworthy solicitude, for not attributing evil to God, certain thinkers have thought of two different gods; a god of the good and a god of the evil. But the question is whether the two would act in mutual accord, or there would arise conflict between them? In the first case, the Duality becomes redundant and superfluous; and if the god of the good consents to the evil, then he becomes even an accomplice in the evil, thus vitiating the very purpose of the Duality. In the second case, one will have to admit that the god of evil would be more often victorious and obtain the upper hand. Should one believe then, in a weakling, the god of the good as God. Moreover, the evil is a relative thing: with regard to one if something is evil the same thing becomes a good with regard to another person, and since the absolute evil does not exist, there is no attribution of the evil to God (cf. *infra* § 155, 157, 228 also).

134. Monotheism alone, pure and unmixed can satisfy reason. God is One, though He is capable of doing all sorts of things. Hence the multiplicity of His attributes. God is not only the creator, but also the master of all: He rules over the Heavens and the earth; nothing moves without His knowledge and His permission. The Prophet Muhammad has said that God has ninety-nine "most beautiful names," for ninety-nine

principal attributes: He is the creator, the essence of the existence of all, wise, just, merciful, omnipresent, omnipotent, omniscient, determinant of everything, to Whom belongs life, death, resurrection, etc., etc.

135. It follows that the conception of God differs according to individuals: a philosopher does not envisage it in the same manner as a man in the street. The Prophet Muhammad admired the fervour of the faith of simple folk, and often gave the example of "the faith of old women," that is, unshakable and full of sincere conviction. The beautiful little story of the elephant and a group of blind men is well known: They had never before heard of an elephant; so on its arrival, each of them approached the strange animal: one laid his hand on its trunk, another on its ear, a third on its leg, and a fourth on its tail, another on its tusks, etc. On their return, each one exchanged impressions and described the elephant in his own manner and personal experience, that it was like a column, like a wing, something hard like a stone, or soft and slender. Everyone was right, yet none had found the whole truth which was beyond his perceptive capacity. If we replace the blind men of this parable by searchers of the Invisible God, we can easily realize the relative veracity of individual experiences. As certain mystics of early Islam have remarked: "There is a truth about God known to the man in the street, another known to the initiated, yet another to the inspired prophets, and lastly the one known to God Himself." In the expose given above, on the authority of the Prophet of Islam, there is enough elasticity for satisfying the needs of different categories of men; learned as well as ignorant, intelligent as well as simple, poets, artists, jurists, mystics, theologians and the rest. The point of view and the angle of vision may differ according to the individual, yet the object of vision remains constant.

136. Muslim savants have constructed their entire system on a juridical basis, where rights and duties are correlative, God has given us the organs and faculties which we possess.

and every gift implies a particular obligation. To worship God, to be thankful to Him, to obey Him, to shun all that does not suit His universal Divinity — all these constitute the individual duties of everyone, for which each one shall be personally responsible.

THE ANGELS

137. God being invisible and beyond all physical perception, it was necessary to have some means of contact between man and God; otherwise it would not be possible to follow the Divine will. God is the creator not only of our bodies, but also of all our faculties — which are diverse and each capable of development. It is He Who has given us the intuition, the moral conscience and the means we employ to guide us in the right path. The human spirit is capable of both good and evil inspirations. Among the common folk it is possible that good people sometimes receive evil inspirations (temptations) and bad · people good inspirations. Inspirations may come from someone other than God also, such as the evil suggestions coming from the Devil. It is the grace of God which enables our reason to distinguish between that which is celestial and worthy of following, and that which is diabolic and fit to be shunned.

138. There are several ways of establishing contact or communication between man and God. The best would have been incarnation; but Islam has rejected it. It would be too degrading for a transcendent God to become man, to eat, drink, be tortured by His own creatures, and even be put to death. However close a man may approach God, in his journeying towards Him, even in his highest ascension, man remains man and very much remote from God. Man may annihilate himself, as say the mystics, and efface completely his personality, in order to act according to the will of God, but still — and let us repeat that — man remains man and subject to all his weaknesses, and God is above all these insufficiencies.

139. Among other means of communication between man and God, which are at the disposal of man, the feeblest perhaps is a dream. According to the Prophet, good dreams are suggested by God and guide men in the right direction.

140. Another means is *ilqa* (literally, throwing something towards someone) a kind of auto-suggestions, of intuition, of presentiment of solutions in case of impasses or insoluble or difficult problems.

141. There is also the *ilham*, which may be translated as "Divine inspiration". Things are suggested to the heart (mind) of a man whose soul is sufficiently developed in the virtues of justice, charity, disinterestedness, and benevolence to others. The saints of all epochs in all countries have enjoyed this grace. When someone devotes one's self to God and tries to forget one's self, there are moments — of very short duration — when the state of the presence of God flashes like lightning, in which one understands without effort that which no other effort would have succeeded in making him aware. The human spirit — or his heart as the ancients said — is thus enlightened; and then there is a sentiment of conviction, contentment and realization of truth. It is God Who guides him and controls him and his thoughts as well as his actions. Even the prophets — the human messengers of God — get this kind of direction, among others. Anyhow there remains the possibility of error of judgement or of comprehension on the part of man. The mystics affirm that sometimes even the most pious men are led astray by their imperceptible ego, not being able to distinguish the base inspirations that come as a Divine trial.

142. The highest degree of contact, the surest and the most infallible means of communication between man and his Creator is called *wahy* by the Prophet Muhammad. It is not an ordinary inspiration, but a veritable revelation made to man on the part of the Lord, a celestial communication. Man is matter,

God is on the contrary above even the spirit, and therefore beyond all possibility of direct physical contact with man (Quran 6/103). God is omnipresent, and, as says the Quran (50/16) : "nearer to man than his jugular vein"; yet no physical contact is possible. Therefore it is a *malak* — literally a messenger, i e. a celestial message-bearer, commonly translated as "angel" — who serves as intermediary, or the channel of the transmission of the message of God to His human agent or messenger, i e , the prophet. None except a prophet receives such a revelation through the intermediary of a celestial messenger. It ought to be remembered that in Islam, prophet does not mean one who makes prophecies and predictions, but only an envoy of God, a bearer of Divine message intended for his people. As to the angel, it does not enter in the scope of our studies here to discuss whether it is a spiritual being, distinct from the material beings in the universe, or something else.

143. According to the Quran, the celestial messenger, who brought revelations to the Prophet, is called Jibril (Jibrail, Gabriel), which etymologically means "the power of God". The Quran cites also Mikal (Mikail, Michael), without indicating his functions. The functionary in charge of hell is named Malik (literally 'master" or "owner"). It speaks also of other angels without name and without attributes, all of whom execute the orders of the Lord. The Islamic belief is that Jibril, also termed by the Quran "trustworthy spirit (*al ruh al-amin*), stands above all. In the sayings of the Prophet Muhammad, as distinct from the Quran, we read that this celestial messenger, Jibril, did not appear to the Prophet always in the same form. The Prophet saw him sometimes like a being suspended in the air, sometimes in the shape of a man, sometimes like a being having wings, etc. In a narration (cf. § 129) preserved by Ibn Hanbal (I, 53 or No. 374), it is reported that one day in the presence of many people, an unknown person came and put some questions to the Prophet Muhammad, and thereafter

went away. Several days afterwards, the Prophet told his companions : I am persuaded to believe that the person who put to me questions on that day was none other than Gabriel, who had come to teach you your religion; and never was I so tardy in recognizing him. It was so, because he had come to examine the Prophet and not to communicate to him some message of God.

144. The way in which the revelation used to come could be deduced from the following reports in which the Prophet himself or his on-lookers have described it: "Sometimes it came to me like the beating sound of the bell — and this is the hardest experience for me — and when that ceases, I retain well engraved in my memory all that it has said; but sometimes the angel appears to me in the shape of a human being and speaks to me and I retain what he says" (Bukhari). In the transmission of Ibn Hanbal, this same report reads: "I hear the beating sounds and thereupon I keep silent; there is not an occasion of the revelation to me when I do not fear that my soul will depart." His Companions relate their observations as under: "Whenever a revelation came to him, a sort of rest (immobility) captured him" (Ibn Hanbal). Or "Whenever the revelation came to the messenger of God, he was overwhelmed and remained in this state a while as if he was intoxicated" (Ibn Sa'd). Or "The revelation came to him in the coldest day, and when it ceased, the front of the Prophet perspired with (sweat falling as) pearls" (Bukhari). Or "Once when the moment (of revelation) arrived, he let enter his head inside (a garment?), and lo, the face of the messenger of God had become red, and he snored; later the state vanished" (Bukhari). Or "Whenever the revelation came, he suffered therefrom and his face darkened" (Ibn Sa'd). Or "When the revelation came to him, we heard near him like the humming sound of bees" (Ibn Hanbal and Abu Nu'aim). Or "The Prophet suffered great pain when the revelation came to him, and used to move his lips" (Bukhari). Other series of reports

say that he then felt the weight of a great load, and say: "I saw the Prophet when a revelation came to him while he was on his camel ; the camel began to foam with rage and twist its legs to the point that I feared that they would break with a crack. In fact sometimes the camel sat down, but sometimes it obstinately tried to stand, with legs planted like pegs althrough the time of revelation, and this lasted until the state (of revelation) vanished, and sweat fell from him like pearls" (Ibn Sa'd). Or "The load almost broke the leg of the camel with a crack" (Ibn Hanbal). Zaid Ibn Thabit reports his personal experience of a certain day in the following words : "His leg lay on my thigh and weighed so heavy that I feared that my femur would break with a crack" (Bukhari). In another version, there is this addition: "... had it not been for the Prophet of God, I would have pushed a cry and taken away my leg". Other reports say: "The revelation came to him once while he was standing on the pulpit of the Mosque and he remained immobile" (Ibn Hanbal). Or "He was holding a loaf of meat (during his meal) when a revelation came to him, and when the state ceased, the loaf was still in his hand" (Ibn Hanbal). At such an occasion, the Prophet sometimes lay on his back, sometimes the inmates even covered his face in respect with a piece of cloth, as the circumstance may be. Yet he never lost his consciousness nor control of his self. In the early times of the mission, he used to repeat aloud, during the course of the revelation, what was revealed to him, but soon, while still at Mecca, he abandoned this habit of simultaneous repeating, but began to remain silent till the end of the state of revelation, and then he communicated the message of God to his secretaries to note (as is mentioned in the Quran 75/16) : "Stir not thy tongue herewith to hasten it; upon Us the putting together and the reading thereof". And again (20/114) : "And hasten not with the Quran ere its revelation hath been perfected unto thee and say : my Lord, increase me in knowledge". And when the Prophet returned to his normal state, he used to dictate to his scribes the portion of the Quran which had just been received by him, in order to publish it amongst the Muslims and to multiply the copies (cf. § 50 and 53 *supra*). In his *al-Mab'ath wa'l-Maghazi* (MS of Fes), Ibn Is'haq reports: "Whenever part of the Quran was revealed to the Messenger of God, he first recited it among men, and then among women."

THE REVEALED BOOKS

145. God being the Lord of the earth as well as of the heavens, it is the duty of man to obey Him, more so because in His mercy, He sends His messengers for the benefit of man, God is the sovereign and the source of all law, spiritual as well as temporal. We have just spoken of the revelations and communications of the will of God to man. It is the collection and compilation of these revelations which constitute the Revealed Books.

146. The formula of the creed enunciated by the Prophet Muhammad speaks of the Books, and not merely of the Book which would refer to the Quran only. This tolerance is characteristic of his teaching. The Quran speaks of it in numerous passages. For instance (2/285): "Each one (of the Muslims) believeth in God and His angels and His books and His messengers,—(and says): We make no distinction between any of His messengers." Again (35/24) it declares: ". . and there is not a nation but a warner hath passed among them." And yet again (4/164, 40/78): "Verily We sent messengers before thee (O Muhammad), among them those of whom We have told thee, and some of them We have not told thee about." The Quran names and recognizes the scrolls of Abraham, the Torah of Moses, the Psalter of David and the Gospel of Jesus as the books revealed by God.

147. It is true that there is no trace today of the scrolls of Abraham. One knows the sad story of the Torah of Moses and how it was destroyed by Pagans several times. The same fate befell the Psalter. As for Jesus, he had not had the time

to compile or dictate what he preached; it is his disciples and their successors who gleaned his utterances and transmitted them to posterity in a number of recensions, of which at least 70 recensions or Gospels are known, and excepting four all are declared by the Church to be apocryphal, Be it what it may, it is a dogma for every Muslim to believe not only in the Quran, but also in the collections of the Divine revelations of pre-Islamic epochs. The Prophet of Islam has not named Buddha, nor Zoroaster nor the founders of Indian Brahminism. So the Muslims are not authorised to affirm categorically the Divine character, for instance, of Avesta or of the Hindu Vedas; yet they cannot formally reject either the possibility of the Vedas and Avesta having been in their origin based on Divine revelations, or of having suffered a fate similar to that of the Pentateuch of Moses. The same is true in connection with what appertains to China, Greece and other lands.

MESSENGERS OF GOD (PROPHETS)

148. An angel brings the message of God to a chosen man, and it is this latter who is charged with its communication to the people. In Quranic terminology, this human agent of the message is differently called: *nabi* (prophet), *rasool* (messenger), *mursal* (envoy), *bashir* (announcer), *nadhir* (warner), etc.

149. Prophets are men of great piety, and models of good behaviour, spiritual as well as temporal and social. Miracles are not necessary for them (although history attributes miracles to all of them and they themselves have always affirmed that it is not they but God who did that); it is their teaching alone which is the criterion of their veracity.

150. According to the Quran, there were certain prophets who had received the revelation of Divine Books, and there were others who did not receive new Books but had to follow the Books revealed to their predecessors. The Divine messages

do not disagree on fundamental truths, such as the Oneness of God, the demand for doing good and abstaining from evil, etc., yet they may differ as to the rules of social conduct in accordance with the social evolution attained by a people. If God has sent successive prophets, it is a proof that previous directions had been abrogated and replaced by new ones, and, except for these latter, certain of the old rules tacitly or explicitly retained.

151. Certain prophets had been charged with the Divine mission of educating members of a single house (tribe or clan), or of a single race, or of a single region; others had vaster missions, embracing the entire humanity and extending over all times.

152. The Quran has made express mention of certain prophets, such as Adam, Enoch, Noah, Abraham, Ishmael, Isaac, Jacob, David, Moses, Salih, Hud, Jesus, John the Baptist, and Muhammad, but the Quran is explicit that there have been others also before Muhammad, he being the seal and the last of the messengers of God.

THE ESCHATOLOGY

153. The Prophet Muhammad has also demanded belief in the doomsday. Man will be resuscitated after his death, and God will judge him on the basis of his deeds during the life of this world, in order to reward his good actions and punish him for the evil ones. One day our universe will be destroyed by the order of God, and then after a certain lapse of time, He Who had created us first, would bring us back to life. Paradise as a reward, and Hell as a punishment are but graphic terms to make us understand a state of things which is beyond all notions of our life in this world. Speaking of it, the Quran (32:17) says: "No soul knoweth what is kept hid from them —of joy as a reward for what they used to do." Again (9/72): "God promiseth to the believers, men and women, Gardens

underneath which rivulets flow, wherein they will abide—blessed dwellings in Gardens of Eden—and the pleasure of God is grander still; that is the supreme triumph". So this pleasure on His part is over and above even the Gardens of Eden. In yet another passage of the Quran (10/26) we read: "For those who do good is what is the best, and more (thereto)". Al-Bukhari, Muslim etc. report, that the Prophet used to refer to this verse saying that, after Paradise there would be the vision of God, ultimate reward of the pious. As far as Paradise is concerned, an oft-quoted utterance of the Prophet Muhammad is: "God says: I have prepared for My pious slaves (-men) things in Paradise the like of which no eye has ever seen, nor ear ever heard, nor even human heart (mind) ever thought of". As to what is beyond Paradise, Bukhari, Muslim, Tirmidhi and other great sources record an important saying of the Prophet: "When the people meriting Paradise will have entered it, God will tell them: 'Ask Me what else can I add to you?' People will wonder, having been honoured, given Paradise and saved from Hell, and will not know what to ask. Thereupon God will remove the veil, and nothing would be lovelier than gazing upon the Lord." (In another version, instead of 'veil'; 'hijab', 'the garb of grandeur' *Rida-al-Kibriya* is used.) In other words, the opportunity of contemplating God would be the highest and the real reward of the Believer, this for those who are capable of understanding and appreciating the abstract notion of the other World. It is in the light of this authoritative interpretation that one should read what the Quran and the Hadith unceasingly describe for the common man with regard to the joys of Paradise and the horrors of Hell in terms which remind us of our surroundings in this world: there are gardensl and rivulets or canals in Paradise, there are young and beautifu girls, there are carpets and luxurious garments, pearls, precious stones, fruits, wine, and all that man would desire. Similarly, in hell there is fire, there are serpents, boiling water and other tortures, there are parts extremely cold; and in spite of these sufferings, there will be no death to get rid of. All this is easily explained when one thinks of the vast majority of men, of the masses, to whom the Divine message is addressed. It is necessary to speak to every one according to his capacity of understanding and of intelligence. One day, when the Prophet Muhammad was speaking to a company of the faithful about Paradise and its pleasures (including its flying horses), a Bedouin rose and put the question: "Will there be camels also?" The Prophet smiled and gently replied: "There will be everything that one would desire." (Ibn Hanbal and Tirmidhi). The Quran speaks of Paradise and Hell simply as a means of persuading the average man to lead a just life and to march in the path of truth; it attaches no important to details whether they describe a place or a state of things? That should not interest us either; a Muslim believes in them, without asking: "how?"

154. It goes without saying that Paradise will be eternal: once meriting it, there would be no question of being ejected from it. The Quran assures (15:48): "Pain will not touch them, and there is no expulsion from it." Some would enter it forthwith, others would suffer longer or shorter periods of detention in Hell, before meriting Paradise. But the question is whether Hell is eternal for the unbelievers? The opinions of the Muslim Theologians have differed on the points although a great majority of them affirm, on the basis of the Quranic verses (4:48, 4:116) that God may pardon every sin and every crime except disbelief in God, and that the punishment that would be meted out for this last sin would be eternal. Others opine that even the punishment of disbelief may one day terminate by the grace of God. These theologians deduce their opinions, also from certain verses of the Quran (11:107, etc.). We need not pursue further this discussion here, but hope God's unlimited mercy.

PREDESTINATION AND FREE-WILL

155. In his expose, the Prophet Muhammad has lastly demanded the belief that the determination (*qadr*) of all good

and evil is from God. Does this phrase signify that everything is predestined for man, or does the statement merely imply that the qualification of good and evil in a given act depends on God? In other words, nothing is good or evil in itself, but it is so only because God has declared it to be such; and man has to do nothing but observe it.

156. Here is in fact a dilemma for the theologian. If we declare that man is responsible for his acts, it would be incompatible with the predestination of his acts. Similarly, if we declare that man is free in his acts, this would imply that God has neither power over nor the knowledge of what man is going to do in his worldly life. The two alternatives create an embarrassment. One would like to attribute to God not only justice, but also omnipotence and omniscience. The Prophet Muhammad ridicules this discussion, which will ever remain inconclusive: and he has formally ordered his adherents not to engage in it, adding: "people before you have been led astray by this discussion". He recognizes for God, in all respect and reverence, the attribute of omnipotence-omniscience, and affirms also that man shall be held responsible for his acts. He does not want to tie up one of these things with the other. In a way, he relegates this discussion to the level of the futility of knowing whether the egg came first into existence or the hen?

157. Moreover good and evil are but relative terms. A tiger hunts a rabbit for food. What is good (sustenance) for one is evil (death) for the other. That is why the evil that seems to reach us is on account of our own nature, which merits or requires that "evil". That is also why it is for God to determine, for whom a given act is good and for whom evil. Furthermore it should be remembered that the conception of "responsibility" is a this-worldly thing, whereas the "Divine reward and punishment" belong to the other-worldly matters. We are shocked only when we relegate them both to the same level. To do so would be a fallacy.

158. Let us remember that it is this double belief in the omnipotence of God and the absolute individual responsibility of man, which rouses a Muslim to action, even as it enables him to support easily an unavoidable misfortune. Far from creating in him an immobility, it gives him a dynamism. We have to refer to the exploits of the early Muslims, who were the best practitioners of the teaching of the Prophet, in order to convince ourselves of the truth of this statement.

CONCLUSION

159. This is a resume practically of all that a Muslim has to believe. The whole formula of the creed is succinctly summed up in the two expressions : "There is no God if not God Himself, and Muhammad is the messenger and slave - servant of God." This would serve to remind us that Islam is not only a belief, but also a practice, spiritual as well as temporal. It is in fact a complete code of human life.

CHAPTER V

Devotional Life and Religious Practices of Islam

IT is the aim of Islam, to offer a complete code of life, without neglecting any one or the various domains of human activity. Its objective is a co-ordination of all these aspects. The concern for "centralization" is displayed in the fact that all Islamic practices touch simultaneously the body and soul. Not only do temporal practices acquire sacred moral character, when they conform to Divine prescriptions, but the spiritual practices also possess a material utility. The rules of conduct, whether spiritual or temporal, emanate from the one and the same source, the Quran, which is the Word of God The ineluctable result is that according to the Islamic terminology the *imam* (supreme director or leader of the Muslim world) signifies not only the leader of the service of prayer in the mosque, but also the head of the Muslim State.

161. In a well-known saying, the Prophet Muhammad has defined the faith (*Iman*), the submission (*Islam*) and the best method (*Ihsan*), leading thereto. In the preceding chapter the Beliefs have been explained. For elucidating the subject under discussion, it would admirably suit our purpose to quote and comment on what he has said on the second point. He declared : Submission to God (*Islam*) is, that one should celebrate the services of worship, observe annual fasting, perform the *Hajj* (pilgrimage) and pay the zakat-taxes.

SERVICE OF WORSHIP

162. "Worship is the pillar of religion" is a saying of the Prophet Muhammad. The Quran speaks of it more than a

hundred times, and calls it variously *salat* (inclination), *du'a* (prayer, appeal), *dhikr* (remembering), *tasbih* (glorification), *inabah* (returning, attachment), etc.

163. In its concern for creating an atmosphere of the sovereignty of God on earth, Islam has prescribed five services of worship daily: one should pray when one rises—and one should rise early—again early in the afternoon, late in the afternoon, at sunset, and at night before one goes to bed. This requires abandoning, during the few minutes spent in each service of worship, all material interests, in order to provide proof of one's submission and gratitude to God our Creator. That applies to every adult, man or woman.

164. The service of early afternoon is transformed every Friday into a weekly congregational service, with greater solemnity, in which the *imam* of the locality delivers also a sermon before prayer. Islam has instituted two annual feasts: one at the end of the fasting month, and the other on the occasion of the pilgrimage to Mecca. These two feasts are celebrated by two special services or worship, in addition to the daily five. Thus, early in the morning people assemble for a collective service of prayer, after which the *imam* delivers a sermon. Another service of prayer, of restricted obligation, is held for the deceased before burial.

165. Speaking of the hidden meaning and mysterious effects of the service of worship, the great mystic Waliullah ad-Dihlawi says:

"Know that one is sometimes transported, quick as lightning, to the Holy Precincts (of the Divine Presence), and finds one's self attached, with the greatest possible adherence, to the threshold of God. There descend on this person the Divine transfigurations (*tajalli*) which dominate his soul. He sees and feels things which the human tongue is incapable of describing. Once this state of light passes away, he returns to his previous condition, and finds himself tormented by the loss of such an ecstasy. Thereupon he tries to rejoin that which has escaped him, and adopts the condition of this lowly world which would be nearest to a state of absorption in the knowledge of the Creator. This is a posture of respect, of devotion, and of an almost direct conversation with God, which posture is accompanied by appropriate acts and words . . . Worship consists essentially of three elements: (1) humility of heart (spirit) consequent on a feeling of the presence of the majesty and grandeur of God, (2) recognition of this superiority (God) and humbleness (of man) by means of appropriate words, and (3) adoption by the organs of the body, of postures of necessary reverence . . . To show our honour to somebody we stand up, with a fulsome concentration of attention, turning our faces, towards him. Even more respectful is the state when we bend and bow our heads in reverence . . . Still greater respect is displayed by laying down the face — which reflects in the highest degree, one's ego and self-conscious-ness — so low that it touches the ground in front of the object of reverance . . . As a man can reach the top of his spiritual evolution only gradually, it is evident that such an ascension must pass through all the three stages; and a perfect service of worship would have three postures, Standing up, Bowing down, and Prostrating by laying the head on the ground in the presence of the Almighty; and all this is performed for the necessary evolution of the spirit so that one might feel truly the sublimity of God and the humbleness of man." (*Hujjatullah al Balighah*, vol. I, Secrets of Worship).

166. In a passage (22:18), the Quran says: "Hast thou not seen that before God are prostrate whosoever is in the heavens and whosoever is on the earth, and the sun, and the moon, and the stars, and the hills, and the trees, and the beasts, and many of mankind.. ?" Again (17/44) : "The seven

heavens and the earth and all that is therein praise Him, and there is not a thing but hymneth His praise; but ye understand not their praise..." The Islamic service of worship combines in fact the forms of worship of all creatures. The heavenly bodies (sun, moon, stars) repeat their act of rising and setting (like rak'at after rak'at of the service); the mountains remain standing (like the first act in the service); the beast remain bowed and bent (like the ruku' in the service); as for trees, we see that they get their food through their roots, which are their mouths and this in their words signifies that the trees are perpetually prostrate (like the sajdah or prostration in the Islamic service of worship). Further, according to the Quran (8/11) one of the principle functions of the water is to purify (and compare the need of ablutions for the service). Another passage (13/13) says : "The thunder hymneth His praise," and this makes us think of the loud pronunciation of Allaahu akbar, so often repeated during the service, even if we disregard the loud recitation of the Quran during the service which is done during certain services and not in others. The birds flying in flocks worship God (Quran 24/41), as also Muslims do when celebrating their congregational service. Just as the shadow stretches and shortens in the course of its daily life, (which is its particular way of submission to and worship of God, cf. Quran 13/15, 16/48), so too the human worshipper stretches or shortens himself while standing, bowing prosterating or sitting in the course of the service. (See pictures of the different postures of Muslim worship in the last chapter. The above-mentioned acts of different creatures have been adapted and assimilated therein, adding thereto what is particular to man and not found in other creatures). (cf § 167, infra.)

166/a. It may be recalled that the Islamic word for the service of worship is 'ibaadah, which is from the same root as abd, i.e., slave. In other words, worship is what the slave does, the service the master desires of him. God demands of the mountains to remain standing, of beasts and birds to remain bent, and of plants to remain prostrate before Him, that is their service, their worship. To everyone what suits him and what his Lord desires of him. Of course to man also what becomes of him as a rational being, as the foremost of the creatures, as the vicegerent of God.

166/b. Ablution or ritual washing and physically being clean is a pre-requisite of the validity of a Service of Worship, as will be detailed later (§ 549 ff). A saying of the Prophet (cf Muslim, *Sahih*, II, N°4, 32, 41) has nicely brought into relief its significance. For this ritual purification one has to wash the hands, the mouth, the nose, the face, the arms, the head, the ears and the feet. Washing them is not merely the outward cleanliness; it is a repentance for the past and a resolution for the future. Repentance washes away the past sins, and resolution through invoking the help of God concerns what is yet to come in life; and this relates to our principal organs of mischief. The hand attacks, the mouth talks, the nose smells, the face or presence abuses the prestige and exerts influence and pressure, the arms hold, the head thinks and plots, the ears hear, the feet march in the way of evil, forbidden by God. Not to speak of the sexual sin, from which one gets rid even before beginning the ablutions, and one has to cleanse oneself in the W.C. This symbolical and mystical aspect or purification is evident in the formulas of invocations which accompany washing each organ. In the W.C. we say : "O God, purify my heart from hypocrisy, and my sex from shameful acts and fornication." One begins the formulation of the intention of the ablution by saying: "Praise be to God Who has made water pure and purifying." When washing the face, one prays to God: "Brighten my face on the Doomsday, and do not darken it", for washing the arms: "Employ me in good deeds and not in evil one, give me my Rolls on Doomsday in my right hand and not in my left, and facilitate me my reckoning and do not make it difficult;" for the head: "Teach me useful knowledge;" for the ears : "Let me listen to Thy word and the word of Thy messenger;" and for the feet : "Make my feet firm on the path when crossing over the Hell, and do not let them stumble on the day when the feet of Thy friends will remain firm and the feet of Thy enemies will stumble."

167. The five daily services were made obligatory for Muslims on the occasion of the ascension of the Prophet (mi'raj). The Prophet Muhammad has moreover declared that the service of worship of a believer in his own ascension, in which he is raised into the presence of God. These are no empty words; let us look at what a Muslim does in his worship. First of all, he stands up, holds up his hands, and proclaims t "God alone is great"; thus he renounces all except God, and submits himself to the will of his Lord alone. After having hymned and recalled the merits of God, he feels so humble before the Divine majesty, that he bows low and puts down his head as a sign of reverence, proclaiming "Glory to my Lord Who alone is Majestic." Then he stands erect to thank God for having guided him, and in his mind of minds he is struck so much by the greatness of God that he feels impressed to prostrate himself and to place his forehead on the ground in all humility, and declare "Glory to my Lord Who alone is High". He repeats these acts so that the body gets accustomed to the spiritual exercise and gradually becomes worthier and worthier so as to be lifted from the world of matter and pass through the heavenly atmosphere, and enter the presence of God. There he salutes God, and receives the answer to his greetings. In fact, he employs for the purpose the very formulae that were used during the Ascension of the Prophet Muhammad, when he exchanged greetings with God : "The blessed and purest of greetings to God — Peace with thee, O Prophet, and the mercy and blessings of God — Peace with us and with all the pious servants of God." Without material, idol-like symbols, the believer travels, so to say, towards the transcendent God, on a spiritual journey, which, in certain communities, is termed "communion."

168. Such is the spiritual significance of the service of worship. As for its material utilities, these again are numerous. It assembles five times daily the inhabitants of a locality, provides the opportunity of relaxation for some minutes in the course of the monotonous duties of individual avocations, and gathers the highest as well as the lowest personalities of the place in perfect equality (for it is the chief of the locality, who is to conduct the prayer; and in the metropolis, at the central mosque, it is the head of the State himself who performs this duty). Thus one meets not only other members of the community, but also the responsible functionaries of the place and approaches them directly without formality or hindrance. The social aspect of the service of prayer is that the believer feels around him the sovereignty of God, and lives in a state of military discipline. At the call of the *muezzin*, all rush to the place of assembly, stand in serried ranks behind the leader, doing acts and carrying on movements in common with others, in perfect uniformity and co-ordination. Further, the faithful, in all parts of the globe, turn their faces, during the service of worship, towards the same focal point, the Ka'bah or the House of God in Mecca. This reminds them of the unity of the world community of Muslims, without distinction of class, race, or region.

169. The preferable and more formal way of worship is the congregational service. In the absence of such a possibility, or lacking adequate facility, one prays alone and individually, man or woman. The five prayers of the day mean rather a minimum duty of passing about 24 minutes, during 24 hours, in the presence and remembrance of God; but the believer must actually remember God, every instant, in weal and in woe, at work or in bed or while engaged in any occupation. The Quran (3 : 190-91) says : "... men of understanding, who remember God standing, sitting, and reclining, and consider the creation of the heavens and the earth, (and say) Our Lord ! Thou didst not create this in vain..." God has made

the universe subservient to the use and benefit of man; but the enjoyment must be accompanied by recognition (gratitude) and obedience, and not by rebellion against God and injustice against other fellow-beings.

170. It may here be mentioned, that at the very moment when the service of prayer was instituted, the Quranic verse (2/286) was revealed : "God tasketh not a soul beyond its scope." It is the intention and will that counts in the eyes of God, and not the quantity or the exterior method of accomplishing a thing. If a devout man honestly believes that he is unable to perform five times daily the service of prayer, let him observe it four times, thrice, twice or even a single time every day, according to his opportunities and circumstances, and the duration of the hindrance. The essential point is that one should not forget one's spiritual duty in the midst of material and mundane pre-occupations. Such a reduction is permitted in abnormal conditions, such as when one is ill and has fits of unconsciousness, or unavoidable duties in the service of God as we infer from the practice of the Prophet himself. In fact it is reported that in the course of the battle of Khandaq, it happened that the Prophet himself performed the *zuhr*, *'asr*, *maghrib* and *'ishaa* services, all these four late in the night, for the enemy had not allowed a single moment's respite during the day to attend to prayer. (Maqrizi, *Imta'*, I, 233). This means twice the prayer during the day. Again on the authority of Ibn 'Abbas, it is reported (see Bukhari, Muslim, Tirmidhi, Ibn Hanbal, Malik, and particularly *Sahih* of Muslim, kitab as-salaat, bab al-jam' bain as-salatain fi'l-hadr, No. 49, 50, 54) that "sometimes the Prophet combined *zuhr-'asr* and *maghrib-'ishaa* having neither fear (of enemy) nor (inconvenience of) travel; adding : and the Prophet wanted thereby that there should be no inconvenience for his community." This narration implies thrice the prayer during the day. Evidently all depends on the conscience of the individual faithful who is personally responsible to God Whom

one cannot dupe and from Whom one can conceal nothing
There is again the question of the timings. We know that
there is a great difference in the risings and settings of the sun
between normal (equatorial-tropical) countries and the regions
situated beyond and extending to the two poles. Al-Biruni
(cf. *al-Jamahir*) has observed that at the poles the sun
remains set for six months continually, and then rises to shine
continuously for six months (excepting the two days of the
equinox) The jurist-theologians of Islam affirm in general
that the hours at 45° parallel remain valid upto 90° parallel,
i.e., upto the poles; and in the regions, comprised between 45°
and 90°, one is to follow the movement of the clock and not
that of the sun. This applies to worship as well as fasts and
other like duties.

171. Women are exempted from prayer-services during
their monthly indisposition and accouchement.

THE FAST

172. The second religious duty of a believer is the fasting
for one month every year. One must abstain during every day
of the month of Ramadan from eating, drinking and smoking
(including inoculations and injections) from dawn to sunset in
the equatorial and tropical countries (and for an equivalent
period in regions situated far away from the centre of the
globe, calculated on the basis of the hours at 45° parallel, as
we have just mentioned). Of the sick we shall speak later on,
§ 174. It goes without saying that one must likewise abstain
from thinking of carnal and other pleasures, incompatible with
the spiritual regimen. It is quite a rigorous discipline, which
may appear very difficult to the adherents of other religions;
yet even the new converts get accustomed to it very soon if
they show good will, and inclination as is evidenced by the
experience of centuries.

173. The fast extends over a whole month; and as is well
known, it is the purely lunar month which counts in Islam. The

result is that the month of fasting, Ramadan, rotates turn by turn through all the seasons of the year, autumn, winter, spring and summer; and one gets accustomed to these privations in the burning heat of summer as well as the chilling cold of winter, and one undergoes all this as a spiritual discipline, in obedience to God. At the same time one derives from fasting temporal advantages connected with hygienic, military training, development of will power, among others, even as those resulting from the services of worship. More than anybody else, it is the soldiers who have, during sieges and other occasions of a war to support the privations of food and drink and still continue their duty to defence. So the most stupid ruler or commander-in-chief would be the one who hinders his militia from fasting in the month of Ramadan. But it must be repeated that the aim is, essentially and chiefly a religious practice and a spiritual exercise enabling proximity to God. If one fasts for temporal motives only — under the prescription of a doctor for instance — he will be far from accomplishing his religious duty, and will not benefit spiritually at all.

174. As in the case of prayer, women do not require to fast during their feminine indispositions, yet with this difference that the defaulting days are to be made up later by an equal number of days of fasting. The same applies to the sick. As to the very old, he need not fast, yet if he has means he must feed a poor for each day of the fasts of Ramadan.

175. It may be recalled that the Prophet forbade fasts extending over several days continuously (for 48 hours or 72 hours for instance), over the whole year, or during the whole life, even to those who longed to do so in their zeal for spiritual practices to obtain increased benefit. He remarked : "Thou hast obligations even with regard to thine own self." In addition to the obligatory fast of Ramadan, one may fast, as a work of supererogation, if one likes, from time to time; and for

this voluntary fast, the Prophet has recommended fasting for two days at a time. From the medical point of view, one notes that fasting eternally becomes a habitude, which does not produce the same effect as fasting at intervals. To fast for less than a month does not produce great effect, and a fast for more than 40 days becomes a habitude.

175/a. It is a myth to say that fasting, in the sense of the privation of food and drink, in a cold climate is contrary to the requirements of human health. Biological observations show that wild beasts get practically nothing to eat especially when it snows. They sleep or otherwise pass their time "fasting", and get rejuvenated on the approach of spring. The same is true of trees also, in winter they lose completely their leaves, and sleep, and are not even irrigated; and after a few months of "fasting", they are rejuvenated in spring and get more vigorous than ever, as everybody can see in their luxuriant new foliage and blossoming. In fact like all animal organs, the digestive apparatus also require rest. Fast is the only conceivable method for it. Now-a-days a new school of medicine has come into existence in all the western countries, which treats, particularly chronic diseases, by short or long periods of fasting.

175/b. It is an antique notion in human society to offer the tithe of one's gains to God; the tithe of the harvest is an example. Fasting is offering the tithe of our meals to God. A parallel notion (endorsed by the Quran 6 / 160 : "Whoso bringeth a good deed will receive tenfold the like thereof") is that a good deed is rewarded ten times as much by God. That explains the saying of the Prophet : "Whoever fasts the month of Ramadan and six more days in the following month, Shauwal, is as if he has fasted the whole year." In fact the lunar year employed in Islam, has 355 days, and the lunar month sometimes 29 and sometimes 30 days. So a Muslim fasts every year for 35 or 36 days, which is worth tenfold, i.e., 350 or 360 days, the average being 355 which is the number of the days in the lunar year.

176. The mystics observe, that an ebullition of animal nature hinders the perfection of the human spirit. In order to subjugate the body to the spirit, it is necessary to break the force of the body and increase that of the spirit. It has been found that nothing is as efficacious for this purpose as hunger, thirst, renunciation of carnal desires and the control of the tongue, the heart (mind) with its thought and other organs. One of the aspects of individual perfection is the sub-ordination of animal nature to reason and the spirit. Nature sometimes rebels, and its behaviour at other times is one of submissiveness. One therefore needs the practice of hard exercises, such as fasting, in order to keep in check animality. If one commits sins, penitence and mortification through fasting may bring solace and purify the soul, even as they fortify the will so as not to indulge again in vices. It has also been remarked that neither eating nor drinking is a trait of the angels; and in imposing this regimen, man makes himself resemble more and more the angels; and since his actions are intended to conform to the behests of God, in the result, he approaches nearer to Him and obtains His pleasure ; and that is the ultimate aim of man.

THE HAJJ

177. *Hajj* literally means a travel (i.e towards God) as also an effort to dominate something (the self, in this connection). Conventionally this term is translated as pilgrimage, although it is far from giving the exact significance of the word *hajj*. This is the third of the religious duties of a Muslim. It is obligatory on every adult, man or woman, to go once in his or her life-time to Mecca in order to perform there the great *Effort* for annihilating the ego (*fana'*), i.e., assimilating one's self with the will of God. Those who do not possess the material means of travel, are exempted from it. But which Muslim would not collect, little by little, the necessary amount for being one day able to visit the centre of his religion, the Ka'bah or the House of God? The Quran (3 : 96) does not

exaggerate when it says that this is the oldest House in the world dedicated by mankind to God and to the cult of monotheism. If one were to think only of Abraham— who according to the Islamic tradition, was but the restorer of the edifice erected originally by Adam — it would still be older than the temple of Jerusalem, constructed by Solomon. No other place of worship older than the Ka'bah of Mecca, is known to be still functioning.

178. The rites of the Hajj may briefly be noted: At the borders of the sacred territory, around Mecca, one puts off the ordinary dress, and puts on by way of a religious uniform two sheets of cloth-a loin cloth and a shoulder cover, a dress required only of men, not of women. He is bare-headed, and one tries to forget one's self during the several days of the Hajj. He goes to 'Arafat, in the suburbs of Mecca, to pass there the day in meditation. Towards evening, he returns, passes the night at Muzdalifah, and early next morning arrives at Mina which is on the outskirts of Mecca. There he passes three days, during which he lapidates Satan every morning, sacrifices a goat, pays a short visit to the Ka'bah for performing the ritual sevenfold circumambulation and running between the hills of Safa and Marwah in front of the Ka'bah. The symbolic background may also be described here :

179. After their fall from Paradise, Adam and Eve were separated and lost. They searched for each other, and by the grace of God met together at 'Arafat. In gratitude to God, the descendants of Adam and Eve turn to Him, make an effort to forget themselves and be assimilated with the Divine Presence, with a view to entreat His pardon for their shortcomings in the past and His help for the future.

180. As to the lapidation of Satan, it may be recalled that when Abraham claimed to love God above everything else, God demanded of him as a proof the immolation of his beloved son. To add to this trial, Satan went first to Abraham to

dissuade him from his resolution — and they say that this happened at Mina—but Abraham chased Satan away every time by pelting stones at him. Then he went to Hagar, and lastly to Ishmael himself; each one of them did the same. So one repeats the acts symbolically, and resolves to fight diabolic temptations.

181. The visit to the "House of God" is self-explanatory. To give evidence of obedience, one goes there with respect and in humility. It is a very old custom to circumambulate a thing for showing one's readiness to sacrifice one's self for the object of devotion and care and love.

181/a. The Black Stone requires a particular mention on account of the many misunderstandings on its score. It is not a meteorite, but a black stone. Its practical importance is to show the starting point of the circumambulation, and by its colour it is conspicuous in the building. Secondly, this stone is not worshipped, nor do Muslims even prostrate in the direction of this stone, prostration being done towards any and every part of the building of the Ka'bah, and more often than not one turns to directions other than the Black Stone (al-Hajar al-Aswad). It may be recalled that when the Qaramitah ravaged Mecca in 318 H./930, they carried the Black Stone to their country as booty and it remained there for 21 long years. In the course of this absence of the Black Stone, no Muslim turned to the place where it was kept (in 'Uman), but continued to turn towards the Ka'bah in Mecca. Even the building of the Ka'bah is not essential: if it is demolished, for instance for repairs and new construction, Muslims turn to the same spot, whether the Ka'bah with its Black Stone is there or not. As said, the practical importance of the Black Stone is that it indicates the point from which the circumambulation begins and at which it ends; but it has a symbolical significance too. In the Hadith, the Prophet has named it the "right hand of God" (yamin-Allah), and for a purpose. In fact one poses there one's hand to conclude the pact, and God obtains there our pact of allegiance and submission. In the Quranic terminology, God is the king, and He has not only His treasures and His armies, but also His realm; in the realm there is a metropolis *(Ummal qurra)* and in the metropolis naturally a palace (Bait-Allah, House of God). If a subject wants to testify to his loyalty, he has to go to the royal palace and conclude personally the pact of allegiance. The right hand of the invisible God must be visible symbolically. And that is the al-Hajar al-Aswad, the Black Stone in the Ka'bah.

182. As to the act of covering seven times the ground between Safa and Marwah, it is related that when Abraham left his wife Hagar and the suckling Ishmael in the desolate and un-inhabited site of Mecca, the provision of water was soon exhausted. So Hagar ran hither and thither, driven by maternal affection, to search for some water for the thirst-stricken baby; and then the spring Zamzam gushed forth. So one repeats this act in the same place where Hagar did it, to pay homage to maternal love and in thanksgiving for the mercy of God.

183. The social aspect is not less striking. The world brotherhood of Muslims manifests itself there in the most vivid manner. The believers, without distinction of race, language, birthplace or even class feel the obligation to go there, and to mix with one another in a spirit of fraternal equality. They camp together in the desert, and perform their religious duties in common. For several days, at fixed hours, they march, make a halt, pass the night under tents or in bivouac,—all this, to an extent greater even than the five daily prayer-services, trains the soldier of God for a life of discipline.

183/a. When the Prophet Muhammad performed his own hajj, a few months before his demise, he uttered then from above the *Hill of Mercy* (Jabal ar-Rahman) a sermon which constitutes the charter of Humanity in Islam. Some 140,000 Muslims had come that year from all parts of Arabia, to listen to this testament of their Prophet, which may be analysed as follows: He reminded the basic elements of Islam. viz., belief in the One God with no icons or other material representation; Equality of all Muslims without discrimination on account of race or class, and there being no superiority to one over any other except by the individual excellence in the matter of piety and fear of God; Sacrosanct character of the three fundamental rights of each and every human being concerning his person, his property and his honour; Prohibition of transaction on interest, be the interest big or small; Prohibition of vendetta and private justice, obligation of treating well the womenfolk; Constant re-distribution and circulation of the private wealth to avoid its accumulation in the hands of a few (by means of the law of obligatory inheritance, restrictions on wills and prohibition of interest etc.); and Emphatic restatement that the Divine Revelation alone should be the source of law for our conduct in all walks of life:—The pilgrims are made to hear this same sermon every year, recited from above the same sacred Hill of Mercy, at 'Arafaat.

184. There is a reason to believe that a pre-Islamic practice was continued, at least in the early generations of Muslims, during the Hajj festivities: Profiting by the occasion provided by such a vast assembly, an annual literary congress was organized, where poets "published" their new compositions, orators made harangues before the spell-stricken masses to demonstrate their talents, professional wrestlers fascinated the spectators, and traders brought merchandises of all sorts. Caliph 'Umar gave it a most salutary administrative character. For this was an occasion for him to hold the sessions of an appeal court against his governors and commanders as also of public consultation on important projects in view. Let us recall once again, that in Islam the sacred and the profane, the spiritual and the temporal live in co-existence and even in harmonious collaboration.

THE ZAKAT-TAX

185. In modern times, the man in the street understands by zakat a certain percentage of his hoarded cash which is to

be given to the poor every year. But in the Quran, in the Hadith and in the practice of the early centuries of Islam the zakat (also called *sadaqat* and *haqq*)° meant all sorts of tax perceived by the Muslim State on its Muslim subjects: tax on agricultural product, on sub-soil exploitation, on commercial capital, on herds of domesticated animals lying on public pastures, on hoarded cash, etc. In the beginning all these taxes were paid directly to the government, but later, during his caliphate, 'Uthman decided that Muslims could spend directly the tax on the hoarded cash to its beneficiaries prescribed by the Quran (9:60) without the intermediary of the government.

185/a. The Quran (4/5) recognizes that wealth is the basis and the essential means of the subsistence of humanity. Therefore it should not be surprising that the payment of tax to the government has been raised by the Prophet to the dignity of an article of faith and one of the four fundamental rites of religion, along with prayer, fasting and pilgrimage. In Islam one does not pay a "tribute" to the chief of the city for his personal luxury and vanity, but one pays his dues, as a right connected with the collectivity, and more particularly in favour of the needy; and this for the purpose of "growing" and "purifying" one's self, as is the etymological sense of the term *zakat*. The Prophet Muhammad said: "The chief of a people is in fact their servant." In order to demonstrate the truth of this saying, and the absolute disinterestedness with which he had assumed the direction of his people— both as a spiritual guide and the head of the State — the Prophet formally declared that the revenues of the Muslim State, coming from

---

Chronologically speaking, the Quran has used the terms **nasib** *(6:136, 16:56) and* **haqq** *(6:141, 70:24) in the Meccan surats, and* **zakat** *(2:43 passim),* **infaq** *(2:267),* **sadaqat** *(9:60), and* **sadaqah** *(9:103) in the Madinan period. Later the word* **zakat***, to the exclusion of all else became the technical term used by the jurists.*

Muslim tax payers, were religiously forbidden to him and to all members of his tribe. If the head of the State does not abuse public confidence it follows that his subordinates cannot but be scrupulous in the performance of their duties.

186.   In the time of the Prophet and the Orthodox Caliphs, there was in the Muslim State no tax on Muslims other than the *zakat*. Far from being an almsgiving, it constituted a State-tax, an obligatory contribution fixed in quantity and in epoch, levied by sanctions and coercion from the recalcitrants In order better to inculcate the importance of these payments in the spirit of the faithful, the Prophet declared that the *zakat* was a religious duty and a Divine prescription, on par with belief in One God, the service of prayer, the fasting and the *Hajj*. If belief is a spiritual duty, and prayer, fasting and *Hajj* are bodily duties, the payment of the *zakat* is a fiscal duty. The jurists call it *'ibadat maliyah* (worship of God by means of property).   This is another proof — if there is need of one — of the fact that Islam co-ordinates the entire human life into a single whole, for the purpose of creating a harmonious equilibrium between the body and soul, without either favouring or treating with disdain these two elements of the human constitution.

187.   The Quran indifferently employs several terms to designate the tax: *zakat*, used in numerous verses which means both growth and purification.   It connotes that one must pay part of one's growing wealth in order to purify it; *sadaqat* (Quran 9/60) which signifies both truth and charity, implying that to be true to humanity, one must be charitable towards the less fortunate; and *haqq* (cf. 6/141) or right. If it is the right of others, it also entails a duty on the one who possesses,— rights and duties being correlative terms, and collaboration being the basis of all functioning of society.

188.   There are taxes on savings, on harvests, on merchandise, on herds of beasts pasturing in public meadows, on mines,

on maritime products, etc. The tariffs differ, yet all are called *zakat*, *sadaqat* and other synonymous names indifferently.

189. The tariffs of the time of the Prophet seem not to have been considered rigid and incapable of modification. We have seen above (§ 88) that the Prophet himself exempted the inhabitants of Ta'if from the zakat, (with some other examples for other regions also). The great caliph 'Umar reduced, as Abu 'Ubaid records, the duties on the importation of victuals in Madinah. In the life-time of the Prophet, there were occasions when he was obliged to appeal for extra-ordinary contributions, for instance, the defence of the country against foreign menace. This has enabled the jurists to conclude that the government may impose new provisional taxes, called *nawa'ib* (cf Sarakhsi, *Mabsut*, X, 21) or augment the rates, for the duration of the crisis. The silence of the Quran on the items and rates of taxation confirms the deduction of the jurists.

190. But the Quran speaks in detail of the expenditure of the State, and the principal heads of the government budget:

"The *sadaqat* (taxes levied on Muslims) are only for the needy and the poor, and those who work (for these State revenues), and those whose hearts are to be won, and for (freeing) the necks, and the heavily indebted, and in the path of God, and for the wayfarers;—a duty imposed by God, and God is the Knower, the Wise." (Q. 9:60).

As stated above, *sadaqat* and *zakat* are synonymous, meaning: What is perceived on a Muslim subject. What is perceived on a non-Muslim, such as kharaj, jizyah, ghanimah etc., is not included in zakat; the beneficiaries of the two also differ considerably.

191. While other legislators would rather prescribe rules for income, Quran, on the contrary, formulates the principles of State expenditure only. In the eight categories of beneficiaries

of zakat, of whom the verse speaks, it will be noted that there is no mention of the Prophet. Some remarks may be useful for the better understanding of the range and extent of this verse, which speaks of certain exclusive recipients:

192. According to so great an authority as the Caliph 'Umar, (cf. Abu Yusuf, *Kharaj*, ch. Fi man tajib alaihi al-jizyah), the needy *(fuqara)* are those of the Muslim community, and the poor *(masakin)*—almost an equivalent—are the poor among the non-Muslim inhabitants (the protected persons). (cf. § 353 *infra*). It is to be noted that the *sadaqat* do not include the revenues coming from non-Muslims, yet Islam includes them among the beneficiaries of the taxes paid by the Muslims.

193. Those who work for the revenues are the collectors, accountants, those in charge of the expenditure, controllers and auditors, which list practically embrace, the entire administration, both civil and military, of the State, in view of the fact that the beneficiaries of these revenues include practically all departments of administration.

194. Those whose hearts are to be won are of many kinds. The great jurist, Abu Ya'la al-Farra' (al-Ahkam as-Sultaniyah, p 116), points out: "As for those whose hearts are to be won, they are of four kinds: (1) those whose hearts are to be reconciled for coming to the aid of the Muslim; (2) those whose hearts are to be won in order that they might abstain from doing harm to Muslims; (3) those who are attracted towards Islam; and (4) those by whose means conversion to Islam becomes possible for the members of their tribes. It is lawful to benefit each and every one of these categories of 'those whose hearts are to be won, be they Muslims or polytheists."

195. By the term "freeing the necks," one has always understood the emancipation of the slaves and the ransoming of the prisoners of war made by an enemy. A word about the

slaves may not be out of place. No religion before Islam seems to have paid attention to the amelioration of the condition of the slaves. The Prophet of Islam forbade altogether the enslavement of the Arabs as Sarakhsi records; as to other peoples, the Quran (24:33) orders that if a well-behaving slave is prepared to pay off his value to his master, this latter cannot refuse the offer; in fact, he will be constrained by the court to grant his slave opportunities to earn and save the necessary amount for obtaining manumission (and be exempted from serving his master in the meanwhile). Further, as we have just seen, the Muslim government allots a sum in the annual budget for the aid of the slaves desiring emancipation. The object of permitting slavery in Islam is not the exploitation of an unfortunate fellow-being. Far from that, its aim is first to provide shelter to the prisoners of war who have lost everything, and for some reason or other are not repatriated; and secondly to educate them and give them the opportunity of acquiring culture in Islamic surroundings, under the government of God. Slaves are obtained only in legitimate war, waged by a government. Private razzias, kidnapping or even the sale of infants by their parents have no legal sanction whatsoever.

196. Aid to those-who are heavily indebted or have too great a charge may take different shapes We see Caliph 'Umar organizing a service of interest-free loans also

197. "In the path of God" includes every charitable cause; and the jurists have not hesitated to start with military equipment for the defence of Islam, since Islam struggles only and solely for the establishment of the Kingdom of God on earth.

198. As for the "wayfarers," one can help them not only by giving them hospitality, but also by ensuring them health and comfort, security of routes and adoption of measures for the well-being of such who have to pass through a place other than their own, whether they be natives or aliens, Muslims or non-Muslims.

CONCLUSION

198/a. After having detailed the facts concerning the religious practices, it may not be out of place to repeat, that the development of the whole and the co-ordination of all parts—is the basic principle governing the Islamic way of life. The Quran has repeated scores of times: "establish worship and pay zakat-tax." What can be a better manifestation of this unity of the body and soul than the fact that the worship of the One God and payment of the duty towards society are commanded in one and the same breath! The spiritual duties are not devoid of material advantages, and temporal duties have also their spiritual values; all are dependent again on the intentions and motives that govern one's performance of those duties.

CHAPTER VI

The Cultivation of Spiritual Life

ISLAM envisages for man a discipline for his life as a whole, material as well as spiritual. But there is no denying the fact that, owing to differences of individual temperaments, certain people would specialize in certain domains and not in others. Even if one were to concentrate on the spiritual side of one's existence, he still remains more or less attached to the other occupations of life, for his nourishment, for the sake of the society of which he is a member, and so on.

200. In his celebrated expose of his teaching on faith, submission and the best method of this submission, the Prophet Muhammad defined this last point in the following terms: "As to the embellishment (*ihsan*) of conduct, so render thy service unto God as if thou seest Him; even though thou dost not see Him, yet He seeth thee." This beatification, this best and most beautiful method of devotion or service unto God, is the spiritual culture of Islam. "Service unto God" is a most comprehensive term, and includes not merely the cult, but also relates to human conduct throughout life. The most cultured from the spiritual point of view, are those who abide most closely by the will of God, in all their acts.

201. Questions concerning this discipline form the subject matter of mysticism. The term mysticism has in Islam several synonyms: *Ihsan* (which we find also used in the above-mentioned expose of the Prophet), *Qurb* (or approaching God), *Tareeqat* (road, i.e., of the journey unto God), *Sulook* (journey, i.e., unto God), *Tasauwuf* (which etymologically means: to put on a woollen cloth). This last term is, curiously enough, the most currently used.

202. It is true that Muslim mystics—even as their counterparts in other civilizations—are not very eager to divulge their practices and their peculiarities to those outside the restricted circle of their disciples or conferers. This is not because there are scandalous secrets, but probably because of the fear that the man in the street may not understand why they undergo so much "useless" pain by renouncing the amenities of life; and also because the commoners do not believe in the personal experiences of the mystics. So the mystics think, it is better to conceal them from those who are unable to appreciate them Incidentally it also happens that if a thing is enshrouded in secrecy, it becomes so much the more cherished by those who ignore it, yet are in search of it.

203. Differences of individual temperaments have existed in the human race at all times. It goes to the credit of Islam, that it has discovered certain things which it could impose on each and everybody, irrespective of temperament, a minimum necessary to be shared and practised in common; and this minimum necessity touches not only the spiritual but simultaneously also the material needs. In order to understand it well, it may be noted that all are agreed that the best Muslims were the immediate disciples of the Prophet, namely his companions. A study of their lives shows that from the very outset they were possessed of a variety of temperaments. There was Khalid, a warrior, an intrepid soldier, on whom the Prophet was pleased, in admiration, to confer the title of "the Sword of God"; there were 'Uthman and Ibn 'Awf, who were rich merchants, and the Prophet had announced the good tidings that they belonged to the people of the Paradise; there was also Abu Dharr, who detested all property, and preferred an ascetic life of mortification. We may recall the Bedouin nomad, who had visited the Prophet one day, in order to learn what were the minimum duties to merit Paradise. The Prophet had replied: Faith in the One God, prayers five times a day, fast during the whole month of Ramadan, and the pilgrimage

and payment of zakat-tax if one had means thereto. The Bedouin embraced Islam, and burst forth: By God! I shall do nothing more and nothing less. When he departed, the Prophet remarked: Whoever wishes to see a man of Paradise, let him look at him! (cf. Bukhari and Muslim). Be it the warrior Khalid, or the wealthy 'Uthman, they never neglected the essential duties of Islam and its spirituality; similarly Abu Dharr, Salman, Abu'd-Darda' and others who liked asceticism, did not obtain permission from the Prophet to lead, for instance, lives of recluses, to fast perpetually, to get castrated in horror of carnal pleasures, etc. On the contrary, the Prophet enjoined on them to marry, and added: "Thou hast obligations even with regard to thy own body" (cf. Ibn Hanbal).' According to Islam, one does not belong to one's self, but to God; and it is not permitted to misuse the trust which God has reposed in us in the shape of our persons.

THE SUFFAH

204. In the grand mosque of Madinah, there was in the time of the Prophet a special portion, called *Suffah* somewhat away from the prayer hall. This was a centre of training and education, functioning under the personal supervision of the Prophet himself. A considerable number of Muslims occupied it. They devoted part of their time, during the day, to learn the Islamic way of life, not only in matters of man's relation with God, but also with other members of society. They also worked to earn their bare necessaries of life, so that they might not become parasites and a burden on others. During the night, they passed their time, like the best mystics, in the observance of supererogatory *(nafal)* prayers and in meditation on God. Call this institute a convent (a *Tekkeh*, a *Khanqah*) or by any other name, there is no doubt that the inmates of the *Suffah* were more attached to spiritual practices than to material avocations. Perhaps one will not be able to know the details of the practices which the Prophet had enjoined on these early Muslim mystics, which practices must have varied

according to the temperament and capacities of each individual. Yet the object being determined, there was enough liberty to select lawful means leading thereto. It may be recalled, by the way, that the Prophet once said: "Wisdom is the lost-property of the believer; wherever he should find it, he should recover it" (cf. Tirmidhi, Ibn Majah).

THE ESSENCE OF MYSTICISM

205. Through mysticism, Islam envisages a rectitude of beliefs, embellishment or beatification of the acts of devotion, taking the life of the Prophet as a model to be followed in all activities of life, the amelioration of personal conduct, and the accomplishment of duties imposed by Islam.

206. It has nothing to do with the power to know invisible things, with performing miracles, or imposing one's will on others by mysterious psychic means; not even with asceticism, mortification, seclusion, meditation and the consequent sensations (which may sometimes be means, yet not ends); or even with certain beliefs regarding the person of God (pantheism, etc.); much less with what the charlatans assert, that a mystic is above the Islamic law and the necessary minimum duties imposed by it.

207. For want of a better term, one might use the word "mysticism" which in Islam means the method of the best individual behaviour, i e , the means by which one acquires control over one's own self, the sincerity, the realization of the constant presence of God in all one's acts and thoughts, seeking to love God more and more.

208. In the Islamic teachings, there are certain "external" duties, such as prayer-service, fast, charity, abstaining from evil and wickedness, etc. There are also "internal" duties, such as faith, gratitude to God, sincerity and freedom from egoism. Mysticism is a training for this latter aspect of life. However, even the external duties are motivated for purifying the spirit,

which is the only means of eternal salvation. In general, the mystic develops by his spiritual practices certain of his faculties and talents, which appear to the commoners as miraculous; but the mystic does not seek them; he even despises them. To know invisible things, even if that becomes possible for certain persons by certain practices, is not desirable for the mystic; for these constitute the secrets of God and their premature divulgation is harmful to man in the long run. That is why the mystic does not utilize such powers even if he comes to acquire them; his aim remains always the purification of the spirit, in order to become more agreeable to the Lord. The perfect man is he who beautifies not only his outer but also his inner self, or—as mystics say—his body and his heart. For the external aspect, there is the *Fiqh* or body of Muslim law which consists of rules for the entire outer life, such as cult, contractual relations, penalties, etc. It is however the internal aspect which is the true subject matter of mysticism. The acts of prayer-service belong to the domain of the *Fiqh*, but sincerity and devotion are inner things, and belong to mysticism. Let us recall in this connection two verses of the Quran: "Successful indeed are the believers who are devout in their prayer-service" (23: 1-2), and "Lo, the hypocrites... ... ...when they stand up to worship they perform it languidly and in ostentation so as to be observed by men" (4:142). The good and bad services of worship, indicated therein, give us a clue to the understanding of what Islam requires of its adherents in all activities of life.

208/a. Islamic tradition reserves to the caliph or the head of the Muslim State not only politics (including administration of justice),but also cult, i.e. the outward practice of the religion, such as service of worship, fasting, pilgrimage. All this falls under the purview of the *Fiqh* (Muslim law) developed by the different schools (see *infra* § 563/a). In this realm, monopoly of power has been jealously imposed, although this concerns rather the less important part of our life. Sectarian differences exist among Muslims, since the death of the Prophet, as to who had the right to succeed to the Prophet in the exercise of the power regarding politics and cult. Let us leave the decision to God on Doomsday, and let us occupy ourselves with our future and the defence against the enemies of God. As to the inner life, which alone determines the salvation in the everlasting Hereafter, in this sphere there are no jealousies : several persons could and did succeed the Prophet simultaneously. If the Naqshbandiyah Order of mystics seeks its authority from the Prophet through Abu Bakr, the Qadriyah and Suhrawardiyah orders for instance, do the same through 'Ali, and all this among the Sunnis, to whom Abu Bakr alone was the immediate successor of the Prophet in the political field. This spiritual Realm, which unites Sunnis and Shi'as, is no vapid abstration : it has its own full-fledged administrative organisation. The existence of *abdal* and *autad* or spiritual governors and administrators is known on the authority of the Prophet himself, as we read by as early an author as Ibn Sa'd. A monograph of Suyuti has collected all the traditions of the Prophet on the subject of qutb, abdal and autad. One need not enter into details here.

PLEASURE OF GOD

209. The common folk desire that God should love them, in a sort of one way traffic, without their loving Him : that He should give them well-being without their obeying Him. The Quran (2/165) teaches : "...... those who believe are stauncher in their love for God." Again, it indicates the traits of the best men and says (5/54): "... a people whom He loveth and who love Him."

210. Obtaining Divine pleasure is not analogous to the enjoyment of material comforts, which God may give a man in order to test his gratefulness. Sometimes a man remains deprived of these comforts so that his endurance and constancy may be tested. In both cases, man must show his devotion and attachment to God. This necessitates, on the one hand,

abnegation of the ego by getting absorbed in the will of God, and on the other, a constant feeling of the effective presence of God.

211. The philosophic conception of pantheism emanates from the necessity of "self-abnegation in God". For a mystic, the mere affirmation of this belief has no value: he aspires to assimilate it and feel it as a reality. Thus it is that the learned distinctions between pantheism in the sense of the unity of existence, and that of the unity of vision, or any other, are for a true mystic mere logomachy, which makes the eager traveller lose his track, and retards his arrival at his destination.

212. It may be recalled here that the Islamic notion of pantheism does not lead to the reunification of man with God. However close a man may approach God, there is still a distinction, a separation, and a distance between the Creator and the created. One abnegates one's ego, but not one's person. The higher the level we attain, the more does God speak with our tongue, act with our hand, and desire with our heart° (cf. Bukhari). There is an ascension and a journey of man towards God, but there is never a confusion of the two. Thus it is that a Muslim does not use the term "communion", which may imply a union and a confusion. The Muslims designate the spiritual journey by the term *mi'raj*, which means a ladder, an ascension, which varies according to individuals and their capacities. The highest imaginable level a human being can attain is the one that has been reached by the holy Prophet Muhammad; and this experience of his is also called *mi'raj* So, in a state of consciousness and wakefulness, the Prophet had the vision (*ru'ya*) of being transported to heaven and graced with the honour of the Divine Presence. Even there, in this state beyond time and space, the Quran (53:9) indicates formally that the distance between God and the Prophet, "was of

° *Literally: "I become his ear with which he hears, his eye with which he sees, his hand with which he seizes, his feet with which he walks.*

two bows' length or even nearer," and this graphic description lays emphasis simultaneously on the closeness of proximity as well as the distinction between the two. The Prophet himself employed the term *mi'raj* in connection with the common faithful, when he indicated that "The service of worship is the *mi'raj* of the believer." Evidently to each according to his capacity and his merit.

213. The spiritual journey has a whole series of stages, and it is only gradually that one traverses them. In the life of the Prophet Muhammad, we see that he began with retreats in the cave of Hira'; then came the Meccan period, in which there was in store for him suffering and self-abnegation for the sake of the Divine cause. It is only after the Hijrah that he permits himself, — under Divine instructions always — to oppose injustice with force. It is quite possible that someone, who pretends to be a derwish, should only be so in appearance, being in reality a wolf disguised, as a sheep; similarly it is quite possible that a king, with all the powers and treasures accumulated in his hands, should still be in practice a saint, who does not at all profit by these things, but makes a great self-sacrifice, in the course of accomplishing his duties, by renouncing his personal comforts.

214. To break the ego, the first requirement is a feeling of humility, which should be developed. Pride is considered as the greatest sin against God. In the words of al-Ghazali, ostentation is the worship of self, therefore really a kind of polytheism.

215. Temperaments differ, that is why the roads also are various. One insists on the need of a guide and master. One who has studied medicine privately, without passing through a period of apprenticeship or even attending the courses of study with proficient doctors, is not allowed to practise medicine. The cases are rare where one sees all one's defects; rarer still are instances of people who correct themselves immediately.

A master is necessary in the first instance to indicate to us our defects and also the way in which these are to be removed. There is a constant development and a perpetual evolution in the individual, and the master spares us many an unnecessary effort. If one were not to profit by the experience of the past, and if each new-born were tor ecommence all of the task and to fall back on his own individual self, there would be no growth of culture and civilization which may be defined as the accumulated knowledge and practice of generations of our ancestors. The pupil has a regard for the judgement and counsel of his master, which he never has for his comrades and equals. After theoretical studies, one passes through a probationary period, for learning their practical application. This is as true of the material sciences as of the spiritual ones. There are many things which one can never learn by mere reading or listening; their practical application under the supervision of an experienced master is always useful, if not indispensable. Further, mere knowledge does not suffice: it should be assimilated and become a second nature.

216. Mystics recommend four practices: eat less, sleep less, speak less and frequent people less. "Less" does not mean complete abnegation, which is sometimes impossible (such as in eating and sleeping), and always undesirable; there must always be a moderation. One should eat to live, and not live to eat. To eat for the purpose of obtaining the energy to accomplish the will and the commandments of God, is an act of devotion; and to diminish the nourishment and get weakened to the extent of diminishing the spiritual productivity is a sin. Sleep is necessary for health, and is a duty imposed on man; but laziness, which makes us remain in bed for long, affects our spiritual progress. Sleeping less does not mean passing time in material needs, but finding more time for the practices of devotion and piety. Speaking less means diminution of frivolous talks, and avoidance, if possible, of all evil talk. It is often our habit to give good counsel to others, but forget to practise

it ourselves. To frequent people less, means refraining from unnecessary talk and wasting time in needless contacts. To do a good turn to others, and to be occupied with the realization of things which could procure the pleasure of the Lord are rather desirable frequentations. However, it should not be forgotten that the needs of the individuals differ according to their stage of evolution; one does not give the same advice to an expert master as to a young novice. Mundane frequentations often occasion temptations, waste of useful time, and the forgetting of our more important obligations. It may be permitted to add a fifth counsel: spend less, meaning on luxury, on flirtation, on personal pleasure; the amount thus saved could be used for purposes dear to us but for which we have no money — in our spend-thrift habits — to contribute our mite. The five counsels may constitute five principles of economy in Islam both spiritual and material..

SPECIAL PRACTICES

217. One has to remember God all the time. The essential feature is the remembering by the heart. But concentration not being constant, one employs physical methods for strengthening the presence of the spirit, and focusing of thought on the Divine person. The Quran (33:41-2) says: "O ye who believe! Remember God with much remembrance. And glorify Him early and late." Again (3/191): "such as remember God, standing, sitting and reclining and meditate on the creation of the heavens and the earth (and say:) our Lord, Thou createdst not this in vain; glory be to Thee; Preserve us from the doom of Fire." There are litanies, in which some formulas are repeated a number of times; there are prayers which one pronounces every day as a habit This is done aloud or in a low voice, but all should be related invariably and always to God, to His person or to His attributes, and never to created beings. Even if the subject be the Prophet Muhammad, for gratitude and admiration, the approach should be always through God, and never praying to Muhammad himself indepen-

dently to do something for us. For instance "O God, incline to Muhammad and take him into Thy protection," or "O God resuscitate Muhammad in the glorious place which Thou hast promised him, and accept his intercession in our favour," etc. For developing concentration of thought, the mystics sometimes live in seclusion, or retreat, stop respiration for moments. close the eyes, and concentrate on the throbbing of the heart while thinking of God, etc. They also say that there are three grades of remembrances of God: to remember only His name, to remember His person by means of and through His name, and to remember His person without having the need of His name or any other means. That these practices were recommended by the Prophet himself and that they are not of a foreign origin, it may be recalled that Abu Hurairah had a rosary made of a thread, with 2,000 knots to serve as many beads, and he repeated a certain prayer on it every night. (Ibn Fadlallah al-'Umari, *Masalik al-Absar*, vol. 5, MS of Istanbul).

218. Among other practices, one may mention a life of asceticism, self-mortification, and meditation particularly on death and the final judgement. For Islam these are not ends, but only the means, rather temporary and provisional, for the purpose of mastering and breaking the ego. Everything that one permits to one's self in this world is divided into two categories : necessaries and luxuries. One can never renounce the necessaries, for it would be suicide. To commit suicide is religiously forbidden in Islam, for we do not belong to ourselves, but to God; and to destroy something before its full-fledged realization is to go against the will of God. As for luxuries, if they are not made the aim of our existence in this world, they are lawful. One can renounce them in order to dominate over one's animality; one can also do so in order to help those who do not possess even the necessaries of life, or perhaps as a penitence. But it is not permitted to act in an exaggerated manner or out of all proportion. A verile man who makes an effort to lead a chaste life has greater merit than the one who

destroys his desires by means, for instance, of a surgical operation. One who has no capacity for evil has no merit in comparison with the one who has the most perfect capacity for it and yet abstains voluntarily from it, for fear of God.

219. Self-mortifications, abstinences and other spiritual practices enhance certain faculties, yet the acquisition of such faculties, however miraculous they might be, is not the aim of one who travels towards God. One seeks to realize acts, but not the sensations which are produced thereby automatically. Even an infidel may acquire certain of the faculties of saints, yet without the ultimate salvation. The mystic is continually directed towards his destination, and does not think of, much less profit by, these incidents of the saintly journey.

220. The life of a Sufi, derwish or mystic begins with repentance for the past sins and the reparation, as far as possible, of the harms done to other people. God pardons harms done to His own rights, but not those to the rights of other creatures; it is these latter who alone can pardon. It is only then that one can march on the path leading to the Lord. It is not the monopoly of any person or class or caste; it is within the reach of everybody, and it is the duty of each and everyone to take this road. The provisions for this journey are two-fold: obedience to God and constant remembering of Him. Obedience is easier in the sense that one knows what one has to do and what the will of the Lord is. He has revealed His will and His prescriptions through His chosen prophets, in order that they communicate them to the common folk.

221. God has sent innumerable prophets. If their teachings have differed in details, it is not because God has changed His opinion, but only because, in His mercy and wisdom, the evolution or deterioration of the human capacities necessitated a change in the rules of conduct and in the details. Although in the essentials of their teachings, particularly in those which concern the relation of man with God, prophets do not differ,

— and the Quran lays a strong emphasis on it, — it is part of the obedience of man to God's orders to abide by the latest disposition of His will. If God taught men something through the prophet Abraham, for instance, it will not be disobedience to abandon it for abiding by the teachings of the prophet Moses, because he brought in his time the latest disposition of the orders of the same Law-giver; what is more, to neglect the directions of Moses and continue to practise the teachings of Abraham would be flagrant disobedience to God. It is thus that man should practise, turn by turn, the messages of God brought by successive prophets, the latest of whom being Muhammad of holy memory. It is thus that, with all his respect for the previous prophets, a Muslim cannot abide except by the latest disposition of the will of God communicated to man. A Muslim venerates the Torah, the Psalter and the Gospel as the word of God, yet he abides by the latest and the most recent of the words of God, namely the Quran. Whoever remains attached to the preceding laws, cannot be considered, by the Legislator, as law-abiding and obedient.

CONCLUSION

222. Man being composed simultaneously of body and soul, of an outer and an inner existence, the harmonious progress and balanced evolution towards perfection require that attention should be paid to both these aspects of man. Mysticism or spiritual culture in Islam envisages the diminution of the Ego and the ever-increasing realization of the presence of God. To be absorbed in the will of God does not at all mean an immobility; far from that. In innumerable verses, the Quran urges man to action and even to compete in the search for the Divine pleasure by means of good actions. Not to follow one's own evil desires, but to abide by the will of God alone, does not lead to inaction. Only that happens which God wills; yet not knowing the will of God, which remains concealed from men, man must always continue his effort, even though failure

follows failure, when trying to attain the goal which he conscientiously believes to be good and in conformity with the revealed commandments of God. This notion of a dynamic predestination, which urges one to action and resignation to the will of God, is well explained in the following verses of the Quran (57:22-3): "Naught of disaster befalleth on the earth or in your souls but it is in a Book (Prescription) before We bring it into being — lo! that is easy for God — that ye grieve not for the sake of that which hath escaped you, nor ye exult because of that which ye had been given; God loveth no prideful boasters." Man should always think of the grandeur of God, and vis-a-vis this, of his own humility, as well as of the day of the Resurrection when the Lord will demand individual accounts. The Quran says (29:69): "As for those who strive in Us, We surely guide them to Our paths, and lo! God is with the good."

CHAPTER VII

The System of Morality

MEN may be divided into three principal categories: (1) Those who are good by nature, and incorruptible in the face of temptations, whose very instinct suggests to them whatever is good and charitable; (2) Those who are just the contrary and are incorrigible; and (3) Those who belong to the intermediary group, and behave suitably if they are constrained thereto by supervision or sanction, but who otherwise lapse into a state of carelessness or do injustice to others.

224. This last category comprises the immense majority of the human race, the members of the other two extreme categories comprising but a few individuals. The first kind (of the human-angels) does not require any direction or control; but it is the second kind (of the human-devils) which must be controlled, and prevented from doing evil. Great attention has to be devoted to the third kind (of the human-men).

225. The members of this third category resemble in certain respects the beasts: they are calm and content with what they possess, so long as they perceive nothing better in the possession of others, or do not suspect some mischief on the part of others. This evil propensity in the face of temptations has been, at all times, the object of intense preoccupation on the part of human society. Thus the father controls his children; the head of the family, of the tribe, of the city-state, or of any other group of men, tries to force those who are placed under his authority to be content with what they possess, and not to usurp that which others have obtained in an honest and legitimate way. Perhaps the very aim of human society is no

other than controlling temptations and remedying the damage already done. All men, even members of the same nation, are never developed alike. A noble spirit is willing to sacrifice and do works of charity. An intelligent spirit sees very far; and the consequences which would compromise the immediate gain prevent it from doing evil, even if it should not be persuaded to sacrifice on its own initiative. As to the ordinary spirit, not only does it not willingly consent to sacrifice, but even permits itself to thrive at the expense of others, unless there be a fear of violent and immediate reaction on the part of its victim, or society, or any other superior power. And the obtuse spirit is not deterred even by this fear, and persists till the last in its criminal intent, struggling against all opposition, until it is placed by society in a state where it can no more have a nuisance value, such as a punishment by death or imprisonment.

226. All laws, all religions and all philosophies try to persuade the masses, or the intermediary category, to behave in a suitable manner and even to offer voluntary sacrifices in order to help the poor, the destitute and those who have needs and yet cannot satisfy them, for no fault of theirs.

CHARACTERISTIC TRAITS OF ISLAM

227. Islam is an all-embracing mode of life. Not only does it prescribe beliefs but also the rules of social behaviour, moreover, it occupies itself with the nicer application and functioning of its laws. We know that Islam does not believe in the life of this world as an end in itself, or in body without any relation to soul. On the contrary, it teaches belief in the Hereafter. Its motto, as enunciated by the Quran, is "The best in this world as well as the best in the Hereafter." It is thus that not only does it praise the good and condemn the evil, but also provides rewards and sanctions, both spiritual and material. As far as its injunctions and prohibitions are concerned, Islam inculcates in the spirit, the fear of God, the last judgement after the Resurrection, and the punishment of the Hell

fire. Not content with this, it takes all possible precautions in the realm of material sanctions, in order to deter man from permitting himself acts of injustice and violation of the rights of others. It is thus that the believer prays and fasts even when he is not coerced to do that; he pays the tax even when the government ignores fixation of the amount or finds itself unable to obtain payment by force.

THE BASIS OF MORALITY

228. Often it so happens that motives or circumstances bring about a profound change in the import of acts which outwardly seem to resemble one another. For instance, the death occasioned at the hands of a brigand, of a hunter mistaking his victim for a game, of a fool, or a minor, in self-defence, by a headsman executing the capital punishment ordered by a tribunal, a soldier defending his country against an aggressive invasion, etc. — in all these cases the killing is sometimes punished more or less severely, sometimes pardoned, sometimes considered a normal duty entailing neither praise nor condemnation, and sometimes obtains high praise and honour. Almost all human life is composed of acts whose good and evil are relative. This is why the Prophet Muhammad has often declared: "Acts will be (judged) only according to intentions."

229. Islam is based on the belief of a Divine revelation sent to men through prophets as intermediary. Its law and morality, even as its faith, are therefore based on Divine commandments. It is possible that in the majority of cases human reason also should arrive at the same conclusion, but essentially it is the Divine aspect which has the decisive significance in Islam, and not the reasoning of a philosopher, a jurist or a moralist, the more so because the reasonings of different individuals may differ and lead to completely opposite conclusions. Sometimes the motive of discipline is found underlying an obligation and practice which is apparently superfluous.

230. One may divide human actions, first of all, into good and evil, represented by orders and prohibitions. The acts from which one must abstain are also divided into two big categories: Those against which there is temporal sanction or material punishment in addition to condemnation on the day of the Final Judgement, those which are condemned by Islam without providing a sanction other than that of the Hereafter.

231. In a saying attributed to the Prophet (and reported by Qadi 'Iyad, in his *Shifa,* ch. 2) we see the conception of life envisaged by Islam: "Ali asked the Prophet one day about the principles governing his general behaviour, and he replied: Knowledge is my capital, reason is the basis of my religion, love is my foundation, desire is my mount for riding, remembrance of God is my comrade, confidence is my treasure, anxiety is my companion, science is my arm, patience is my mantle, contentment is my booty, modesty is my pride, renunciation of pleasure is my profession, certitude is my food, truth is my intercessor, obedience is my sufficiency, struggle is my habitude and the delight of my heart is in the service of worship."

232. On another occasion, the Prophet Muhammad said : The sum-total of wisdom is the fear of God. Islamic morality begins with the renunciation of all adoration outside God, be it adoration of the self (egoism), or adoration of our own handicrafts (idols, superstitions), etc.; and the renunciation of all that degrades humanity (atheism, injustice, etc.).

233. Abolishing the ineluctable inequalities — based on race, colour of skin, language, place of birth — Islam has proclaimed (and realized more than any other system) the superiority of the individual based solely on morality, which is a thing accessible and open to everybody without exception. Thus it is what the Quran (49:13) has said: "O mankind, lo! We have created you of a male and a female, and have made

you nations and tribes that ye may know one another; verily the noblest of you in the sight of God is the one who is the most pious; lo! God is Knower, Aware."

234. In a beautiful passage (17:23-9), the Quran gives twelve commandments to the Muslim community, and says:

1. Thy Lord hath decreed, that ye worship none save Him.

2. And that (ye show) kindness to parents. If one of them or both of them were to attain old age with thee, say not 'Fie' unto them nor repulse them, but speak unto them a gracious word. And lower unto them the wing of tenderness through mercy, and say: My Lord! Have mercy on them both, as they did care for me when I was little. Your Lord is best aware of what is in your minds. If ye are righteous, then lo! He is ever Forgiving unto those who turn (unto Him).

3. Give the kinsman his due, and the poor, and the wayfarer, and squander not (thy wealth) in wantonness. Lo! the squanderers are ever brothers of the devils, and the Devil was an ingrate to his Lord. But if thou turn away from them, waiting mercy from thy Lord, for which thou hopest, then speak unto them a convenient word.

4. And let not thy hand be chained to thy neck nor open it with a complete opening, lest thou sit down rebuked, denuded. Lo! thy Lord enlargeth the provision for whom He will, and straineth (it from whom He will). Lo! He is ever Knower, Seer of His slaves.

5. Slay not your children, fearing a fall to penury; we shall provide for them and for you. Lo! the slaying of them is great sin.

6. And come not near unto fornication. Lo! it is an abomination and an evil way.

7   And slay not the life which God hath forbidden save with right. Whoso is slain wrongfully, we have given power unto his rightful representative, but let him not commit excess in slaying. Lo! he will be helped.

8.   Come not near the property of the orphan save with that which is better till he comes to strength;

9.   And keep the covenant. Lo! of the covenant it will be asked.

10.   Fill the measure when ye measure, and weigh with a right balance ; this is meet, and best refuge.

11.   Follow not that whereof thou hast no knowledge. Lo! the hearing and the sight and the heart — of each of these it will be asked.

12.   And walk not in the earth exultant. Lo! thou canst not rend the earth, nor canst thou stretch to the height of the hills. The evil of all that is hateful in the sight of thy Lord. This is part of the wisdom wherewith thy Lord hath inspired thee (O Muhammad). And set not up with God any other god, lest thou be cast into hell, reproved, abandoned.

These commandments, comparable to and more comprehensive than those given to Moses, were revealed to the Prophet during the *mi'raj*.

235.   It would be too lengthy to cite here all the Quranic exhortations. However, we may quote a passage (4 : 36-8), in which it speaks of the social behaviour of the average man : "And serve God; ascribe nothing as partner unto Him: (show) kindness unto parents, and unto near kindred, and orphans, and the needy, and unto the neighbour who is of kin (unto you) and the neighbour who is not of kin, and the fellow-traveller and the wayfarer, and (the slaves) whom your right

hands possess; lo! God loveth not such as are proud and boastful, who hoard their wealth and enjoin avarice on others, and hide that which God hath bestowed upon them of His bounty; for disbelievers, We prepare a shameful doom. And (also) for those who spend their wealth in order to be seen of men, and believe not in God nor the Last Day; whoso taketh Satan for a comrade, a bad comrade hath he."

236. In another passage (49:10-12), the Quran describes the characteristics of Muslim society. "The believers are naught else than brethren; therefore make peace between your brethren and observe your duty to God, that haply ye may obtain mercy. O ye who believe! Let not a folk deride a folk who may be better than they are, nor let women (deride) women who may be better than they are; neither defame one another, nor insult one another by nicknames; bad is the name of lewdness after embracing the faith; and whoso turneth not in repentance, such are evil-doers. O ye who believe! Shun much suspicion; for lo! some suspicion is a crime; and spy not, neither backbite one another; would one of you like to eat the flesh of his dead brother (by backbiting)?; ye abhor that (so abhor the other); and keep your duty to God; lo! God is Relenting, Merciful."

THE FAULT AND ITS EXPIATION

237. Nobody could object to good counsel, offered in the above-mentioned verses; but man has his weaknesses. He is constituted simultaneously of the elements of good and evil By his innate defects, he gets angry; he is subject to temptations, and is driven to do harm to those who are weaker and have no means of defending or avenging themselves. Similarly, his noble sentiments make him repent afterwards; and in proportion to the force of his repentance, he tries more or less to rectify the harm he had done.

238. Islam divides faults into two big categories : those which are committed against the rights of God (unbelief, neglect of worship, etc.), and those against the rights of men. Moreover, God does not pardon the harm done by a man to his fellow-being : it is the victim who alone can pardon. If one does harm to another creature, be it man, animal or any other one commits in fact a double crime : a crime against one's immediate victim, and also a crime against God, since the criminal conduct in question constitutes a violation of the Divine prescriptions. It is thus that, when there is an injustice or crime against another creature, one has not only to try to repair the damage, by restituting to the victim of one's violation the right which had been taken away from him, but he has also to beg pardon of God. In a famous saying of his, the Prophet Muhammad gave a warning, that on Doomsday, a certain person would be thrown in Hell because he had tied up a cat with a rope, giving it neither to eat nor to drink, nor letting it go and seek itself the food, thus causing the death of the poor animal in inanition. In another Hadith, the Prophet spoke of Divine punishment to those men who did not fulfil their duty against even the animals, by not giving them sufficient food, or loading them beyond their strength, etc. The Prophet prohibited even the hewing down of trees without necessity. Men should profit by what God has created, yet in an equitable and reasonable measure, avoiding all dissipation and waste.

239. When one causes damage to another and wishes to repair it, there are several ways he could adopt. Sometimes by merely asking pardon everything is set right; at other times it may be necessary to restitute the rights which were taken away, or replace them if the original rights could not be restituted, and so on.

240. To show clemency to others and pardon them is a noble quality, and upon this Islam has often insisted. In eulogizing it, the Quran (3/133-4) says : ''And vie one with

121

another for forgiveness from your Lord and for a Paradise as wide as the heavens and the earth, prepared for the pious, who spend (as charity) in case and in adversity, who control their wrath and are forgiving towards mankind; and God loveth the doers of good."

241. Pardon is recommended, yet vengeance is also permitted (for the average man). In this respect, the Quran (42/40) says : "The guerdon of an ill-deed is an ill the like thereof. But whoever pardoneth and amendeth, his wage is the affair of God. Lo ! He loveth not the oppressors" This is one of many similar verses.

242. God is incomparably more forgiving and merciful than the most merciful of men. Among the names with which Islam calls God, there is *Rahman* (Most Merciful), *Tauwab* (Most Pardoning) 'Afu (one who effaces faults), *Ghaffar* (Most Forgiving), etc. Those who commit a sin against God, and then repent, find God full of indulgence. Two verses of the Quran may show the Islamic notion of the bounty of God :

(a) "Verily God pardoneth not that partners should be ascribed unto Him, while He pardoneth all else to whom He will (4/116).

(b) ".........O My slaves who have been prodigal to your own hurt ! despair not of the mercy of God; Verily God forgiveth all sins; verily He is the Forgiving, the Merciful. (39/53).

243. If one gives up disbelief and turns to God to beg pardon of Him, one can always hope for His clemency. Man is weak, and often breaks his resolutions ; but true repentance can always restore the grace of God. There is no formality, no buying of Divine pardon by the mediation of other men; but one must turn directly to God, present Him one's sincere regrets in a tete-a-tete conversation (*munajat*); for He is the knower of all and nothing could be concealed from Him. "The

Love of God for His creatures is a hundred and more times greater than that of a mother for her child," as has once been remarked by the Prophet. For the Prophet Muhammad has said : "Mercy has been divided by God into one hundred portions, of which He has retained Himself 99 and distributed the one portion among all the beings living on the earth; the mutual mercy found among the creatures comes from the same". In a saintly saying (*hadith qudsi*) the Prophet reports God as saying : "Whoever tries to approach Me by a span, I approach him by a cubit, whoever approaches Me by a cubit, I approach him by a fathom, whoever comes towards Me walking, I run to meet him". The Quran (11/114) announces no doubt : "Verily the good deeds carry away evil deeds." Alms and charities are no doubt recommended, yet they do not buy automatically the Divine pardon for a given sin ; each has an independent existence, and God's freedom is absolute.

THE INJUNCTIONS

244. The Quran often employs two characteristics terms to designate the good and the evil. Thus it refers to *ma'ruf* (the good known to everybody and recognized as such), and *munkar* (the evil denounced by everybody and recognized as such). In other words, the Quran has confidence in human nature, in the common sense of man: "There will never be a unanimity in favour of the evil, even if some people permit it to themselves" is the purport of a well-known saying of the Prophet. The Quran (3/110) calls the faithful "the best community" and explains that this is so because they "enjoin the good (*ma'ruf*) and forbid the evil (*munkar*) and believe in the One God." Another passage (103:1-3) is still more emphatic: "By the Time! Lo! Man is in a state of loss, save those who believe and do good works, and exhort one another to truth (or right) and exhort one another to endurance (or constancy)."

245. But there are also injunctions against particular evils. As has already been remarked, there are those which accompany a sanction and a public punishment, and those regarding which there is only a warning of punishment in the Hereafter, and except in cases of extra-ordinary gravity, the public authorities do not take cognizance of them.

246. In his celebrated speech, on the occasion of the Farewell Pilgrimage, the Prophet declared the inviolability of the rights of a man in all the three categories of person, property and honour. In fact the Muslim penal law takes it into account, declaring that the principal crimes are the following: murder, damage to body, fornication and adultery (which are all crimes against the person), theft and highway robbery (which are crimes against property), and calumny against chastity, and consumption of alcoholic drinks (constituting crimes against honour). All these are punished.

247. As for the damages against person, the punishment is in principle retaliation: life for life, eye for eye, tooth for tooth. But there is first of all the great principle of motive and intention. Has one caused damage voluntarily or only by accident? Again, there is the choice for the victim (or the heirs of his rights) to agree to a pecuniary reparation, or even pardon completely. If the judicial proof establishes that the crime was intentional, the public authorities have no right to pardon; the matter rests with the sufferer.

248. Entirely different is the case of fornication and adultery. For the consent of the parties does not attenuate its gravity. The Prophet had so greatly succeeded in developing justice and -self-criticism among his companions that they preferred the severest public punishment in this world to the one in the Hereafter; and they presented themselves voluntarily before the Prophet, to confess their sins and submit themselves cheerfully to the legal sanctions. Outside confession, it is always very difficult to prove illicit sexual relations if the

parties were willing. In order to diminish the temptation, Islam has taken other precautions also: prohibition of promiscuity, of easy and unsupervised meetings between the young of opposite sexes if they are not near relatives, and even the recommendation of the veil to cover the face of the woman if she goes out in the street or meets strangers. Far from attracting the gaze of the amorous strangers by her coquetry, it is the duty of a Muslim woman to reserve her beauty and her attraction only for her husband. The veil has other advantages also for the woman. One knows the great difference between the exterior of those women who work in the fields, for instance, and of those who are not exposed to the sun. One knows also the difference between the outer and inner feathers of a bird. In fact the veil preserves for a longer time the charm and freshness of the skin. One can see that plainly on comparing the skin of the face or hands with that of other parts of the body which are habitually covered by the dress. The veil does not at all signify seclusion, but it does diminish the temptation that could attract strangers. It is abusing the credulity of the simpleton to make-believe that covering the face with a veil generates tuberculosis. This disease is as prevalent among people where womenfolk never uses the veil, not only in Black Africa, but even in the most highly developed societies from Finland to Italy, as the latest research has brought to light. In passing, it may be mentioned that there is no legal penalty for the neglect of this Quranic recommendation.

249. We do not require to enter into the details of the different aspects of the injunction against theft and highway robbery, or other crimes against property.

250. It is characteristic of Islam to have imposed a penalty on the defamation of women in the matter of their chastity. When one thinks of the numerous occasions when one indulges in conjectures against neighbours or other women

and the case with which one gives liberty to one's tongue, in the company of friends, one will admit that this Islamic break is well founded in the interests of society. If someone intends to accuse a woman, one should produce judicial proofs; otherwise, conjectures touching the honour of a woman will be punished with severe sanctions.

251. The prohibition of alcoholic drinks is one of the most well-known traits of Islam. It was by gradual steps that the Quran had enforced it: "They question thee about alcoholic drink and games of chance; say: In both there is great sin and certain profits for men, yet the sin of them is greater than their usefulness" (2: 219). Again (4:43): "O ye who believe ! Draw not near unto service of worship when ye are drunk, till ye know that which ye utter..." And finally (5:93-94): "O ye who believe! Verily the wine, and games of chance, and idols, and divining arrows are only an infamy of Satan's handiwork; leave it aside, haply ye may prosper. Satan seeketh only to cast among you enmity and hatred by means of wine and games of chance, and to turn you from remembrance of God and from (His) worship; will ye then abstain?" It will not pass unnoticed that in this last verse, the Quran includes alcoholic drinks and idolatry in the same category. During his life, the Prophet Muhammad administered forty stripes to those who violated the injunction. The caliph 'Umar doubled the punishment, arguing that drunkenness leads to obscene loquacity in which one calumniates the chastity of women, for which latter crime the Quran (24/4) has imposed the punishment of eighty stripes therefore alcoholic drinks should also have the same sanction. What enormous economic loss would be avoided, and how many homes would recover peace, if drink, so dangerous to health and morality, were given up !

252. Among the acts for which no definite penalty has been prescribed but which are left to the discretion of the judge, we may mention games of chance of all kinds (including

126

lotteries, gambling on the results of races, etc.). Who does not know the tragedies of casinos? How many homes have not been ruined in the vain hope of easy gain—and therefore illicit gain? Lotteries, on national scales, gradually upset the equitable distribution of the country's wealth, and prove to be the source of all economic ills. They affect politics too.

253. In his anxiety for cleansing society, and above all public administration, from corruption, the Prophet employed the severest terms of condemnation : "One who takes as well as one who offers bribe, would both go to Hell." One day, a tax-collector submitted his accounts to the Prophet, saying: These are the public revenues, and these are gifts which people have offered me. Getting furious, the Prophet mounted the pulpit of his mosque and addressed: "Let these tax-collectors remain in the house of their mothers and see if gifts come to them!" Without the knowledge of her husband, one day the wife of the caliph Umar sent through an official envoy, proceeding to Byzantium, a present to the wife of the emperor who in her turn, sent a precious necklace. When the caliph learnt this news, he confiscated the necklace in favour of the Public Treasury, and paid his wife the value of her original present to the empress as has been recorded by Tabari.

254. In order to ameliorate public morality, the Prophet said one day: "Don't insult time; it is God that you insult, because the succession of nights and days comes from Him." This is an admonition that deserves to be considered by our contemporaries even today. After all what avails our malediction of the weather so many times every day, if not to prove our own stupidity?

255. Islam does not exact the impossible; it seeks only to bring a constant betterment of human morals, in all walks of life, by means available to individuals and collectivities. And the responsibility will always remain personal. So the Quran (2/286) says: "... for each soul, it is only that which it hath

earned, and against it only that which it hath deserved —". A noble spirit does not permit itself evil on the pretext that others also indulge in the same. Instead of imitating the vices of others, one should rather set others an example of good and of integrity of character.

256. Some remarks may be made on social conduct in general. Regarding the rights of good neighbourliness, the Prophet Muhammad declared: "Gabriel has so often and so greatly insisted upon the rights of neighbours, that I feared that he was going to accord them the right to heritage even as to the near relatives of a deceased." It is related that there lived a Jew in the neighbourhood of the Prophet in Madinah, and the Prophet himself set an example to show how a Muslim should treat his non-Muslim neighbours. Among other daily acts of courtesy, the Prophet used to go to the house of this Jew if he fell ill, in order to inquire about his health, and to be otherwise of help to him. As regards daily relations with others, the Prophet declared: "None of you is a believer if he does not like for his brother exactly that which he likes for his own self." Or again: "The best of men is he who does good to others." The Quran (59/9) has spoken of a concrete case, that of the first Muslims of Madinah, who had extended their hospitality to the Meccan refugees, and it cites them as an example of practical Islam: ". . . they prefer (the Refugees) above themselves though poverty be their (own) lot . . ."

257. To conclude: "O ye who believe! Be ye staunch in justice, witnesses for God, even though it be against yourselves or (your) parents or (your) kindred, whether (the case be) of a rich man or a poor man . . . ." (Quran 4/135).

CHAPTER VIII

The Political System of Islam

THE Islamic conception of life being a co-ordination between the body and the soul, it was natural that a very close relationship should have been established between religion and politics, between the mosque and the citadel. In its social conception, Islam is "communal." It prefers a social life, demands worship in collectivity and congregation, in which every one turns towards the same centre (the Ka'bah), fasting together at the same time in all parts of the world, and visiting the House of God (the Ka'bah) as one of the principal duties of all Muslims, men and women. It lays emphasis on strictly personal responsibility, and does not forget the development of the individual, and yet it organizes all individuals in a single whole, the world Muslim community. The same law regulates the affairs of all, whatever the class or country; and as we shall see, the same chief, Caliph, receives the allegiance of all the faithful of the world.

NATIONALITY

259. One finds in human society, turn by turn, two contradictory tendencies: centripetal and centrifugal. On the one hand, separate individuals group themselves in wedlock, families, tribes, city-states, states and empires, sometime willingly and at other time under compulsion. On the other hand, descending from the same couple and ancestors, groups detach themselves from bigger units in order to lead separate and independent lives, away from their relatives; and this separation is occasioned sometimes amicably, for the purpose of finding the means of livelihood elsewhere and lightening the

charge on a locality too restricted to furnish food for all; while at other times, it is dictated by passions, quarrels and other motives.

260. In spite of the almost unanimous concept that all human races have the same common origin, two factors have powerfully contributed to accentuate the diversity: death and distance. Man is instinctively attached to close relatives and ancestors, yet the cementing factor disappears with the death of the common parent; and the notion of relationship among the surviving members, whose number multiplies every day, bears an importance and an influence which gradually become less and less effective. As regards distance, not only does it make us forget the ties of relationship, but also, as history has shown, creates insurmountable obstacles. One ceases to speak the same language, uphold the same interests or defend the same values.

261. At the dawn of Islam, in the 7th century of the Christian era, differences and prejudices arising from race, language, place of birth and other things had become the rule rather than the exception; they developed deep-rooted notions, which grew to be almost natural instincts. It was so everywhere in the world, in Arabia, in Europe, in Africa, in Asia, in America and elsewhere. Islam came to class these notions among the evil traits of humanity, and tried to bring about a cure.

262. The unifying ties of family, of clan, and even of tribe proved too weak to serve the needs of defence and security in a world where egoism and cupidity had rendered inevitable wars of everybody against everybody else. But groups bigger than tribes were created sometimes by the use of force by warriors and emperors. Failing however to create an identity of interests among the totality of the subjects, these artificial unions were constantly menaced by disintegration.

263. Without entering into the history of the several thousand years of the development of this aspect of human society, it would suffice to consider the idea of nationality prevalent in our own time in order to illustrate the point. If nationality is based on the identity of language, race, or place of birth, it goes without saying that it will make the problem of aliens of strangers exist perpetually, and such a nationality will be too narrow, ever to be able to embrace the inhabitants of the entire world; and if the aliens are not assimilated, there will always be the risk of conflicts and wars. In fact, the tie of nationality is not a very sure bond at all. For two brothers may be enemies, and two strangers, having a common ideology, may be friends.

264. The Quran (30/22, 49/13) has rejected all superiority on account of language, colour of skin or other ineluctable incidences of nature, and recognizes the only superiority of individuals as that based on piety. A common ideology is the basis of "nationality" among the Muslims, and Islam is this ideology. We shall not speak of religions which do not admit conversion. Among the religions of universal application, Islam distinguishes itself by the feature that it does not exact the renunciation of the world, but insists on the body and soul growing and operating simultaneously. The past has shown that Muslims have assimilated this supra-racial and supra-regional ideal of brotherhood; and this sentiment is a living force among them to this day.

265. Naturalization is a feature now admitted among all "nations" but to be naturalized in a new language, in a new colour of skin, and in a new land is not as easy as to adhere to a new ideology. For others nationality is essentially an ineluctable accident of nature; in Islam it is a thing depending solely upon the will and choice of the individual.

MEANS OF UNIVERSALIZATION

266. Apart from the means already mentioned, namely the same law for all, the same direction to turn to in the service of prayer the same place for meeting in the universal pilgrimage, etc., the institution of the universal caliphate plays a particular role.

267. Muhammad of holy memory had proclaimed himself to be a messenger of God, sent towards the totality of human beings (cf. Quran 34/28) and also the last of such messengers (cf. Quran 33/40), and therefore for all time, till the end of the world. His teaching abolished the inequalities of races and classes. Moreover, the Prophet himself exercised all powers, spiritual as well as temporal and others, in the community which he had organised into a state and endowed with all its organisms. Thus cumulation of powers was passed in heritage, after his death, to his successors in the state, with this difference that these successors were not prophets, and so did not receive the Divine revelations. The Prophet Muhammad had always insisted on the necessity of community life, and he went so far as to declare that "Whoever died without knowing his imam (caliph), dies in paganism." He had also insisted on unity and solidarity inside the Muslim community, saying that "Whoever separates himself from it goes to Hell." reported by Muslim, Tirmidhi etc.)

268. Even in the time of the Prophet, there were individuals and even groups of Muslims, who lived voluntarily or under constraint, outside the frontiers of the Islamic State, for example in Abyssinia, and in Mecca (before its conquest by the Prophet). Some of the non-Muslim regions did not know religious tolerance, and persecuted the Muslims (as in the city-state of Mecca and the Byzantine empire). Others, like the Christian Abyssinia, practised a liberal policy in matters of conscience.

269. As we have just seen, the caliph inherited from the Prophet the exercise of the double power, spiritual-temporal, and he presided over the celebration of the service of worship in the mosque, and he was the head of the State in temporal affairs.

270. To recognize the Prophet, one used to take the oath of allegiance, (*bai'ah*, or contract of obedience); and one did the same for the caliphs at the moment of their election. The basis of the statal organization is a contract concluded between the ruler and the ruled. In practice, only persons who are the most representative of the population take this oath of allegiance. This nomination under a contract of course implies the possibility of the annulment of the contract and the deposition of the ruler by the same representative personalities.

271. It was by virtue of being the messenger of God, that the Prophet Muhammad commanded his community; and the law which he promulgated and left to posterity was equally of Divine inspiration. For his successors, the sovereignty of God continued to exist as a reality, in the sphere of their competence; therein they were the successors of the Prophet of God. But for them there was no possibility of receiving Divine revelations; and thus their power in the matter of legislation was restricted: they could not abrogate the laws established by the Prophet in the name of God; they could however interpret these laws, and legislate in cases where the law of the time of the Prophet was silent. In other words, the caliph could not be a despot, at least in matters of legislation: he is a constitutional head, and as much subject to the laws of the country as any ordinary inhabitant of the State. The tradition created by the Prophet himself is responsible for the fact that the head of the Muslim State should not be above the law; and history shows that the caliphs could always be cited, even by the humblest of the subjects, also by non-Muslims, to appear before

the courts of the country, from the time of Abu-Bakr (the first caliph) to our day.

272. The theory and practice of the caliphate have how-ever not always been indentical in Muslim society. A rapid sketch of this history would be useful for understanding the actual position.

THE CALIPHATE

273. The Quran speaks of kings, both good and bad, and never refers to other forms of government, such as a republic. The fact that there have been differences of opinion, at the death of the Prophet, shows that he had not left positive and precise instructions regarding his succession. Certain groups wanted that the statal power should rest, as a heirloom, in his family; and as he had left no male issue, his uncle 'Abbas, or his cousin 'Ali were the next of kin to succeed him. Others wanted an ad hoc individual election; and inside this group, there were differences as to the candidate to be chosen. An overwhelming majority rallied in favour of an election. The form of government thus established was intermediary between hereditary monarchy and a republic: the *caliph was elected for life*. If the fact of election makes it resemble the republic, the duration of the power was like that of a monarchy. From the very beginning, there have been dissidents to the elected caliphs; later there have been even rival claimants and these caused bloodshed in the community from time to time. Later power was held by some dynasty. Thus came the Umaiyads, who in their turn were replaced by the 'Abbasids; these latter did not succeed in obtaining the homage of the far-off province of Spain, where independent dynasties of Muslim rulers exer-cised sovereign powers, without however daring to assume the title of "caliph." It required two more centuries before the Muslim world knew the multiplicity of caliphs, at Baghdad, Cordova, and Cairo (Fatimids). The Turks, when converted to Islam, brought a new element. First they furnished soldiers

and then commanders who became the real governing power in the State. Side by side with the caliphs, there appeared a "commander of the commanders," and later a "sultan," and the State authority became divided and administration went into the hands of the Sultan who governed in the name of the caliph. This excited greed and aroused jealousies; several provinces became independent, producing "dynasties" of governors, who in their turn were replaced by other adventurers; and the caliph had no choice but to ratify the fait accompli whenever it arose. The Fatimid caliphate of Cairo disappeared first; and this kingdom was acquired by a dynasty of Turkish-Kurdish governors, who recognized the caliphate of Baghdad. When this latter was devastated by the pagan Tatars, the seat of the caliphate was moved to Cairo. Later the Ottoman Turks conquered Egypt, and abolished the neo-'Abbasid dynasty of caliphs there. After some time, the Spanish caliphate surrendered the country to Cristian conquerors, and reconstituted a caliphate in Morocco. The Turkish Istanbul, and the Mughal Delhi also pretended to the caliphate; but however big their empires might have been, their claims were recognized only inside their respective jurisdictions. Prior to these two, there had at least been the obligatory qualification of a caliph being a Quraishite, i.e., a descendant of the Meccan Arabs of the time of the Prophet. The Turks and the Mughals did not fulfil this condition; but we shall revert to the point later. The Mughals were removed from their Indian power by the British; the Turkish caliph of Istanbul was later deposed by his own subjects, who not only chose a republican form of government, but would not even preserve the dignity of caliphate for the head of the state. The powers and privileges of the caliph were nominally conferred on the Grand National Assembly, which however neither claimed them nor exercised them. The last Turkish caliph 'Abdulmajid II, the 100th after the Prophet, died in exile as a refugee in Paris. In the meanwhile the caliphate of Morocco became a protectorate of France.

274. Some observations suggest themselves in this connection. The Prophet had predicted that after him, the caliphate would continue only for thirty years and that afterwards a "biting kingship" would follow (cf. Ibn Athir's *Nihayah*, Tirmidhi, Abu Dawud). Another saying is attributed to the Prophet to the effect that the caliphate belongs to the tribe of Quraish. The context of this last direction is not known; but the practice of the Prophet himself does not seem to confirm the obligatory character of this qualification. For history shows that since his arrival in Madinah and the founding of a City State there, the Prophet left his metropolis at least 25 times, in order to go on military expéditions to defend the state territory as well as for pacific avocations (such as contracting alliances, making a pilgrimage). On all such occasions, he nominated a vicegerent in Madinah, yet it was not the same person that he chose always for carrying on the interim government. We find among these vicegerents, called *khalifah* or caliph, Madinans, Quraishites, Kinanites and others; there was even a blind person. At the time of his last journey when he went on pilgrimage, just three months before his death, it was a blind person who was the "caliph" in the metropolis. Another point to be noted is that, at the election of Abu-Bakr as caliph, there was a proposal for a sort of joint-rule, with two caliphs operating simultaneously.[1] For

---

1. *This is the narration of Ibn Hisham. As for Ibn Sa'd (III/i. p. 151), he gives details and refers even to the practice of the Prophet, and says: "Abu Sa'id al-Khudri reports: When the Prophet breathed his last, the orators of the Ansarites stood up and one of them said: O Muhajirites, whenever the Prophet nominated some person as 'aamil (governor), he attached to him someone from amongst us, so we are of opinion that this power (caliphate) should also be exercised by two persons, one from among you and one from among us." The report of Diyarbakri (Khamis, 2/168-9) seems to concern a further compromise. In*

(Contd. on next page)

practical reasons, the proposal was rejected. It is nevertheless one of the possible form of Muslim government, as it is recognized by the Quran (20/32), which speaks of Aaron as the associate of Moses in the statal power, and because this form was preserved by the Prophet himself in 'Uman where Jaifar and 'Abd, who ruled conjointly, had embraced Islam.[2]

275. The universal caliph does not exist now-a-days among the Muslims; nevertheless the masses continue to aspire for it. The very independent existence of Muslims is also subject to fragmentary reconquest. Before restoring the institution of a universal caliphate, it may be that they could have recourse to the precedents of the time of the Prophet, in order to avoid regional rivalries and susceptibilities : one may have for instance a "Council of Caliphate" composed of the heads of all the Muslim States, Sunnites as well as Shi'ites, Quraishites as well as non-Quraishites; and by rotation every member could preside over the Council, say for a year.

DUTIES OF THE STATE

276. The duties and functions of a Muslim state seem to be four: Executive (for the civil and military administration), Legislative, Judicial, and Cultural.

(Contd. from the previous page)

fact according to this historian, the Ansarites had proposed to the Muhajirites the following formula : "If you nominate for the caliphate today someone from amongst you, on his death we shall nominate someone from amongst us as his successor; and after the death of this latter, a Muhajirite shall be elected. And we shall do this kind of (alternate) succession so long as the Muslim community subsists."

2. The letter of the Prophet inviting them to Islam is preserved, and says: "If you both embrace Islam, I shall maintain you both as rulers, but if you refuse to embrace Islam, your kingdom will vanish."

277. The Executive does not require elaborate examination; it is self-evident, and obtains everywhere in the world. The sovereignty belongs to God, and it is a trust which is administered by man, for the well-being of all without exception.

278. We have already mentioned the restrictions of legislative competence in the Islamic society, in the light of the fact that there is the Quran, Word of God, which is the source of law in all walks of life, spiritual as well as temporal. (cf. below § 318/v).

279. In the domain of judiciary, we have already pointed out the equality of all men before law, in which the head of the state is not exempt even vis-a-vis his subjects. The Quran (5/42-50, 5/66) has ordained another important disposition: The non-Muslim inhabitants of the Islamic State enjoy a judicial autonomy, each community having its own tribunals, its own judges, administering its own laws in all walks of life, civil as well as penal. The Quran says that the Jews should apply the Biblical laws, and the Christians those of the Gospel. It goes without saying that in the case of conflict between laws, where parties to a litigation belong to different communities, special disposition would solve the difficulties for the choice of the law as well as of the judge; and it is a kind of private international law which regulates such cases.

280. By cultural duty, we mean the very raison-d'etre of Islam, which seeks that the Word of God alone should prevail in this world. It is the duty of each and every individual Muslim, and *a fortiori* that of the Muslim government, not only to abide by the Divine law in daily behaviours, but also to organize foreign missions in order to make others know what Islam stands for. The basic principle, as the Quran (2/256) says, is that "There is no compulsion in religion." Far from implying a lethargy and indifference, a perpetual and disin-

terested struggle is thereby imposed to persuade others for the well-foundedness of Islam.

FORM OF GOVERNMENT

281. Islam attaches no importance to the external form of government; it is satisfied if the well-being of man in both the worlds is aimed at, and the Divine law applied. Thus the constitutional question takes a secondary place, and as we have already mentioned, a republic, a monarchy, and a joint-rule, among other forms, are all valid in the Islamic community.

282. If this aim is realized by a single chief, one accepts it. If at a given time, in a given surrounding, all the requisite qualities of a "commander of the Faithful" or caliph are not found united in the same person, one admits voluntarily the division of power also for the purpose of the better functioning of the government. We may refer to the famous case cited by the Quran (2/246-7): A former prophet was solicited by his people to select for them a king beside his own prophetic self, so that they might wage war under his leadership, against the enemy which had expelled them from their homes and families. The designation of a king in the presence of and in addition to a prophet, and even by the intermediation of the latter, shows the lengths to which one can go in this direction. A division is thus made between the spiritual and temporal functions, yet no arbitrary power is tolerated for either of them: the politics and the king remain as much subject to the Divine law as the cult and the prophet. The source of authority and codes of law remain the same; only the application of law and the execution of necessary dispositions relate to different persons. It is more a question of specialization than a divorce between the two aspects of life.

CONSULTATIVE DELIBERATIONS

283. The importance and utility of consultation cannot be too greatly emphasized. The Quran (3/159, 27/32, 42/38,

47/21) commands the Muslims again and again to take their decisions after consultation, whether in a public matter or a private one. The practice of the ·Prophet has reinforced this disposition. For, in spite of the exceptional quality of his being guided by the Divine revelations,the Prophet Muhammad always consulted his companions and the representatives of the tribes of his adherents, before taking decision. The first caliphs were not less ardent defenders of the consultative institutions.

284. In this respect also, the Quran does not prescribe hard and fast methods. The number, the form of election, the duration of representation, etc., are left to the discretion of the leaders of every age and every country. What is important is that one should be surrounded by representative personalities, enjoying the confidence of those whom they represent and possessing integrity of character.

285. The Quran has also spoken of a kind of proportionate representation, while describing the selection of 70 representatives from among his people by Moses, to be received in the presence of God (cf. Q. 7/155). Further (in 7/160) one may discern even a sort of proportionate representation, since twelve springs of water were allotted to as many tribes accompanying Moses in the desert. Anyhow we know that the aim of all representation, selected or elected, is that the government should always remain in touch with ·public opinion. This aim is realized in Islam in a perfect manner through the institution of the congregational services of worship. So five times every day — and even on Friday which is the weekly holiday — every Muslim, man and woman, has to gather in the mosque of the street or locality where he resides (or is otherwise present), and it is the highest government official of the locality who leads the service of worship. This provides the possibility of meeting the highest responsible authority and complaining to him of any injustice or hardship befalling any individual. If that proves of no avail, the individual goes to a higher official,

even to the head of the State who also leads the service of worship in the public mosques of their locality or street and is accessible to every commoner.

FOREIGN POLICY

286. The relations with foreign countries are based on what is called international law. The rules of conduct in this domain have had an evolution very much slower than those of the mutual behaviour inside a social group. In pre-Islamic antiquity, international law had no independent existence : it formed part of politics and was dependent on the will and pleasure of the head of the State. Few were the *rights* recognized for foreign friends, still less for enemies.

287. We may bring into relief the historic fact, that it was the Muslims who not only developed international law, the first in the world, as a distinct discipline, but also made it form part of law (instead of politics). They composed special monographs on the subject, under the name of *siyar* (conduct, i.e,, of the ruler), and they also spoke of it in the general treatises of law. To the very first originators of these studies (of the early second century of the Hijrah/8th century of the Christian era), the question of war formed part of penal law. So after discussing brigandage and highway robbery of the local people, the jurists logically spoke of similar activities by foreigners, demanding a greater mobilization of the forces of order. But the very inclusion of war under the heading of penal law means unequivocally that it had to do with legal matters, in which the accused had the right of defending himself before a judicial tribunal.

288. The basic principle of the system of international relations in Islam, in the words of jurists, is that "the Muslims and non-Muslims are equal (*sawa'*) in respect of the sufferings of this world." In ancient times, the Greeks, for instance, had the conception that there was an international law which

regulated the relations amongst only the Greek city-states; as for the Barbarians, i.e. non-Greeks, nature had intended them, as was said by Aristotle, to be the slaves of the Greeks. Therefore it was an arbitrary conduct, and no law, which was the rule with regard to relations with them. The ancient Hindus had a similar notion, and the dogma of the division of humanity into castes together with the notion of untouchability rendered the fate of the defeated still more precarious. The Romans recognized a few rights in respect of foreign friends; yet for the rest of the world there was nothing but discretion and arbitrary rule, changing with the whims and fancies of individual commanders and ages. The Jewish law asserted (cf. *Numbers*, 31/8-9, 17-18, *Deuteronomy* 20/16, *I Samuel* 15/3) that God had ordained the extermination of the Amalecites ('Amaliqah, Arab inhabitants of Palestine); and that the rest of the world might be allowed to live on payment of tribute to and as servants of the Jews. Until 1856, the Westerners reserved the application of international law to Christian peoples; and since then they have made a distinction between the civilized and non-civilized peoples, the latter having still no rights. In the history of International law, Muslims have been the first—and so far also the only—to admit the right of foreigners without any discrimination or reserve both during war and peace.

289. The first Muslim State was founded and governed by the Prophet. It was the city-state of Madinah, a confederacy of autonomous villages, inhabited by Muslims, Jews, pagan Arabs, and possibly a handful of Christians. The very nature of this State demanded a religious tolerance, which was formally recognized in the constitution of this State, which document has come down to us. The first treaties of defensive alliance were concluded with non-Muslims, and were always scrupulously observed. The Quran insists in the strongest of terms on the obligation of fulfilling promises and on being just in this respect (otherwise imposing punishment in the Hereafter).

290. The different sources of the rules of international conduct comprise not only internal legislation, but also treaties with foreigners, etc.

291. The jurists have so greatly insisted on the importance of the given word, that they say that, if a foreigner obtains permission and comes to the Islamic territory, for a fixed period, and if in the meanwhile a war breaks out between the Muslim government and that of the said foreigner, the security of the latter would not be affected: he may stay in tranquility until the expiration of his visa of sojourn: and not only may he return home in all safety and security, but also take with him all his goods and gains. Moreover during the sojourn, he would enjoy the protection of the courts even as before the outbreak of the war.

292. The person of the ambassador is considered immune from all violation, even if he brings a most unpleasant message. He enjoys his liberty of creed, and security of sojourn and return.

293. The question of jurisdiction has also certain peculiarities. Foreigners residing in the Islamic territory are subjected to Muslim jurisdiction, but not to Muslim law, because Islam tolerates on its territory a multiplicity of laws, with autonomous judiciary for each community. A stranger would belong therefore to the jurisdiction of his own confessional tribunal. If he is a Christian, Jew, or anything else, and if the other party to the litigation is also of the same confession—no matter whether this other party is a subject of the Muslim State or a stranger — the case is decided by the confessional court according to its own laws. Generally no distinction is made between civil and criminal cases with respect to this jurisdiction. As for cases where the litigants belong to different communities, the question has already been discussed above. However, it is always permissible under Muslim law (cf. Quran 5/42-50) for

a non-Muslim to renounce this privilege and go before the Islamic tribunal, provided both parties to the suit agree. In such an eventuality, the Islamic law is applied. It is permissible for the Muslim judge to apply even foreign law, personal law of the parties to the case, as is evident from the practice of the Prophet: Two Jews, guilty of adultery, were brought by their co-religionists; and the Prophet caused to bring the Bible (Book of Leviticus) and administered Jewish law to them, as is reported by Bukhari. It may be mentioned by the way that the concern for legality has forced the Muslim jurists to admit that if a crime is committed, even against a Muslim, who is the subject of the Muslim State, by a foreigner in a foreign country, and this foreigner later comes peacefully to the Muslim territory, he will not be tried by the Islamic tribunals, which are not competent to hear a case that had taken place outside the territory of their jurisdiction. Muslim jurists are unanimous on the point. Muhammad ash-Shaibani, pupil of Abu Hanifah, has recorded even a saying of the Prophet in support of this law: "Átiyah Ibn Qais al-Kilabi relates that the Prophet has said: If a man takes refuge in enemy country after having committed murder, sexual immorality or theft, and later returns after obtaining safe-conduct, he would still be judged for what he fled from; but if he has committed murder, illicit sexual intercourse or theft in the enemy territory and later came on safe-conduct, no punishment would be inflicted on him for what he had committed in the enemy territory". (Sarakhsi, *Sharh as-Siyar al-Kabir*, IV, 108).

294. Islamic law does not admit exemptions in favour of the head of the State, who is as much subject to the jurisdiction of the courts as any other inhabitant of the country. If the head of the Muslim State does not enjoy such privileges (of injustice, remnant of class discriminations) in his own country, one should not expect them in favour of foreign sovereigns and ambassadors. All regard, appropriate to their

quality as guest and their dignity, is paid to them, yet they are not held to be above law and justice.

295. Several cases of classical times bring to relief another peculiar feature of Islamic justice. Hostages were exchanged to guarantee the faithful execution of treaties, stipulating expressly that, if one of the contracting parties should murder the hostages furnished by the other party, this latter would have the right to be avenged on the hostages in its hands. Cases of this kind happened in the time of caliph Mu'awiyah and al-Mansur, and the Muslim jurists unanimously observed that the enemy hostages could not be put to death, because the perfidy and treachery was employed by their ruler and not by these hostages in person; and the Quran (16/64, 55/38, etc.) forbids formally vicarious punishment and inflicting reprisals on one for the crime of another.

296. The Muslim law of war is humane. It makes a distinction between belligerents and combatants; it does not permit the killing of minors, women, the very old, sick, and monks; debts in favour of the citizens of the enemy country are not touched by the declaration of war; all killing or devastation beyond the strict indispensable minimum is forbidden; prisoners are well treated, and their acts of belligerency are not considered as crimes. In order to diminish the temptation of the conquering soldiers, booty does not go to the one who seizes it, but to the government, which centralizes all spoils and redistributes them, four-fifths going to the participants of the expedition one-fifth to the government coffers; the share of a soldier and of the commander-in-chief are alike and equal.

297. In an interesting passage (47/35), the Quran enjoins peace and says : "Do not falter, and cry for peace when ye are the uppermost : God is with you and He will not forget your (praiseworthy) actions." It reverts to it again (8/61) and says : "If they incline to peace, then incline to that and have

confidence in God." So did the Prophet on the conquest of Mecca, and told its inhabitants : "Go, you are freed."

298. The Quran attaches so great an importance to the given word, that it does not hesitate (8/72) to give it preference over the material interest of the Muslim community. It teaches us the Islamic law of neutrality even in the case of religious persecution, in the following terms : ".......with regard to those who believe (in Islam) but do not immigrate (into Islamic territory), ye have no duty to protect them till they immigrate; but if they seek help from you in the name of religion then it is your duty to help (them) *except against a folk between whom and you there is a treaty of peace* (*mithaq*) : and God is Seer of what ye do."

CONCLUSION

299. To sum up, Islam seeks to establish a world community, with complete equality among peoples, without distinction of race, class, or country. It seeks to convert by persuasion, allowing no compulsion in religious beliefs, every individual being personally responsible to God. To Islam, government signifies a trust, a service, in which the functionaries are the servants of the people. According to Islam, it is the duty of every individual to make a constant effort for spreading the good and prevent evil; and God judges us according to our acts and intentions.

CHAPTER IX

The Judicial System of Islam

SPECIAL CONTRIBUTION OF MUSLIMS

LAW exists in human society from time immemorial. Every race, every region, and every group of men has made some contribution in this sphere. The contribution made by Muslims is as rich as it is worthy and valuable.

SCIENCE OF LAW

301. The ancients have all had their particular laws, yet a science of law, abstract in existence and distinct from laws and codes, does not seem to have ever been thought of before Shafi'i[1] (150-204 H./767-820). The work of this jurist, *Risalah* designates this science under the expressive name of *usul al-fiqh* "Roots of Law," from which shoot the branches of the rules of human conduct. This science called ever since *Usul al-Fiqh* among the Muslims, treats simultaneously with the philosophy of law, sources of rules, and principles of legislation, interpretation and application of legal texts. These latter, i.e., laws and rules are called *furu'* (branches) of this tree. Apparently these authors were inspired in the choice of the terms by the Quranic verse (14/24-25): "the example of a goodly word is like a goodly tree: its roots set

---

1. *He died in (204 H/820). He has had some predecessors, such as Abu Hanifah (d. 767) with his Kitab ar-Ra'y (i.e. on the Juridical opinion), and this latter's two pupils Muhammad as-Shaibani and Abu Yousuf each of whom with a Kitab Usul al-Fiqh (i.e. on the Roots of Law). Yet none of them has come down to us in order to judge them on the basis of their contents.*

firm, its branches reaching into heaven, giving its fruit at every season by permission of its Lord".

INTENTION IN ACT

302. Among the novelties in the domain of fundamental notions of law, may be pointed out the importance given to the conception of motive and intention (niyah) in acts. This notion is based on the celebrated saying of the Prophet of Islam (d. 632 of Christian era): "The acts are not (to be judged) except by motives." Ever since an intentional tort or crime, and one caused involuntarily, have not been treated alike by Muslim tribunals.

WRITTEN CONSTITUTION OF STATE

303. It is interesting as well as inspiring to note that the very first revelation (Quran 96/1-5) received by the Prophet of Islam, who was an unlettered person himself, was the praise of the pen as a means of learning unknown things, and as a grace of God. It is not surprising that, when the Prophet Muhammad endowed his people with a statal organism, created out of nothing, he promulgated a written constitution for this State, which was a City-State at first, but only ten years later, at the moment of the demise of its founder, extended over the whole of the big Arabian Peninsula, and the southern portions of Iraq and Palestine.[1] After another fifteen years, during the caliphate of 'Uthman, there was an astonishing penetration of Muslim armies to Andalusia (Spain) on the one hand, and the Chinese

---

1. *Among those who received invitation of the Prophet Muhammad to embrace Islam, there is also the King of Samawah, in Iraq. As to Palestine, the campaign of Tobuk attached Ailah, Jarba and Adhruh to the Islamic territory.*

Turkistan[1] on the other, they having already occupied the countries that lay in between. This written constitution, prepared by Prophet Muhammad, comprising 52 clauses, has come down to us *in toto* (cf. Ibn Hisham, for instance). It treats a variety of questions, such as the respective rights and duties of the ruler and the ruled, legislation, administration of justice, organization of defence, treatment of non-Muslim subjects, social insurance on the basis of mutuality, and other requirements of that age. The Act dates from 622 of the Christian era, i.e., the first year of the Hijrah.

UNIVERSAL INTERNATIONAL LAW

304. War, which unfortunately has always been very frequent among the members of the human family, is a time when one is least disposed to behave reasonably and do justice against one's own self, and in favour of one's adversary. As it is really a question of life and death, and a struggle for very existence, in which the least mistake or error would lead to dangerous consequences, the sovereigns and heads of States have always claimed the privilege to decide, at their discretion, the measures they take in regard to the enemy. The science relating to such behaviour of independent sovereigns has existed from very old times; but it formed part of politics and mere discretion, at the most guided by experience. The Muslims seem to have been the first to separate this science of public international law from the changing whims and fancies of the rulers of the States, and to place it on a purely legal basis. Moreover, it is they who have left to posterity the oldest extant works on international law, developed as an independent science. Among authors of such treatises, we

---

1. For the conquest of part of Spain in the year 27 H., cf. Tabari, Baladhuri, etc.; and for that of Transoxiana or Chinese Turkistan in the same year, see Baladhuri, which fact is corroborated by Chinese historians also.

find names of such eminent personalities as Abu Hanifah, Malik, al-Auza'i, Abu Yousuf, Muhammad ash-Shaibani, Zufar, al-Waqidi, etc. They all called the subject *siyar* (conduct, i.e., of the sovereign). Further, in the ordinary codes of law — the oldest extant work hails from Zaid ibn 'Ali who died in 120 or 122 H., and also by every subsequent author—one speaks of this subject as forming part of the law of the land. In fact one speaks of it immediately after the question of highway robbery, as if war could be justified for the same reason as police action against highwaymen. The result is that belligerents have both rights and obligations, cognizable by Muslim courts.

GENERAL CHARACTERISTICS OF MUSLIM LAW CODES

305. The first thing which strikes the imagination of the reader of a manual on Islamic law is that this law seeks to regulate the entire field of human life, in its material aspect as well as the spiritual one. Such manuals begin usually with the rites and practices of cult, and discuss under this rubric also the constitutional question of sovereignty, since the *imam*, i.e., the head of the State is ex-officio leader of the service of worship in the mosque (cf. Kitab al-Umm of Shafi'i, ch. *salaat*). One should not therefore be astonished that this part of law books deals also with the subject of the payment of taxes; since the Quran has often spoken of worship and the zakat-tax in the same breath, worship being bodily worship and tax the worship of God by means of money. Thereafter the law manual discusses contractual relations of all sorts; then the crimes and penalties, which include laws of war and peace with foreign countries, i.e., international law and diplomacy also; and finally the rules governing heritage and wills. Man is composed both of body and soul; and if government with the enormous resources at its disposal attends exclusively to material affairs, the spirit would be famished, being left to its own private resources, very meagre in comparison with those available in temporal affairs. The unequal developments of body and soul will

150

lead to a lack of equilibrium in man, the consequences of which will in the long run be disastrous to civilization. This treatment of the whole, both of body and soul, does not imply that the uninitiated should adventure in the domain of religion, even as a poet, for instance, should not be allowed to perform surgical operations; every branch of human activity must have its own specialists and experts.

306. Another feature of the Islamic law seems to be the emphasis laid on the correlativity of right and obligation. Not only the mutual relations of men among themselves, but even those of men with their Creator are based on the same principle; and cult is nothing but the performance of the duty of man corresponding to the rights to the usufruct of worldly things that Providence has accorded him. To speak only of the "rights of man," without simultaneously bringing into relief his duties would be transforming him into a rapacious beast, a wolf or a devil.

PHILOSOPHY OF LAW

307. The classical jurists, among Muslims, place laws on the double basis of good and evil. One should do what is good and abstain from what is evil. The good and evil are sometimes absolute and self-evident, and at other times merely relative and partial. This leads us to the five-fold division of all judicial rules, both orders and injunctions. Thus, all that is absolutely good would be an absolute duty, and one must do that. Everything which has a preponderant good would be recommended and considered meritorious. Things where both these aspects, of good and evil, are equal, or which have neither of them, would be left to the discretion of the individual to do or abstain from, at will, and even to change the practice from time to time; this category would be a matter of indifference to law. Things absolutely evil would be objects of complete prohibition, and, finally, things which have a prepon-

derance of evil would be reprehensible and discouraged. This basic division of acts or rules into five categories may have other sub-divisions with as minute nuances as the directions on a compass dial in addition to the four cardinal points of north, south, east and west.

308. It remains to define and distinguish between the good and the evil. The Quran, which is the Word of God and a revered Book to Muslims, speaks of these on many occasions, and says that one must do the *ma'ruf* and abstain from the *munkar*. Now, *ma'ruf* means a good which is recognized as such by everybody and which is considered by reason to be good, and therefore is commanded. And *munkar* means a thing which is denounced by everybody as not at all being good, an evil which is recognized as such by everybody; and that which is considered by reason to be evil would be forbidden. A very great part of Islamic morality belongs to this domain; and the cases are very rare in which the Quran forbids a thing and in which there is a divergence of human opinion, such as the prohibition of alcoholic drinks, or games of chance; but to tell the truth the raison-d'etre of law even in such cases is not concealed from thinking and mature minds. In practice, this is a question of confidence in the wisdom and intelligence of the Legislator, whose directions in all the other cases have occasioned nothing but universal approbation.

THE SANCTIONS

309. One meets among the members of the human race most varied temperaments, and these could be divided into three big categories : those who are good and resist all temptations of evil, without in the least being compelled by anybody thereto; those who are bad, and seek, by all means, to escape even from the most strict supervision; and finally those who behave in a suitable manner so long as they have a fear of reprisals, but who permit themselves injustice also when there

are temptations with more or less probability of escaping from detection. Unfortunately the number of individuals of the first category is very restricted; they need neither guides, nor sanctions against violation of laws. The other two categories require sanctions in the interests of society. The disposition of the spirit to do harm to others may be a sickness, a remnant of the criminal animality, a result of bad education, or due to other causes. An attempt will be made to control and counteract the possible harm done by men of the second category, whose number fortunately is also not very great. There remains the third or the intermediate category of the very vast majority of men. They require sanctions, but of what kind ?

310. It goes without saying that if a chieftain has himself a bad conscience, having committed a prohibited thing, he would have little courage to reproach others about that thing. Therefore Islam has struck at the root and the source of this kind of evil, and declared that nobody is exempt from obligations, not even the sovereign, not even the prophet. The teaching as well as the practice of the Prophet Muhammad, followed by his successors, requires that the head of the State should be fully capable of being cited before the tribunals of the country, without the least restriction. The Islamic tradition has been that judges never hesitated in practice to decide even against their sovereigns in cases of default.

311. It is needless to mention in detail the material sanctions which exist in Islam as in all other civilizations. Thus there are services which are charged with the maintenance of law and order, watch and ward, peace and tranquillity in the mutual relations of the inhabitants of the country and if anybody is victim of violence he can complain before the tribunals, and the police would drag the accused to appear before the judges, whose decision is finally executed.

312. But the conception of society, as envisaged by the Prophet of Islam, has added another sanction, perhaps more efficacious than the material one, and that is the spiritual sanction. Maintaining all the administrative paraphernalia of justice, Islam has inculcated in the minds of its adherents the notion of resurrection after death, of Divine judgement and salvation or condemnation in the Hereafter. It is thus that the believer accomplishes his obligations even when he has the opportunity of violating them with impunity, and he abstains from doing harm to others in spite of all the temptations and the enjoyment of security against the risk of retaliation.

313. This triple sanction — of rulers being equally subject to the general law, material sanctions and spiritual sanctions, each element of which strengthens the efficacy of the other, — tries to secure in Islam the maximum observance of laws and the realization of the rights and obligations of all. It is more efficacious than a system in which only one of these sanctions obtains.

THE LEGISLATION

314. In order to better understand the implication of the affirmation that God is the supreme Legislator, we have to think of the different aspects of the question.

315. Islam believes in One God, Who is not only the Creator of all, but also the Sustainer, the *sine qua non* of the very existence of the universe. He is not "placed on the retired list" after having created what He has created. Islam believes further that God is transcendent and beyond all physical perception of man, and that He is omnipresent, omnipotent, just and merciful. Moreover, in His great mercy, He has given man not only reason but also guides, chosen from among men themselves, instructed in the directions which are most wise and most useful to human society. God being transcendent

He sends His messages to His chosen men by means of intermediate celestial message-bearers.

316. God is perfect and eternal. Among men, on the contrary, there is constant evolution. God does not change His opinions, but He exacts from men only that which accords with their individual capacities. That is why there are divergences, at least in certain details, among legislations, each of which claims to be based on Divine revelations. In legislative matters, the latest law abrogates and replaces all the former ones; the same is true of Divine revelations.

317. Among Muslims, the Quran, which is a book in the Arabic language, is the Word of God, a Divine revelation received by the Prophet Muhammad and destined for his adherents. Moreover, in his quality of being the messenger of God, Muhammad, of the holy memory, has explained the sacred text, and given further directions; and these are recorded in *Hadith*, or the collection of the reports on the sayings and doings of the Prophet Muhammad.

318. It goes without saying that the laws promulgated by an authority can only be abrogated by itself or by a superior authority, but not by an inferior one. So a Divine revelation can be abrogated only by another posterior Divine revelation. Similarly the directions of the Prophet can be modified by himself or by God, but not by any of his disciples or others. But this theoretical aspect of rigidity becomes in practice quite elastic in Islam, in order to permit men to adapt themselves to exigencies and circumstances:

(i) The laws, even those of Divine origin or emanating from the Prophet, have not all the same range. We have just seen that only some of these are obligatory; others are only recommended, while in the rest of the cases, the law allows great latitude to individuals. A study of the sources shows that the rules of the first category, i.e., the obligatory ones, are very few in number; those rules which are recommended are a bit more numerous; and cases where the text is silent are innumerable.

(ii) An inferior authority does not change the law, yet it may interpret it. The power of interpretation is not the monopoly of any person in Islam : every man making a special study of the subject has the right of doing that. A sick man would never consult a poet, not even a laureate who has gained a Nobel prize; to construct a house, one does not consult a surgeon, but an engineer; in the same way, for legal questions one must study law and perfect one's knowledge of the subject: the opinion of persons outside the profession will only be a venture. The interpretations of the specialists show the possibility of adapting even the Divine law to circumstances; for Muhammad being the last of the prophets and having left this world as all mortals, there is no more possibility of receiving a new revelation from God to decide problems in the case of divergence of interpretations. There must evidently be divergences of opinion, since all men do not think in the same manner. It may be pointed out that judges, jurisconsults or other experts of law are all human beings; and if they differ among themselves, the public follows the one who appears to be more authoritative. In a judicial litigation, the judge is obeyed; in other cases, the schools of law obtain preference in the eyes of the adherents of the respective schools and so on.

(iii) The Prophet Muhammad himself has enunciated the rule. "My people shall never be unanimous in an error," (reported by Ibn Hanbal, Tirmidhi, Ibn Majah and others): Such a negative consensus has great possibilities of developing the Islamic law and adapting it to changing circumstances. The spirit of investigation is never strangled; on the contrary this Hadith seems to lay down that every opinion which is not rejected unanimously will not entail excommunication.

(iv)   A celebrated incident of the life of the Prophet Muhammad reported by a large number of sources, deserves mention: Mu'adh ibn Jabal, a judge-designate of Yaman, paid a visit to the Prophet to take his leave before departure to take up office. The following conversation took place: "On what basis shalt thou decide litigation ?—According to the provisions in the Book of God (the Quran)! — And if thou dost not find any provision therein ?   Then according to the conduct of the Messenger of God (i.e., Muhammad)! — And if thou dost not find a provision even therein ? — Well, then, I shall make an effort with my own opinion !'' The Prophet was so delighted at this reply, that far from reproaching him, he exclaimed : "Praise be to God Who hath guided the envoy of His envoy to what pleaseth the envoy of God!" This individual effort of opinion and common-sense on the part of an honest and conscientious man is not only a means of developing the law, but also a recipient of the benediction of the Prophet.

(v)   It may be remembered that, in legislation on a new problem, in the interpretation of a sacred text, or in any other case of development of the Islamic law, even when it is occasioned on the basis of a consensus, there is always the possibility that one rule adopted by a process would later be replaced by another rule, by later jurists using the same process. Opinion of an individual by the opinion of another individual, a consensus by another consensus (cf. al-Bazdawi, *Usul*). (This refers to opinions of jurists only, and has nothing to do with the Quran or the authentic Hadith. For God's order can be abrogated by God Himself, and by nobody else; a Prophet's order by a Prophet or by God, and not by an inferior authority of a jurist or a parliament.

319.   History has shown that the power of "legislation" has been vested in Islam in private savants, who are outside official interference. Such legislation would neither suffer from the influence of daily politics, nor serve the interests of particular

persons, even if they were heads of States. The jurists being all equal, each of them can freely criticise the opinion of the other, providing thus the possibility of bringing into relief all the aspects of a problem, either immediately or in the course of generations to come, and so arriving at the best solution.

320. Thus one sees that the Divine origin of legislation in Islam does not render it rigid out of all proportion. What is more important still is that this quality of the Divine origin of law inspires in the believers an awe for the law, in order that it may be observed conscientiously and scrupulously. It may be added that the jurists of classical times have unanimously declared — that "All that the Muslims consider good, is good in the eyes of God." — even if it does not concern a saying of the Prophet himself. (To Sarakhsi it is a Hadith of the Prophet; Ibn Hanbal has known it as a saying of Ibn Mas'ud the Companion of the Prophet). The consensus, in the light of this interpretation, implies that even the deduction of lay savants, entails Divine approval, a fact which adds to the respect of law in the eyes of men.

ADMINISTRATION OF JUSTICE

321. A characteristic feature of the Quranic legislation in this respect is the judicial autonomy accorded to the different communities comprising the subjects. Far from imposing the Quranic law on everybody, Islam admits and even encourages that every group, Christian, Jewish, Magian or other should have its own tribunals presided over by its own judges, in order to have its own laws applied in all branches of human affairs, civil as well as criminal. If the parties to a dispute belong to different communities, a kind of private international law decides the conflict of laws. Instead of seeking the absorption and assimilation of everybody in the "ruling" community, Islam protects the interests of all its subjects (cf. § 293 supra).

322. As for the administration of justice among Muslims, apart from its simplicity and expedition, the institution of the "purification of witnesses" is worth mentioning. In fact, in every locality tribunals organize archives regarding the conduct and habits of all the inhabitants, in order to know, when necessary, whether a witness is trustworthy. It is not left only to the opposite party to weaken the value of an evidence. The Quran (24/4) has said that, if someone accuses the chastity of a woman and does not prove it according to the judicial exigencies, not only is he punished, but is also rendered, for ever, unworthy of testimony before tribunals.

ORIGIN AND DEVELOPMENT OF LAW

323. The Prophet Muhammad taught theological and eschatological dogmas to his adherents; he also gave them laws concerning all activities of life, individual as well as collective, temporal as well as spiritual moreover, he created a State out of nothing, which he administered, built up armies which he commanded, set up a system of diplomacy and foreign relations which he controlled; and if there were litigations, it was he who decided them among his "subjects." So, it is to him rather than anybody else that one should look for studying the origin of the Islamic law. He was born in a family of merchants and caravan-leaders, inhabiting Mecca. In his youth he had visited the fairs and markets of Yaman and of Eastern Arabia, i.e. 'Uman, cf. Ibn Hanbal IV, 206 — as well as of Palestine. His co-citizens used to go also to Iraq, Egypt and Abyssinia with the object of trade. When he began his missionary life, the violent reaction of his compatriots obliged him to go into exile and settle down in another town, Madinah, where agriculture was the principal means of livelihood of the inhabitants. There he organized a statal life; first a city - state was established, which was gradually transformed into a State which extended, at the time of his death, over the whole Arabian Peninsula together

with some parts of Southern Iraq and Palestine. International caravans traversed Arabia. It is well known that the Sassanians and the Byzantines had occupied certain regions of Arabia, and established colonies or protectorates. In the fairs, particularly of Eastern Arabia, merchants were attracted every year even from India, China, and "from the East and from the West" as Ibn al-Kalbi and al-Mas'udi have described. There were not only nomads in Arabia, but also settled people, of whom the Yamanites and Lihyanites had developed civilizations dating from before the foundation of the cities of Athens and Rome.

324. The customary laws of the country were transformed, when Islam came, into statal acts of legislation; and the Prophet had, for his adherents and subjects, the prerogative not only of modifying the old customs, but also of promulgating entirely new laws. His status as the messenger of God was responsible for the exceptional prestige he held. So much so that not only his words, but even his acts also constituted law for the Muslims in all walks of life; even his very silence implied that he did not oppose a custom which was practised around him by his adherents. This triple source of legislation, viz., his words, which are all based on Divine revelation, his deeds, and his tacit approval of the practices and customs of his adherents, has been preserved to us in the Quran and the *Hadith*. While he was still alive, another source began to germinate, viz., the deduction and elaboration of rules, in cases where the legislation was silent, and this was done by jurists other than the head of the State. In fact there were judges and jurisconsults, in the time of the Prophet, even in the metropolis, not to speak of the provincial administrative centres. We have already mentioned the instructions given to Mu'adh when he was sent to Yaman as judge. There were cases, when the provincial functionaries demanded instructions from the central government, which also took the initiative and intervened

in cases of incorrect decisions of the subordinates, if and when they came to the notice of the higher authority. The order to change or modify the ancient customs and practices, or the Islamisation of the law of the whole country, could take place only gradually, because the judges did not intervene except in cases brought to their notice, cases not brought to their notice, in which the parties acted, in ignorance of the law, according to their convenience, must have been numerous. For instance, a Muslim had been married to his own german sister; when the case was brought to the caliph Umar and he asked the explanation from the person concerned, this latter replied that he did not know that it was prohibited. The caliph separated them and demanded the man to pay damages to his sister, yet he did not inflict punishment on account of fornication or incest.

325. The death of the Prophet marks the cessation of the Divine revelations which had the force of ordering every law, abrogating or modifying every old custom or practice. Thereafter the Muslim community was obliged to be content with the legislation already accomplished by the Prophet, and with the means of the development of law authorized by this same legislation. "Development" does not mean abrogation of what the Prophet had legislated, but to know the law in case of the silence of the law.

326. Of these the most important were perhaps the following. On several occasions, the Quran (4/24, 5/1) has, after instituting certain prohibitions, expressly added that all the rest was lawful (in the domain concerned). So, all that does not go against the legislation emanating from the Prophet is permissible, and constitutes good law, the laws and even customs of foreign countries have always served as raw material to the Muslim jurists, in order to detach from them those that were incompatible with Islam, the rest being lawful. This source is perennial.

327. Another source, surprising perhaps, is the direction given by the Quran (6/90) that the Divine revelations received by the former prophets — and it has named almost a score of them, such as Enoch, Noah, Abraham, Moses, David, Solomon, Jesus Christ, John the Baptist — are equally valid for Muslims. But its range and scope was limited only to revelations, the authenticity of which was proved beyond doubt, that is, those recognized expressly by the Quran or the *Hadith* to be so. The law of retaliation of Pentateuch is an instance mentioned in the Quran (5/45), when it is precisely said : "God has prescribed that on Jews", without adding "and on you"

328. Only fifteen years after the death of the Prophet, we see the Muslims ruling over three continents, over vast territories in Asia and Africa and in Andalusia in Europe. Caliph 'Umar had judged the Sassanian fiscality to be good enough to be continued in the provinces of Iraq and Iran; the Byzantine fiscality he found oppressive, and changed it in Syria and Egypt; and so on and so forth. The whole of the first century of the Hijrah was a period of adaptation, consolidation and transformation. The documents on papyrus, discovered in Egypt, inform us of many aspects of Egyptian administration. From the beginning of the second century of the Hijrah, we possess codes of law, copiled by private jurists, one of the earliest of them being Zaid ibn 'Ali, who died in 120 H.

329. The ancients called Yaman "Arabia Felix," — as distinct from Arabia Petra and Arabia Deserta — and not without reason. The physical and other conditions had given it in pre-Christian antiquity an incomparable superiority over other regions of Arabia, as regards culture and civilization; its wealth, as attested by the Bible, was legendary, and its kingdoms mighty. At the beginning of the Christian era, a wave of emigration had led certain Yamanite tribes to Iraq, where they founded the Kingdom of Hirah, which was celebrated for its patronage of letters, and which continued to exist till the dawn

of Islam. In the meanwhile, Yaman knew Jewish rule (under Dhu-Nuwas); Christian domination (under the Abyssinians) followed by the Magian or Parsi occupation of the Iranians, who in their turn yielded place to Islam. The Yamanites influenced by all those successive interactions and strains, were persuaded once again under Caliph 'Umar to emigrate to Iraq and populate it, particularly the part Kufah, which was a new town raised beside the old city of Hirah, 'Umar sent Ibn Mas'ud, one of the most eminent jurists from among the companions of the Prophet, to conduct a school there. His successors at the school, 'Alqamah an-Nakha'i, Ibrahim an-Nakha'i, Hammad, and Abu Hanifa were all, by providential chance, specialists in law. In the meanwhile, 'Ali, another great jurist among the companions of the Prophet, transferred the seat of the caliphate from Madinah to Kufah. It is not surprising therefore that this town became the seat of uninterrrupted traditions, and gained an ever-increasing reputation in matters of law.

330. The absence of all interference from the governmental authority in the liberty of the opinions of the judges and jurists proved greatly favourable for the rapid progress of this science ;but it suffered from certain inconveniences too. In fact, an experienced and high ranking administrator as Ibn al-Muqaffa' complained in his *Kitab as-Sahabah* at the beginning of the second century of the Hijrah, of the enormous quantity of divergences in the Muslim case law, be that penal law, the law of personal status or any other branches of law, particularly in Basrah and Kufah; and he suggested to the caliph the creation of a supreme institution for the revision of the decisions of the judiciary and the imposition of a single, uniform law in all parts of the realm. The suggestion proved abortive. His contemporary, Abu-Hanifah, was jealous of the liberty of science, and solicitous of keeping it aloof from the turmoil of ever-changing politics; and he created, instead, an academy of law. With its forty members, of whom each one was a specialist in a science auxiliary to law — such as the exegesis of the Quran, *Hadith*,

logic, lexicology, etc. — this academy undertook the task of evaluating the case law of the time, and of codifying the laws; it tried also to fill up the gaps in Muslim law on points on which neither the text nor the precedents of the case law had pronounced any opinion. One of his biographers states that Abu-Hanifah (d. 150 H.) "had promulgated half a million rules" (cf. *al-Muwaffaq*, 11, 137). Malik at Madinah, and al-Auza'i in Syria, undertook at the same time a similar task, but they depended on their own solitary knowledge and personal resources. If Abu-Hanifah laid an emphasis on reasoning — notwithstanding the recourse to the Quran and the *Hadith* as the basis of all law — Malik preferred the usage of the population of Madinah — a town impregnated with the traditions of the Prophet — to deduction or logical interpretation.

331. The Quran was "published" only a few months after the death of the Prophet. The task of collecting the data on the sayings and doings of the Prophet as well as his tacit approbation of the conduct of his companions — a material which is called *Hadith* — was undertaken by some persons in the life-time of the Prophet, and later by many others after the Prophet's death. More than a hundred thousand of the companions of the Prophet have left to posterity valuable traditions, based on whatever they remembered on the subject. Some put them down in writing — over fifty, according to the latest research — and others conveyed them by oral communication. These materials of very high legal value were naturally dispersed in the three continents where the companions of the Prophet had gone and settled in the time of the caliphs 'Umar and Uthman. In the following generations, the researchers compiled treatises, even more comprehensive, based on and amalgamating the collections of individual memoirs of the companions of the Prophet.

332. The evaluation of the case law and the codification of the *Hadith* were completed as parallel works at the same time, yet each ignored and was suspicious of the other. Ash-

Shafi'i was born in the year in which Abu-Hanifah died. Mutual differences or polemics led the jurists to take greater cognizance of the *Hadith;* and the specialists of *Hadith* to put in order the data on the sayings and doings of the Prophet, to evaluate the individual merits of the sources of transmission, and determine the context and time of the different sayings of the Prophet, for purposes of deducting the law therefrom. Ash-Shafi'i specialised simultaneously in law and in *Hadith* and thanks to his high intellectual qualities and his efforts, a synthesis was discovered between the two disciplines. Ash-Shafi'i is the first in world history to create an abstract science of law distinct from laws in the sense of rules applied in a country.

333. Another big school (or tradition) of law was founded by Ja'far as-Sadiq, a descendant of 'Ali and a contemporary of Abu-Hanifah. Reasons of rather a political kind were responsible for the development of the law of inheritance in this school in a special manner. Abu-Hanifah, Malik, ash-Shafi'i, Ja'far as-Sadiq and several other jurists each has left his school of law. The adherents of these schools form sub-communities of Islam in our age, yet the differences among them have an influence even less than that of the philosophic schools. With the passage of centuries, it has become common experience to find that some Shafi'ites differ from ash-Shafi'i on certain points and hold the same opinion as Malik or Abu-Hanifah, and *vice versa.*

334. As we have just seen, the Muslim "empire" extended very early over immense territories, which were formerly governed by different legal systems, like the Iranian, Chinese, Indian, Byzantine, Gothic, and others, and to these were added the local contributions of the very first Muslims of Arabia. The possibility of any single foreign legal system having the monopoly of influencing Muslim law is therefore excluded. Among the founders of schools also we find that Abu-Hanifah was of

Persian origin and Malik, ash-Shafi'i and Ja'far as-Sadiq were Arabs. The biographer adh-Dhahabi reports that al-Auza'i was originally of Sindh; and in the subsequent generations there emerged Muslim jurist from all races. The development of Muslim law was therefore an "international" enterprise, in which Muslim jurists of every diverse ethnic origins, speaking different languages, and following different customs, have taken part. There were European Muslims from Spain, Portugal and Sicily, there were Chinese, Abyssinians, Indians, Persians, Turks and many others besides the Arabs.

335. It is a phenomenon observed in all countries that certain Chauvinists and those lacking in independent thought wish to sacrifice the spirit to the letter of the teaching of an old master, while others adventure into non-conformism. But it is the golden means that should always prevail ! A spirit without an inferiority complex, but equipped with the necessary preparation in data, and endowed at the same time with the piety of a practising believer, will never encounter difficulty in finding interpretation practical, as well as reasonable, such as would even modify the opinion held by the ancients. With what confidence and assurance does the great jurist Pazdawi tell us that not only individual opinions, but even the consensus of former times can be replaced by a later consensus !

CONCLUSION

336. Muslim law began as the law of a State and of a ruling community and served the purposes of the community when the Muslim rule grew in dimension and extended from the Atlantic to the Pacific. It had an inherent capacity to develop and to adapt itself to the exigencies of time and clime. It has not lost its dynamism even today, in fact it is obtaining more and more recognition as an agency for good, by Muslim countries which were formerly under foreign political — and therefore juridical — domination, and are trying to reintroduce the Shari'ah in all walks of life.

CHAPTER X

The Economic System of Islam

ISLAM provides guidance to its adherents in all phases and activities of life, in matters, material as well as spiritual. Its basic teaching with regard to economics is mentioned in several passages of the Quran. Far from despising material well-being, it recognizes (4/5) that: "... ...your goods which God has made as the very means of your subsistence... ..."; and it orders: "and neglect not thy portion of this world" (Q. 28/77). It lays however emphasis on the dual composition of man, by reminding: "...... but of mankind is he who saith: Our Lord! give unto us in this world; and he hath no portion in the Hereafter. And of them is also he who saith: Our Lord! give unto us what is good in this world and what is good in the Hereafter, and guard us from the doom of Fire. For these there is in store a goodly portion out of that which they have earned; God is swift at reckoning." (Q. 2/200-2). In other verses we find it stated plainly and definitely that, all that is found on the earth, in the seas and even the heavens has been created by God for the benefit of man; or that all that is on earth, in the heavens, the ocean, the stars and others have been made sub-servient to man by God. It remains for man to know and to profit by the creation of God, and profit in a rational way, paying due regard to the future.

338. The economic policy of Islam has also been explained in the Quran, in most unequivocal terms: "... so that this (wealth) may not circulate solely among the rich from among you......" (Q. 59/7) Equality of all men in wealth and comfort, even if it is ideal, does not promise to be of unmixed good

to humanity. First because natural talents are not equal among different men, so much so that even if one were to start a group of persons with complete equality, soon the spendthrift will fall into difficulties and will again look on the fortune of his comrades with greed and envy. Further, on philosophic and psychological grounds, it seems that in the very interest of human society it is desirable that there should be grades in wealth, the poorer having the desire and incentive to work harder. On the other hand, if everybody is told that even if he works more than what is required of him as his duty, he would get no reward and would remain as those who do not do more than their duty, one would become lazy and neglectful, and one's talent would be wasted to the great misfortune of humanity.

338/a. Everyone knows that human livelihood is in constant progress, through the domination and exploitation one after the other of all those things that God has created, whereas one sees that the rest of animals have changed nothing in their livelihood ever since God has created their species. The cause of this difference as discovered by biologists is the simultaneous existence of a society, a co-operation, and a liberty of competition inside the members of the society, i.e., human beings, whereas other animals suffer from the lack of some or of all of these requisite conditions. Dogs, cats and snakes for instance do not create even a family; they perpetuate their race by means of free and momentary "love". Others, such as crows and pigeons do create a family in the form of couples yet even if the male helps in the construction of the nest, every member of the couple depends on its own gain for its livelihood. Perhaps the most developed social co-operation is found among bees, ants and termites (white ants): they live in a collective way, with complete equality in livelihood, yet without any competition among its members, and consequently it is not possible for the more intelligent or more industrious bee to live more comfortably than others. For this reason there is neither evolution nor change, much less progress in any of these species, as against the human race. The past history of man shows that every advance and every discovery of the means of comfort came into existence through competition and desire for amelioration, and also through the existence of grades of wealth or poverty among men, one above the other. Yes, the absolute liberty would lead devilish men to exploit the needy, and ooze them out gradually. So it was necessary for every progressive civilization and every healthy culture to impose certain duties on its members (such as the order to pay taxes, the interdiction of having recourse to oppression and cheating, etc.), and to recommend certain supererogatory acts (like charity and expenditure for the sake of God), yet nevertheless to have a great deal of liberty of thought and action to its members, so that each one benefits himself, his family, his friends and the society at large. This is the exigency of Islam, and it also conform to nature.

339. It is on the basis of this fundamental principle that Islam has constructed its economic system. If it tolerates the minority of the rich, it imposes on them heavier obligations : they have to pay taxes in the interest of the poor, and they are prevented from practising immoral means of exploitation, hoarding and accumulation of wealth. For this end there will be some orders or injunctions, and also some recommendations — for charity and sacrifice — with the promise of spiritual (other-worldly) reward. Further it makes, on the one hand, a distinction between the necessary minimum and the desirable plenitude, and on the other hand between those orders and injunctions which are accompanied by material sanctions and those which are not so, but for which Islam contents itself with persuasion and education only.

340. We shall describe first in a few words this moral aspect. Some illustrations would enable us to better understand its implications. Most emphatic terms have been employed by Islam to show that to beg charity of others is something

abominable, and it would be a source of shame on the day of Resurrection; yet simultaneously unlimited praise has been bestowed on those who come to the aid of the others, the best of men being in fact those who make a sacrifice and prefer others to their own selves. Similarly avarice and waste are both prohibited. One day the Prophet of Islam had need of considerable funds for some public cause. One of his friends brought a certain sum to offer as his contribution, and on the demand of the Prophet, he replied: "I have left at home nothing but the love of God and of His messenger." This person received the warmest praise from the Prophet. Yet on another occasion, another companion of his, who was seriously ill, told him when he came to inquire about his health: "O messenger of God! I am a rich man, and I want to bequest all that I possess for the welfare of the poor." The Prophet replied: "No; it is better to leave to thy relatives an independent means of livelihood than that they should be dependent on others and be obliged to beg." Even for two-thirds and for a half of the possessions the remark of the Prophet was: "that is too much." When the proposal was submitted to give one-third of the property in charity, he said: "Well, even the third is a large amount." (cf. Bukhari). One day the Prophet saw one of his companions in miserable attire. On enquiry, he replied: "O messenger of God! I am not at all poor; only I prefer to spend my wealth on the poor rather than on my own self." The Prophet remarked: "No; God likes to see on His slave traces of the bounty that He has accorded him!" (cf. Abu Dawud and Tirmidhi). There is no contradiction in these directions; each has its own context and relates to distinct individual cases. We are afforded an opportunity of determining the limits of the discretionary choice in excess of the obligatory minimum, vis-a-vis the other members of society.

INHERITANCE

341. Both the individual right of disposing of one's wealth, and the right of the collectivity vis-a-vis the wealth of

each individual, in as much as one is a member of society, have to be simultaneously satisfied. Individual temperaments differ enormously. Sickness or other accidents may also affect a man out of all proportion. So it is necessary that a certain discipline should be imposed upon him in the interest of the collectivity.

342. Thus Islam has taken two steps; firstly the obligatory distribution of the goods of a deceased person among his close relatives, and secondly a restriction on the freedom of bequest through wills and testaments. The legal heirs do not require any testamentary disposition, and inherit the property of the deceased in the proportions determined by law. A testament is required solely in favour of those who have no right to inherit from a deceased person.

343. There is equality in the parents of the same category, and one cannot award to one son (elder or younger) more than to the other, whether major or minor. The first charges on the property left by the deceased are the expenses of his burial. What remains goes then to his creditors, the debt having priority over the "rights" of the inheritors. In the third place, his testament is executed, to the measure and extent that it does not exceed the third of the available property (after burial and payment of debts). It is only after satisfying these prior obligations that heirs are considered. The (male or female) partner of life, the parents, the descendants (sons and daughters) are the first class heirs, and inherit in all cases. Brothers and sisters, and other remoter relatives inherit from a deceased person only in the absence of nearer relatives. Among these remoter relatives we find uncles, aunts, cousins, nephews and others.

344. Without entering into technical details, certain basic rules may be described. A homicide is excluded from the inheritance of his own victim, even if the court decides that it was a case of death by involuntary accident. The underlying

idea seems to be to prevent all temptations to kill a rich relative in view of earlier inheritance. The Prophet has also prohibited inheritance among relatives of different religions, even between the husband and wife. However, the right of donating gifts and testament can be availed of in this respect; the Muslim husband, for instance, may bequest even on his death-bed a part of his property in favour of his non-Muslim wife. On the strength of the international and political conditions of their times, the classical Muslim jurists have instituted another hindrance, viz., the difference of the territory (i.e., political nationality) as barring inheritance. Evidently the statal treaties may regulate the question of private international law, in a contrary sense, on the basis of reciprocity.

345. In countries where the Islamic law of inheritance is not applied by governments, yet the right of testament is recognized, the Muslim inhabitants can, and must, utilize this facility, in order to fulfil their religious duty with regard to the disposition of their property after their death.

WILLS

346. We have just mentioned that the right of testamentary bequests is operative only within the limits of a third of the property, in favour of persons other than creditors and heirs. The aim of this rule seems to be two-fold: Firstly, to permit an individual to adjust things, in extraordinary cases, when the normal rule causes hardship; and a third of the property is sufficient for fulfilling all such moral duties. Another motive of the law of will is to prevent the accumulation of wealth in the hands of a few, a thing which would happen if one should give all his property, by will, to a single person excluding totally one's near relatives. Islam desires the circulation of wealth among as large a number of people as possible, taking into account the interests of the family.

PUBLIC GOODS

347. One also has obligations as a member of a larger family, viz., society and the State in which one lives. In the economic sphere, one pays taxes, which the government redistributes in the interests of the collectivity.

348. The rates of taxes differ according to the various kinds of the sources of income, and it is interesting to note that the Quran, which gives precise directions with regard to budgetary expenditure, has enunciated neither rules nor rates of the income of the State. While scrupulously respecting the practice of the Prophet and of his immediate successors, this silence of the Quran may be interpreted as giving a latitude to the government to change the rules for income according to circumstances, in the interests of the people.

349. In the time of the Prophet, there were agricultural taxes, and the peasants handed over a tenth of the harvest, provided it was above a certain taxless minimum and irrigated their lands with rain or spring water, and half that rate in the case of wells as the means of irrigation. In commerce and exploitation of mines, one paid 2½% of the value of goods. As for the import taxes, on foreign caravan-leaders there is an interesting fact which should profitably be brought into relief. In the time of the Prophet, these were subject to a tithe as customs duty; caliph 'Umar reduced by half this tax on foreigners, concerning certain categories of victuals imported in Madinah (as reported by Abu 'Ubaid). This precedent of high authority casts light on the essential principles of the fiscal policy of Islam. In the time of the Prophet, there were taxes on herds of camels, sheep and goats, and oxen provided they were fed on public pastures and exceeded in number the taxless minimum. Exemption was accorded further to beasts of burden and those employed for ploughing and irrigation.

350. There was a tax of 2½% on savings and on silver and gold. This obliged people to employ their wealth for increase, and not indulge in idle hoarding.

STATE EXPENDITURE

351. The Quran (9:60) has prescribed the principles regulating the budget of State expenditure in Islam, in the following terms:

"Verily the *sadaqat* (i.e., taxes on Muslims) are only for the needy, and the poor, and those who work for these (taxes), and those whose hearts are to be reconciled, and to free the necks (i.e., slaves and prisoners of war), and the heavily indebted, and in the path of God, and for the wayfarer — a duty imposed by God; God is Knower, Wise."

These eight heads of expenditure which cover practically all the needs of a collectivity, need elucidation to enable the understanding of their exact range and application.

352. The term *sadaqat*, which we translate as the State tax on Muslims, and which is a synonym of *zakat*, signifies all the taxes paid by Muslims to their government, in normal times, whether on agriculture, mines, commerce, industry, pasturing herds, savings or other heads. These exclude the provisional taxes imposed in abnormal times, the revenues levied on non-Muslims, — subjects or foreigners, — and also all the non-obligatory contributions. Juridical literature of early Islam, and particularly the sayings of the Prophet leave no doubt that the term *sadaqat* was employed in this sense. It did not refer at all to alms, which can be neither obligatory nor determined as to the quantity and the time of payment. The equivalent for alms is *infaq fi sabil Allah*, expenditure in the path of God, or *tatauwu'*, voluntary charity.

353. The first two categories of the needy (*fuqara'*) and the poor (*masakin*), which are almost synonymous, have not

been explained by the Prophet; hence there is a divergence of opinion. According to the sayings and constant practice of the caliph 'Umar, (recorded by Abu Yousuf in his *Kitab-al-Kharaj* and Ibn Abi Shaibah in his *Musannaf*), *fuqara'* are the poor among the Muslims, and *masakin* are from among the non-Muslims residing in the Islamic territory, such as Jews. In his *Futuh al-Buldan*, Baladhuri cites another case of the same caliph, who awarded pensions to Christians of Jabiyah (Syria) from the *sadaqat* i.e., zakat revenues. The jurist ash-Shafi'i thought that the terms were absolutely synonymous, and that God, out of his bounty, named them twice in order to make a double provision. According to this authority, as each of the eight heads in the Quranic verse should receive one-eighth of the State income, the poor would receive two-eighths. Be it what it may, the first duty of the State is to see that no dweller on the Islamic soil is deprived of the means of livelihood: food, dress, lodging, etc.

354. The next item concerns the salaries of the functionaries: collectors, accountants, controllers of expenditure, auditors of accounts, etc. If the truth is to be told, this category comprises the entire administration, civil, military and diplomatic, as one can see in the description of the categories of the beneficiaries. The historian al-Baladhuri (in his *al-Ansab*) has preserved a document in which the caliph 'Umar demands of his governor of Syria: "Send us (to Madinah) an expert Greek, who may put in order the accounts of our revenues". (*hisaba fara 'idina*). We require no better authority for asserting that the non-Muslims could not only be employed in the administration of the Muslim State, but also be beneficiaries of the *sadaqat* levied exclusively on Muslims.

355. The category of those whose hearts are to be reconciled can more easily be understood by the modern term "secret funds". In his *al-Ahkam as-Sultanijah*, the jurist Abu-Ya'la al-Farra' says: "As to those whose hearts are to be won, they

are of four kinds: (1) Those whose hearts are to be won for their coming to the aid of the Muslims; (2) or for abstaining from doing harm to Muslims; (3) for inviting them to embrace Islam; and (4) for inviting through them their clans and families to embrace Islam. It is lawful to spend on each and every one of these whether they be Muslims or polytheists."

356. By the term "freeing the necks", one has always understood two kinds of expenditure: the liberation of slaves, and ransoming of the prisoners of war in the hands of the enemy. According to the Islamic law (Quran 24/33), every slave has the right to purchase his emancipation by paying his value to his master; and in order to earn the necessary amount, he may compel his master to give him facilities to work, and during this period he does not require to serve his master; moreover, as we have just seen, it is the duty of the government to allot every year in the budget a certain sum for aiding the slaves to buy their freedom. A document of the time of the Umaiyad caliph 'Umar ibn 'Abdal-'Aziz (reported by Ibn Sa'd), says, that the payment of the ransoms by the Muslim government includes liberating even the non-Muslim subjects who would have been made prisoners by the enemy.

357. The category of those who are heavily indebted has, according to the practice of classical times, a whole series of applications: one helped those who had suffered from calamities such as floods, earthquakes, etc. It does not refer to the poor, who have already been mentioned in the beginning of the verse, but to the well-to-do who have suffered from abnormal conditions, beyond their power. Caliph 'Umar started a special section in the Public Treasury, in order to lend money, free of interest, to those who had temporary needs and provided the necessary guarantees for repayment. The caliph himself had recourse to it for his private needs. It goes without saying

that the "nationalization" of lending without interest was the necessary concomitant of the prohibition of interest in Islam. The same caliph used to lend public money even to merchants for fixed periods, and the Treasury participated with them in a percentage of their business returns, participated not only in gains, but also in the event of losses. Another application of this State expenditure was for a kind of social insurance. If somebody was found guilty of involuntary homicide and was unable to pay the blood money, required by law, out of his own means, the government came to his help under this head of the budget, as is evidenced by several cases of the practice of the Prophet. We shall revert to this, again, later in detail.

358. The expression "in the path of God", in the Islamic terminology, signifies in the first instance military defence and the expenditure for the personnel, equipment, etc. But the term applies in fact to all sorts of charitable works, such as helping students, grants and aids in religious causes such as the construction of mosques, etc.

359. The last category concerns communications and tourist traffic in a wide sense: construction of bridges, roads, hotels, restaurants, security of routes (police included), hygienic arrangements, transport of travellers, and every comfort provided to aliens in the course of their journeying, including extending of hospitality to them without charge and in proportion to the means available. Formerly such hospitality was assured for three days in every place of stay.

360. In order to appreciate the merit of these Quranic dispositions, one must remember that the time was the very beginning of Islam, fourteen centuries ago. There is not much that could be added to these heads of expenditure. They seem to be well applicable to our own times in a progressive and welfare State, having a concern for the well-being of its subjects.

EXCEPTIONAL TAXES

361. The *sadaqat* were the only taxes of the State in the time of the Prophet and the Orthodox Caliphs. In later times, on occasions of extraordinary need, the jurists have admitted the legal possibility of imposing supplementary charges, on a strictly provisional basis, for possible exigencies. Such taxes are called *nawa'ib* (calamities).

SOCIAL INSURANCE

362. Only risks involving heavy charges from objects of insurance, and these differ according to the times and social conditions. Among the Arabs at the commencement of Islam, the daily ailments were unknown, and medical care cost practically nothing; the average man built his house with his own hands, and did not pay even for the major part of the material. Thus it is easy to understand why one had then no need of insurance against sickness, fire, etc. On the contrary, insurances against captivity and against assassination were a real need. Already in the time of the Prophet, this point had received attention; and certain dispositions were made which had the elasticity of further development and adaptation to circumstances. Thus, in the Constitution of the City-State of Madinah of the first year of the Hijrah, this insurance is called *ma'aqil* and it worked in the following manner. If someone was made prisoner of war by an enemy, payment of ransom was needed for purchasing his liberation. Similarly, all bodily torts or culpable homicides required payment of damages or blood money. This often exceeded the means of the individual concerned, prisoner or criminal. The Prophet organized an insurance on the basis of mutuality : the members of a tribe could count on the central treasury of their tribe, to which everybody contributed according to his means; and if the treasury of the tribe proved inadequate, other related or neighbouring tribes were under obligation to render aid. A hierarchy was established for organizing the units into a complete whole. At

Madinah, the tribes of the Ansarites were well known; the Prophet ordered the Meccan refugees there, who belonged originally to the various tribes of Mecca, or were Abyssinians, or Arabs belonging to different regions, should all constitute a new "tribe" of their own, for purposes of the said social insurance.

363. Later in the time of the caliph 'Umar, the mutualities or units of insurance were organized on the basis of professions, civil or military administrations, to which one belonged, or even of regions. Whenever needed, the central or provincial government came to the succour of the units, as we have described above when speaking of State expenditure.

364. Insurance signifies essentially the repartition of the burden of an individual on as many as possible, in order to lighten the burden of each. Instead of the capitalistic companies of insurance, Islam preferred organizing insurance on the basis of mutuality and co-operation, aided by a gradation of the units culminating in the central government.

365. Such a unit could engage in commerce with the help of the unutilized funds remaining at its disposal, so that the capital is augmented. A time might come, when the members of a unit could be fully exempted, from paying further contributions, and might even receive amounts as profits of commerce. It goes without saying that these units of mutual aid could insure against all kinds of risks, such as accidents of traffic, fire, loss in transit, and so on. It goes also without saying that the insurance business is capable of being "nationalized" for all or certain kinds of risks, for instance, for temporary motives such as the despatch of parcels, etc.

366. Without entering into technical details, it may be pointed out that the capitalistic insurances, in which the insured person does not participate in the benefits of the company in

proportion to his contributions, is not tolerated in Islam. For, such an insurance constitutes a kind of a game of chance.

367. In passing, we might mention another social institution of the time of the caliph 'Umar. He had organized a system of pensions for all the inhabitants of the country—and according to the *Kitab al-Amwal* of Ibn Zanjuwaih and *ar-Risalah al-'Uthmaniyah* of al-Jahiz, even the non-Muslim subjects were among the beneficiaries of these pensions—so much so that as soon as a child was born, he began to receive a certain pension. The adults received the minimum necessary for living. In the beginning, the caliph practised a certain discrimination amongst the different categories of the pensioners, and if the minimum was 1, the most favoured person received 40; yet towards the end of his life, he decided to observe complete equality, but he died before this reform could be introduced. This institution, named "Diwan", by 'Umar, seems to have originated in the very time of the Prophet, as the following report implies: "The basis of this practice is the narration that the Prophet named Mahmiyah ibn Jaz' to be in charge of the governmental fifth of the booty captured on the Banu'l-Mustaliq; and in fact Mahmiyah was in charge of the governmental fifths of all booties. The sadaqat (= zakat taxes) were administered separately, and had their particular functionaries. For peaceful revenues from the enemy (*fay'*) were separate functionaries. The Prophet used to spend the sadaqat on orphans, weaklings and poors: if the orphan reached his puberty and military service (*Jihad*) became his duty, he was transferred from the list of the beneficiaries of the *sadaqaat* to that of the *fay'*, yet if he refused to render military service, he benefited no more from the *sadaqat* and was commanded to earn his livelihood himself". (cf. Sarakhsi, *Sharh as-Siyar al-Kabir*, ed. Munajjed, § 1978).

GAMES OF CHANCE

368. In prohibiting these, the Quran (5/90) has characterized them as the "work of Satan"; and this for cogent

reasons. It is recognized that most of the social evils emanate from the bad distribution of the national wealth, some individuals becoming too rich and the others too poor and in the result they fall victim to exploitation by the rich. In games of chance and lotteries, there is great temptation for quick and easy gains, and often an easy gain is bad for society. Supposing that in the races—of horses and others—and in the lotteries, public or private, as well as all other games of chance, the people of a country spend 3 million pounds every week—as is the case in certain countries—in the course of only ten years, a sum of 1,560 millions of pounds will be collected from a very large number of the inhabitants and redistributed among a ridiculously small number. Less than one per cent of the people thrive at the expense of the remaining 99 per cent. In other words, the 99 per cent are impoverished in order to enrich the 1 per cent, and one creates one per cent of millionaires by systematically ruining the 99 per cent. Whether games of chance, including lotteries, are private or nationalized, the evil of accumulating wealth in the hands of the few, at the expense of a very vast majority, works with full force. Hence the total prohibition of games of chance and lotteries in Islam. As in capitalistic insurances, games of chance bear one-sided risks.

INTEREST ON MONEY-LENDING

369. Probably there is no religion in the world which has not prohibited usury. The distinctive trait of Islam is that it has not only forbidden this kind of gain, but also remedied the causes leading to the existence of this evil institution in human society:

370. Nobody pays willingly an interest on what he borrows: he pays only because he requires money and he finds that he could not get it without paying interest.

371. Islam has made a very clear distinction between commercial gains and interest on money-lending. The Quran

(2/275) says: " . . . God permitteth trading and forbiddeth interest . . . " A little later (2/279), it says: "If you do not give up (interest), then be warned of war against God and His messenger; and if ye repent, then ye shall have your principal, (without interest); neither ye wrong nor be wronged."

372. The basis of the prohibition of interest is also the unilateral risk. For when one borrows a certain sum for earning an increase, it is possible that circumstances should not have been propitious enough for earning sufficiently to be able to pay the promised interest, the lender not participating in the risks of the exploitation.

373. It is not possible to compel an individual to deprive himself of his money, in order to lend it to others gratuitously and without interest. We have pointed out that Islam has ordered that one of the charges on State income is the obligation of helping those who are heavily indebted. Hence, the Public Treasury organizes interest-free loans, in addition to and for supplementing the loans offered by charitable men or organizations, to help those who are in need of them. The principle is the mutual aid and co-operation.

374. In the case of commercial loans, there is also the system of *mudarabah*, in which one lends money and participates equally in gains as well as in risks. If, for instance, two individuals form a company, each one furnishing half of the capital and labour, the distribution of the profit is not difficult. However, if the capital comes from one party and the labour from the other, or if the two furnish the capital though only one of them works, or the proportions of the partners' share are not equal, in such cases a reasonable remuneration of the labour, on the basis of the previously agreed conditions is taken into consideration before the distribution of gains and profits is effected. Of course all possible precautions are taken, in order to prevent risks, yet Islam demands that in all contractual

participations, the profit as well as the loss should be participated in by both the contracting parties.

375. As far as banks are concerned, their activities are principally of three kinds: remitting of amounts from one place to another, assuring safety of the savings of the clients, and lending money to others on profit. The expenses of the functioning are borne by those who utilize the service of banks. The question remains of loans for commerce, industry or any other trade motive. If the bank participates in the profit of its debtors as well as in their risks, Islam allows such banking activities, otherwise not.

376. Confidence is borne of confidence. If the savings banks of a government declare at the end of the year, and not at its beginning, that they are in a position to pay such and such percentage of profit to the clients, not only would this be lawful according to Islam, but the public also would have no hesitation in depositing its savings with governmental banks, in spite of the silence in the beginning with regard to the quantity of the expected profit. For one has confidence in the public administration.

377. To sum up, the principle of mutual participation in profits as well as in risks must be observed in all commercial contracts.

STATISTICS

378. In all planning, it is necessary to have an idea of the available resources. The Prophet organized the census of the Muslim population, as al-Bukhari informs us. In the caliphate of 'Umar, the census of beasts, fruit-trees, and other goods was organized; and in the newly-acquired provinces, cultivable lands were measured. With a large spirit, full of concern for the well-being of the public, caliph 'Umar had the habit of inviting representatives of the people of different provinces,

after the collection of taxes, to find out if they had any complaint against the behaviour of the collectors during the year.

THE DAILY LIFE

379. We may end this brief sketch by mentioning two prohibitions of considerable importance, which form in fact characteristic features of the daily life of a Muslim, games of chance and alcoholic drinks. We have had occasions to discuss games of chance, in which one spends sometimes continually during long year without obtaining anything in return. What a loss to those who are economically weak! The use of Alcohol has the peculiarity that its consumption in a small quantity makes one gay and weakens his resolution to drink no more; and when one becomes drunk, one has no more control over one's acts. One may then squander money without noticing it. To these evils may be added the unhygienic effects of alcoholic drinks which are transmitted in the children and the posterity also. One of the Quranic verses (2/219) speaks of it, in interesting terms: "They question thee about wine and games of chance; say: in both is great sin and some profits for men; but the sin of them is greater than their usefulness." (Quran 2/219). The Quran does not deny that there are certain profits in the use of alcohol, yet it declares it a sin against society, against the individual himself, and of course against the Legislator. In another verse (5/90) it relegates it to the same level as idolatry, and declares it to be the handiwork of Satan; and adds, if one would desire to be happy in the two worlds, one should abstain from games of chance and alcoholic drinks.

CHAPTER XI

The Muslim Woman

WHEN studying the principal rights and obligations of women in Islam, it must be pointed out at the very outset that, in spite of the capacity of Muslim law to adapt itself and to develop according to circumstances, there will be no question of recognizing the extreme liberty which a woman enjoys today in fact and in practice, in certain sections of social life, both in the capitalistic and the communistic West. Islam demands that a woman should remain a reasonable being. It does not expect her to become either an angel or a demon. "The golden means is the best of things" said the Prophet Muhammad. If one wants to compare or contrast her position in Islam with that in other civilizations or legal systems, one shold take into consideration all the facts, and not merely isolated practices. In fact, in regard to certain aspects of morality, Islam is more rigid and more puritan than certain other systems of life in our times.

GENERALITIES

381. The position of a mother is very exalted in Islamic tradition. The Prophet Muhammad has gone so far as to say: "Even Paradise lies underneath the feet of your mothers." Al-Bukhari reports: Somebody asked the Prophet which work pleases God most? He replied: "The service of worship at the appointed hour." And when it was continued: "And what afterwards?" the Prophet replied: "To be bounteous to your father and mother." The Quran reverts to this often, and reminds man that he must always keep in mind the fact that it was his mother who had borne him in her womb, suffered much

on his account and reared him up after making all kinds of sacrifices.

382. As regards the woman as wife, the saying of the Prophet is well known: "The best among you is the one who is best towards his wife." In his memorable Farewell Discourse, pronounced on the occasion of the Last Pilgrimage, the Prophet spoke of woman at length, and said in particular:

"Well then, people! Verily there are rights in favour of your women which are incumbent upon you, and there are rights in favour of you which are incumbent upon them. As to what is incumbent upon them in your regard, is that they should not let your beds be trampled by others than you, should not allow those to enter your houses whom you do not like without your authorization, and should not commit turpitude. If they do commit that, then God has given you permission to reprimand them, to separate yourself from them in beds, and to strike them but not hard. If they abstain and obey you, then it is incumbent upon you to provide their food and dress in accordance with good custom. And I command you to treat women well, because they are like captives in your houses, possessing nothing for themselves, and you, on your part, take them as a deposit from God, and permit yourselves the enjoyment of their persons by means of a word of God. Have therefore the fear of God with regard to women, and I order you to treat them well. Attention! Have I communicated? O God, be witness!" (cf. Ibn Hisham).

383. With regard to woman as a daughter, the Islamic attitude can be guessed from the reproaches which the Quran makes against the pagan, pre-Islamic behaviour at the birth of daughters : "And they assign unto God daughters — be He purified (from this) ! — and unto themselves what they desire (i.e., sons); and when if one of them receiveth tidings of the birth of a female, his face remaineth darkened, and he is wroth inwardly. He hideth himself from the folk because of the evil of that whereof he hath tidings, (asking himself) :

Shall he keep it in contempt, or bury it beneath the dust?
Verily evil is their judgement." (Q. 16/57-9). The Quran
reminds ceaselessly that God has created all things in pairs,
and for procreation both the sexes are equally indispensable,
each one having its particular function. And it proclaims:
"...unto men a fortune from that which they have earned, and
unto women a fortune from that which they have earned."
(4/32).

384. To avoid redundance, Nature has not willed
perfect equality among the two sexes, but a complemental
distribution of avocations and functions. For instance, it will
not be possible for man to conceive a baby; similarly the natural attributes of men cannot be exercised by women. She has
a more delicate physical constitution, affecting even the weight
of her brain and bones, and she will have a taste more in conformity with the need of the conservation of this delicacy.
More robust, man will have greater strength and therefore more
endowed to engage in the more painful parts of life. To each
will be according to his (or her) requirements, both natural and
reasonable.

385. If there is a certain natural inequality between the
two sexes, in many other aspects of life they resemble each
other. Therefore their rights and obligations in these domains
will also be similar.

386. This sums up, in a way, the Islamic teaching on
woman: She is considered equal to man in certain respects
and not so in certain others. This could be understood better
in the description of her obligations and her rights:

OBLIGATIONS OF WOMAN

387. In religious matters, her first duty, even as that of
man, is to believe in the oneness of God, which is the only
means of salvation in the Hereafter. One knows that Islam
has formally prohibited the use of compulsion to convert anybody to Islam — and it may be recalled by the way that a non-

Muslim wife of a Muslim husband has the full right to conserve her religion, and to practise it in her individual capacity, even while she is in the wedlock of a Muslim — and one also knows that inside the Muslim community a rigorous discipline is maintained for its conservation as a whole and the preservation of its system of life. Treason in this respect is punished; yet certain cases of the time of the Orthodox Caliphs show that the punishment of women on account of apostasy is less severe than that of men.

388. Among the religious practices, it is incumbent upon women, as also upon men, to celebrate the services of worship, though with certain concessions. An adult woman is exempt during several days every month from performing the daily services of worship. As to the congregational prayer of Friday, it is optional for her, while it is obligatory for man. The rigour of fasts is also lightened to her, and at the moment of child-birth, monthly course etc., she has the right to postpone her fasts of the month of Ramadan. With regard to *Hajj* (pilgrimage of Mecca) also, there are certain rites from which she is exempted, if she cannot perform them for feminine reasons. To be brief, Islam is lenient and considerate to her. As to the last of the basic duties, viz., the payment of her zakat-tax, she has equality with man, though certain schools of law — the Shafi'ite for instance — make her certain concessions. So, there is a tax on the savings, yet the savings converted by a woman into ornaments of personal use are exempt from tax. In spite of the fact that Islam lays emphasis on the constant circulation of the national wealth for the purpose of continually increasing it, and discourages hoarding by subjecting it to a tax, it has nevertheless made a concession in favour of women and their feminine tastes.

389. There are also social duties. With a view to distribute the national wealth equitably, the means leading to the accumulation of wealth in the hands of the few are forbidden,

as in the case of interest and games of chance. A Muslim woman is as much subject to the rules as a man. Lotteries and speculations on racing, etc., are harmful to the economic equilibrium of society, and reamain expressly forbidden, for both men and women.

390. Let us recall another source of numberless misfortunes and that is alcohol. It is the express duty of every Muslim to abstain from it. The Quran (5/90) calls it the work of Satan. Its hygienic, economic, moral and other evils are too well known to require description. Alcoholic drinks have a particular aspect concerning the woman: It is she who nourishes her baby with her blood, and then with her milk, thus transmitting her health or her ailment to her baby, to the new generation and to the future of humanity.

391. A very comprehensive duty is that of morality. If spirituality is our duty in our relations with our Creator, morality has the same place in our mutual relations with our fellow-beings. In his ardent desire to attack the very sources of evil, and not merely certain of its manifestations. Islam has imposed, recommended, or otherwise encouraged certain practices, which astonish us sometimes if we do not take into consideration their profound motives. All religions say that fornication and adultery are crimes, but Islam would go farther and would prescribe means to diminish the temptations. It is easy to hope that every one would develop one's individual morality in order to resist the temptations; but it is wiser to diminish the occasions in which persons with weak characters—who constitute the majority of men—need to engage in a battle where defeat is a foregone conclusion.

392. It is thus that the Quran (33/59) first exhorted "to put on their *jalabib*" (sort of cloak or overall, covering from head to foot), in order to diminish the occasions of attraction and protecting women from the wickedness of men, as the

verse explains. Then came the revelation (24/30-31) for behaviour inside the house with friends and visitors: "Tell the believing men to lower their gaze and be chaste; that is purer for them; lo! God is aware of what they do. And tell the believing women to lower their gaze and be chaste and to display of their adornment only that which is apparent, and to draw their *Khumur* (veils covering the face) over their bosoms......" In every epoch of Islamic history, including the time of the Prophet, one sees Muslim women engaged in every profession that suited them. They worked as nurses, teachers, and even as combatants by the side of men when necessary, in addition to being singers, hair-dressers, etc. Caliph 'Umar employed a lady, Shifa' bint 'Abdallah, as inspector in the market at the capital (Madinah), as Ibn Hajar (*Isabah*) records. The same lady had taught Hafsah, wife of the Prophet, how to write and read. The jurists admit the possibility of women being appointed as judges of tribunals, and there are several examples of the kind. In brief, far from becoming a parasite, a woman could collaborate with men, in Muslim society, to earn her livelihood and to develop her talents.

393. According to the Quran (30/21): "And of His signs is this: He created for you helpmates from yourselves that ye may find rest in them, and He ordained between you love and mercy." Women and men mutually form complements of one another (Q. 2/187); therefore they should accommodate one another for their mutual interest. Two equals cannot be in accord with each other in a hundred per cent of cases; mutual concessions would be needed in the interests of the home and for the better comprehension inside the family. The counsel of the Quran (4/19), given to the husband regarding the treatment of the wife, provides food for thought: "......but consort with them in kindness, for if ye hate them it may happen that ye hate a thing wherein God hath placed much good." In fact the wiser one is, the greater the concession one makes, especially when one is also more powerful.

394. One seeks and prefers for the purpose of marriage the person one loves. But the question of love has quite a gloomy history in the annals of man. The motives of love, especially among the young, are often fantastic and ephemeral: a sweet voice, a delicious manner of smiling, the eyes, the colour, the coiffure or any other passing gesture starts the drama. However, for true conjugal life this does not suffice. The Prophet Muhammad has given us a very wise counsel in this respect: ''Do not marry only for the sake of beauty; may be the beauty becomes the cause of moral degradation. Do not marry even for the sake of wealth; may be the wealth becomes the reason of insubordination. Marry rather on the ground of religious devotion'', (*Ibn Majah*, No. 1859). As the Islamic religion regulates all domains of life, it goes without saying that the one who observes scrupulously one's religious duties is the more apt to create peace at home. On another occasion, the Prophet said: ''The world is an ephemeral thing, of which one takes temporary advantage; and among the worldly things nothing is better than a good (pious) wife.'' (*idem*, No. 1855). At-Tirmidhi and an-Nasa'i report another saying of the Prophet: ''The perfect believer is the one who has a perfect character and is kind to one's wife.''

395. As we have just remarked, Islam attaches particular importance to morality. Hence it is that promiscuity is ordered to be suppressed by every means. According to the Quran (4/34): if one fears immorality (*nushuz*, cf. § 382) on the part of one's wife, one should first admonish, then exert pressure by separating the beds, and finally may even scourge, though not heavily. Is there is no means of reform, divorce — which has been characterized as ''the most detestable among the lawful things,'' by the Prophet — may solve the problem. This obligation of chastity is reciprocal. A little later, the Quran (4 : 128-30) says that if a woman fears immorality (*nushuz*) or indifference, on the part of her husband, she should

try to arrange things, and in the last resort she too has the right to demand judicial separation.

395/a. A good mutual understanding implies identity of views of the couple. This may take place at times spontaneously: both husband and wife arriving at the same conclusions; at others one of the couple will have to make the concession and to renounce his personal opinion. However there is a limit to it, and one should not be astonished that the Quran (29/8) and the Hadith prescribe: "No obedience to a creature in the disobedience of the Creator." One is allowed to make concessions of all sorts, by love or for simple expediency, provided that this does not affect a formal law of Islam, above all the religious injunctions should on no account be violated.

395/b. One thing was very dear to the Holy Prophet, and he talked of it at several occasions, that men should avoid effeminate practices, and that girls should not behave as boys in coiffure, in dress, in the manner of talking and so on. One should rather develop one's self in the natural direction, and not in the opposite way; otherwise it is the "curse of God" which shall befall the person who violates this direction, as a hadith menaces.

RIGHTS OF WOMEN

396. The pre-Islamic Arabs attached less importance to the person of a woman than to that of a man. Thus, if the culprit was a man and the victim a woman, retaliation could not take place. The Quran abolished this inequality, and delicts against the woman were placed on the same level as those against the man, whether they concerned person or property or honour. One may even say that in certain cases the rights of women are held to be more important. For instance the Quran (24/4-5) decrees that if a man accuses a woman of immorality and does not produce proof, he is exposed

not only to the penalty prescribed for a false accusation, but to be declared for perpetuity as unworthy of giving an evidence before a tribunal (this in addition to the Divine punishment in the Hereafter, which however may be effaced in case of repentance). There is almost a consensus of opinion that repentance effaces the sin in the eschatological sense, yet the incapacity of evidence remains constant in spite of the recognized repentance. The Quran seems to require the purging of society from the evil of inconsiderate talk, particularly in matters where injury is easy to inflict and difficult to remedy.

397. The perfect and complete individuality of the person of the woman is manifest in a most striking manner in the matter of property. According to Islamic law, the woman possesses a most absolute right over her property. If she has attained majority, she may dispose of it according to her will without reference to anybody else, whether it be her father, brother, husband or son or any other person. There is no difference in this matter between a man and a woman. The property of a woman cannot be touched even if her husband or father or any other relative has liabilities exceeding his assets. Similarly, these relatives are not held responsible if she contracts debts. A woman has the same rights as man for acquiring property. She may inherit it, receive it in gift or donation, earn it by her own work and toil; and all this remains hers and hers alone. She is absolute mistress of her property to enjoy it or to give it to whomsoever she likes as a gift, or to dispose of it, by sale or any other legal means, at her will. All these rights are inherent in a woman; there is no question of obtaining them through special contracts, with the husband for instance or by an award depending on somebody else.

398. The right to inheritance requires some explanation. A pre-Islamic Arab woman had not the right to inherit from anybody, either her father or even her husband. The Prophet did not pay attention to this question during the first fifteen years

of his mission. The chroniclers mention that in the year 3 H. a rich Ansarite, Aus ibn Thabit died, leaving a widow and four daughters of tender age. According to the Madinan customs, only male adults, capable of taking up arms in a war, had the right to inheritance; and even a minor son had no right to the property of his deceased father. So, the cousins of Aus took possession of all that he had left, and the family became overnight completely destitute and deprived of the means of livelihood. At that moment a passage of the Quran was revealed, promulgating the law of inheritance which is ever since practised by Muslims, and even by some other communities, such as the Christians of the Levant. According to this law (cf. Quran 4/7-12 and 4/176), different female relatives have obtained the right to inheritance: wife, daughter, mother and sister in particular. With regard to inheritance, Islam makes no difference between the movable and immovable property; every thing must be divided among the rightful heirs. In order to avoid evil caprices. Islam has also prohibited the bequest of property by testament to strangers and the deprivation of the near relatives. In fact these latter do not require to be mentioned in a will; they inherit automatically. A will cannot even diminish or increase the rights of individual relatives to inheritance, the rights being fixed and determined by the law itself. The will is valid solely in favour of "strangers," i.e., those who have no right to inherit directly the property of the deceased. Islam has fixed the maximum, which one can bequeath by will, and that is one-third of the whole property, the two-thirds going to near relatives. A will for more than one-third is valid only if the heirs unanimously accept it at the moment of the distribution of the heritage.

399. The law of inheritance is complicated enough, for the shares of different heirs vary according to individual circumstances: the daughter alone or in the presence of a son, the mother alone or in the presence of the father, with children or without them, the sister alone or in the presence of the

brother, father or children of the deceased, inherit in different proportions according to individual cases. It is not our intention to describe it here in all the details. The shares of female heirs may however be mentioned briefly. The wife gets one-eighth if the deceased leaves also a child; otherwise she gets a fourth. The daughter when alone gets a half, several daughters get two-thirds which they divide among themselves in equal proportions;—all this when there is no son. In the presence of a son, the daughter gets half of her brother. The mother, when alone, gets a third, in the presence of father, child or brothers and sisters of the deceased she gets one-sixth. The sister does not inherit if the deceased leaves a son: but when alone, she gets a half; two or more sisters get two-thirds which they divide among themselves equally. In the presence of a daughter, the sister gets one-sixth; in the presence of a brother, she gets the half of what he gets. There are also differences between the shares of full sisters, consanguine sisters and uterine sisters.

400. It is perhaps necessary to give an explanation justifying the inequality between sister and brother, between mother and father, and between daughter and son. It seems that the Legislator has taken into consideration the rights of a woman in their entirety, together with the fact that laws are framed for normal cases of life and not for rare exceptions (for which latter, exceptional means are always provided). We have already mentioned that the woman possesses her property separately, on which neither her father nor her husband nor any other relative exercises any right whatsoever. Further, in addition to this separation of her proprietary rights, she has the right to maintenance (food, dress, lodging, etc.); and the court obliges her father, husband, son, etc., to satisfy on their sole expenses these needs of the woman. Again, the woman obtains from her husband the *mahr* a contractual sum, which went before Islam to the father of the woman, but which in Islam remains vested exclusively in the woman herself. This *mahr* is

not a dowry, which is not an obligatory thing. *Mahr* is a necessary element without which no marriage is valid. Thus it will be seen that a woman has lesser material needs to satisfy on her own account than a man, who has heavier obligations. In such conditions, it is easy to understand that a man has the right to a greater part of heritage than a woman. It should be remembered that, in spite of the fact that the woman has the right to be maintained at the expense of others, Islam accords her a supplemantary right to property in the form of inheritance. It goes without saying that a good household requires mutual co-operation, and the woman also works to increase the income of the family, or to diminish the expenses which would follow if she does not work; but we are speaking of the rights of woman, and not of the social practices which may vary according to individuals. The notion of the maintenance goes so far in Islam that, according to the law, a wife is not obliged even to give her breast to her suckling; it is the duty of the father of the child to procure for it a foster mother at his own expense, if the mother does not want to suckle it.

401. Let us speak of marriage, which also raises numerous questions. Marriage, according to Islam, is a bilateral contract, based on the free consent of the two contracting parties. The parents certainly aid by their counsel and their experience in searching or selecting the companion of life for their child, yet it is the couple who have the last say in the matter. In this respect, there is no difference between man and woman, in so far as the law is concerned. Illegal practices may exist in varying degrees from region to region and class to class; but the law does not recognize the customs which contravene its provisions.

402. It is true that Islam permits polygamy, but on this point Muslim law is more elastic and more in harmony with the requirements of society than the other systems of law which admit polygamy in no case. Supposing there is a case, in which a woman has young children, and falls chronically ill, becoming

incapable of doing the household work. The husband has no means of employing a maid-servant for the purpose, not to speak of the natural requirements of the conjugal life, Supposing also that the sick woman gives her consent to her husband to take a second wife, and that a woman is found who agrees to marry the individual in question. Western law would rather permit immorality than a legal marriage to bring happiness to this afflicted home.

403. In fact, Muslim law is nearer to reason. For, it admits polygamy when a woman herself consents to such a kind of life. The law does not impose polygamy, but only permits it in certain cases. We have just remarked that it depends solely on the agreement of the woman. This is true of the first wife as well as with the second one in prospect. It goes without saying that the second woman may refuse to marry a man who has already one wife; we have seen that no one can force a woman to enter into a marriage tie without her own consent. If the woman agrees to be a "co-wife" it is not the law which should be considered as cruel and unjust with regard to women and as favouring only men. As to the first wife, the act of polygamy depends on her. For, at the time of her marriage, she may demand the acceptance and insertion, in the document of the nuptial contract, of the clause that her husband would practise monogamy. Such a condition is as valid as any other condition of a legal contract. If a woman does not want to utilize this right of hers, it is not legislation which would oblige her to do that. We have just spoken of exceptional cases; and the law must have possible remedies. Polygamy is not the rule, but an exception; and this exception has multifarious advantages, social as well as other — the details would be burdensome here — and Islamic law is proud of this elasticity.

404. In the religious laws of antiquity, there is no restriction to the number of wives a man may have. All the Biblical

197

prophets were polygamous. Even in Christianity which has
become synonymous with monogamy. Jesus Christ himself
never uttered a word against polygamy; on the other hand
there are eminent Christian theologians, like Luther, Melanchthon, Bucer, etc. (cf. *Dictionaire de la Bible* by Vigouroux, §
Polygamie), who would not hesitate to deduce the legality
of polygamy from the parable of the ten virgins, spoken of in
the Gospel of Matthew (25: 1-12), for Jesus Christ envisages
there the possibility of the marriage of one man with as many
as ten girls simultaneously. If the Christians do not want to
profit by the permission (which the founder of their religion
seems to have given them)[1] the law is not changed for all that

---

1. "Monogamy as the unique and exclusive form of marriage, in the
    sense that bigamy is regarded as a grave criminal offence and a sin as
    well as a sacrilege, is very rare indeed. Such an exclusive ideal and
    such a rigid view of marriage is perhaps not to be found outside the
    modern, relatively recent development of Western culture. It is
    not implied in Christian doctrine even." (Encyclopaedia Britannica,
    s. v. Marriage).

    "It cannot be said that Christianity introduced obligatory monogamy,
    into the western world . . . Christianity does not expressly prohibit
    polygyny except in the case of a bishop and a deacon (I Timothy, iii,
    2 and 12 [which is however the recommendation of St. Paul and no
    saying of Jesus Christ himself]) . . . But no Council of a Church in the
    earliest centuries opposed polygyny; and no obstacle was put in the way
    of its practice by kings in the countries where it has occurred in the
    times of [pre-Christian] paganism. In the middle of the sixth century
    Diarmait, king of Ireland, had two queens and two concubines (H. d'
    Arbois de Jubainville, Cours de litterature Celtique, vi, 292). Polygyny
    was frequently practised by the Merovingian kings [of France]. Charles
    rhe Great [Charlemagne] had two wives and many concubines; and
    one of his laws seems to imply that polygyny was not unknown even
    among priests (A Thierry, Recits des temps merovingiens, or its English
    translation] "Narratives of Merovingian Era", p. 17 sqq. v. Hellwald,
    Die menschliche Familie, p. 588 n.L. Hallam, Europe during the Middle
    Ages, 1,420 n. 2). In later times Philip of Hesse and Frederick-

(Contd. on next page)

This is true of the Muslims also, whose law is moreover the only one in history which expressly limits the maximum permissible number of polygamous wives. (For Christian theory and practice, as well as for general discussion, cf. also Encyclopaedia Britannica, under the articles, *Marriage*, and *Polygyny;* Westermark, *History of Human Marriage*, 3 Vols.)

405. The possibility of the annulment of a marriage has also existed in Muslim law since all time. There is the unilateral right acquired by a husband, to divorce his wife. The wife also may acquire a similar right while contracting the

---

(Contd. from the previous page)

William II of Prussia contracted bigamous marriages with the sanction of the Lutheran clergy (Friedberg, Lehrbuch des katholischen und evangelischen Kirchenrechts, i, 436, note to § 143). Luther himself approved of the bigamy of the former, and so did Melanchthon (Koslin, Martin Luther, ii, 476 sqq.). On various occasions Luther speaks of polygyny with considerable toleration. It had not been forbidden by God (ibid i, 693 Sq.) . . . In 1650, soon after the Peace of Westphalia, when the population had been greatly reduced by Thirty Years' War, the Frankish Kriegstag [War Parliament] at Nuremberg passed the resolution that thenceforth every man should be allowed to marry two women (V. Hellwald, Cours de litterature Celtique, p. 599 note). Certain Christian sects have even advocated polygyny with much fervour. In 1531, the Anabaptists openly preached at Munster that he who wants to be a true Christian must have several wives (ibid, p. 558 n. I). And the Mormons, as all the world knows, regard polygyny as a divine institution." (Westermarck, History of Human Marriage, III, 50-51). "In the instructions given by the Landgrave Philip of Hesse to Martin Bucer, regarding questions which he had to ask Martin Luther and, Philip Melanchthon, one reads the following: § 10. I know that Luther and Melanchthon had advised the king of England not to repudiate his marriage but rather to marry a second wife, as one sees in their motivated consultation" (J.-B. Boussuet, "Histoire des variations des eglises protestantes, livre VI, depuis 1573 jusqu'a l'an 1546 in : Oeuvres completes de Boussuet, new edition at Bar-le-Luc, 1877, Vol. III, p. 233-250, in particular p. 244). See also Dictionnaire de la Bible, by F. Vigouroux, Paris, 1912, vol. IV, 513, s. v. polygamie-

marriage. The court of justice also possesses the right of separation of the couple on the plaint of the wife, if the husband is incapable of fulfilling his conjugal duties, or if he is suffering from a particularly serious sickness, or if he disappears for years without leaving a trace, etc. Further, there is also the bilateral separation, when the two mates agree mutually, on conditions, to discontinue their marital tie. The Quran (4/35) insists that the two should refer their quarrels to arbitration, before deciding for definite separation. The saying of the Prophet may be remembered: "The most detestable of the permitted things in the eyes of God is divorce." The law, the ethics, and the exhortations, all complement each other; and the source of all these is the same, namely the Quran and the *Hadith*.

CHAPTER XII

Status of Non-Muslims in Islam

IT is but natural that one should make a distinction, and even a discrimination, between the near and the distant, between the relative and the stranger. With intellectual and moral evolution, there is a tendency in human society to facilitate the assimilation of the foreigner. If society were to group itself solely on the basis of blood relationship, naturalization would be out of the question for ever. The same is true if the basis were the colour of skin, which cannot be concealed. Language as a factor of social unity requires long years for a veritable assimilation. Place of birth is even less perceptible in a stranger; and ever since man has crossed the horizon of city-states, not much importance is attached to this last factor. However, one would remark that in all these various conceptions of social unity, the basis is a mere accident of nature, and belongs more to the animal instinct than to the rationality of man. It is common knowledge that Islam has rejected all these notions of nationality, and selected only the identity of ideas—a thing which depends upon the choice of man and not upon the accidents and hazards of birth—as the basic tie of society and the factor of union. Naturalization and assimilation in such a society is not only easy and accessible to all human races in their entirety, but is also closer to reason and more practical, showing how to live one's life in peace and tranquillity.

407. If a believer in God or a capitalist is considered as a stranger in communist countries, a black-skinned in such white countries as practise social segregation, or a non-Italian in Italy, it should not be surprising if a non-Muslim should be considered as a stranger in the land of Islam. Conceptions or

rather angles of view, differ, yet everybody makes some distinction or other between those who belong to his own group and those who do not.

408. As in every other political or social system, Islam also makes a distinction between its "relatives", and "strangers", but there are two characteisrtics peculiar to it: (1) the facility to cross this barrier, by subscribing to its ideology, and (2) but little inequality between the two categories regarding the affairs of this world. We shall try to throw some light on this last aspect of the question.

DIVINE ORIGIN OF DUTIES

409. One should not forget the great practical importance attached to the fact, that Muslims obey their system of law as something of Divine origin, and not merely the will of the majority of the leaders of the country. In this latter case, the minority enters on a struggle so that its own conceptions may prevail. In the democracies of our time, not only do the majorities often change from election to election, but are also constituted or disintegrated by all sorts of commutations and combinations, and the party in power tries to upset the policy pursued by its predecessors, causing, among other changes, the modification of laws. Without entering here into the question of the adaptability of Islamic laws to the exigencies of social evolution, one might deem it as an incontestable truth that there is greater stability in the Muslim law — due to its Divine origin — than in any other secular legislation of the world with the following result.

410. The Islamic law ordains justice to, and observance of certain rules regarding the non-Muslims. These therefore feel no apprehension in the face of political quarrels and parliamentary elections of the country of their residence, with regard to the Islamic laws in force. The ruler or the parliament cannot modify them.

BASIC NOTIONS

411. The believers and the unbelievers cannot be equals; the former will go to Paradise, and the latter to Hell, but all this concerns the Hereafter. As to the life in this world, Muslim jurists like ad-Dabusi and others have at all times revealed the greatest equality compatible with their system between the "relatives" and the "strangers," as we shall presently see.

412. There is the question of religious tolerance. The Quran (2/256) prescribes that there should be no compulsion in religion. The residing subjects as well as the temporary sojourners have an assurance regarding their safety and the liberty of their conscience.

413. There is the question of hospitality and asylum, regarding which the theoretical position is strengthened by the practice of more than a thousand years. There is the well-known verse of the Quran (9/6): "And if anyone of the pagans seeketh thy asylum (O Muhammad), then give him asylum . . . and afterwards convey him to his place of safety . . . " The victims of racial, religious, political and other persecutions have always found refuge and shelter in the land of Islam.

413/a. What a touching and even stupefying teaching is the commandment that a Muslim should collaborate even with the enemy in a state of war! Says the Holy Quran (5:2): " ... and let not the hatred of a people who have stopped your going to the Inviolable Mosque (of the Ka'bah) incite you to transgress; but help ye one another unto charity and piety. Help not one another unto sin and transgression. Lo! God is severe in punishment." Mutual help is not to be restricted among Muslims alone, but with entire humanity without restriction of religion and race!

PRACTICE OF THE PROPHET

414. When the Prophet Muhammad settled down in Madinah, he found there complete anarchy, the region having never known before either a State or a king to unite the tribes torn by internecine feuds. In just a few weeks, he succeeded in rallying all the inhabitants of the region, into order. He constituted a City-State, in which Muslims, Jews, pagan Arabs, and probably also a small number of Christians, all entered into a statal organism by means of a social contract.

415. The constitutional law of this first "Muslim" State —which was a confederacy as a sequence of the multiplicity of the population groups—has come down to us *in toto*, and we read therein not only the clause 25: "To Muslims their religion, and to Jews their religion," or: "that there would be benevolence and justice," but even the unexpected passage in the same clause 25: "The Jews...are a community (in alliance) *with*—according to Ibn Hisham and in the version of Abu-'Ubaid, a community (forming part) *of*— the believers (i.e., Muslims)."

416. The very fact that, at the time of the constitution of this City-State, the autonomous Jewish villages acceded of their free will to the confederal State, and recognized Muhammad as their supreme political head, implies in our opinion that the non-Muslim subjects possessed the right of vote in the election of the head of the Muslim State, at least in as far as the politilcal life of the country was concerned.

417. Military defence was, according to the document in question, the duty of all elements of the population, including the Jews. This implies their participation in the consultation, and in the execution of the plans adopted. - In fact, §37 laid down: "The Jews would bear their expenses and the Muslims theirs, and there will be mutual succour between them in case an aggressor attacks the parties to this Document." Further, §45 says that war and peace will be undivisible for the parties to the Document.

418. Some months after the establishment of this City-State, we see the Prophet Muhammad concluding treaties of defensive alliance and mutual aid with the pagan Arabs of the neighbourhood of Madinah. Some of these embraced Islam about ten years afterwards. During all these long years, mutual confidence was most complete, as the following incidents would show.

419. In the year 2 H., the pagans of Mecca sent a diplomatic mission to Abyssinia, in order to demand of the Negus the "extradition" of Meccan Muslims who had taken refuge in his country. To counteract their machinations, the Prophet also sent, in his turn, an ambassador for interceding with the Negus in favour of the Muslims who had sought asylum in his country due to religious persecution by their co-citizens. This ambassador of Islam was 'Amr ibn Umaiyah ad-Damri, "who had not yet embraced Islam." In fact, he belonged to one of the allied tribes of the neighbourhood of Madinah just referred to.

420. At a time when there were constant wars on extensive frontiers of the Islamic territory, military service was very far from being an easy means of earning a livelihood; for the risks to life and to the economic situation of the combatants were very real. Even if the exemption of the non-Muslim subjects from this service was motivated by suspicions in regard to their trustworthiness, all non-Muslims who had accepted Muslim domination and did not seek its overthrow in collusion with foreigners welcomed this exemption from military service. They could thus pursue in tranquillity their avocations and prosper, while the Muslims would be engaged in military duties with all the attendant risks. So, the non-Muslims paid a little supplementary tax, the *jizyah* — of which the women, children and the poor from among them were exempt — which was neither heavy nor unjust. In the time of the Prophet, the *jizyah* amounted to ten dirhams annually, which represented the expenses of an average family for ten days. Moreover, if a

non-Muslim subject participated in military service during some expedition in a year, he was exempted from the *jizyah* for the year in question. Some typical cases would show the real character of this tax.

421. In the beginning of Islam, this tax did not exist in the Muslim State, either in Madinah or elsewhere. It was towards the year 9 H., that the Quran ordained it. That it was a question of expediency, and not a matter of dogmatic duty in Islam, is sufficiently shown by the following incidents. It is reported (by Ibn Sa'd on the authority of Zuhri) that at the moment of the death of his son, Ibrahim, the Prophet Muhammad declared: "Had he survived, I would have exempted all the Copts from the *jizyah*, as a mark of esteem for Ibrahim's mother" (who was a Coptic girl). Or again, (cf. Suyuti, *Husn al-Muhadarah*, ch. Khalij Amir al-Mu'minin), when a non-Muslim Egyptian laid before the Muslim government the project of re-digging the ancient canal from Fustat (Cairo) down to the Red Sea, thus facilitating the maritime transport of the food stuffs of Egypt to Madinah—the famous *Nahr Amir al-Mu'minin* —the caliph 'Umar rewarded him by exempting him from *jizyah* during his whole life. There are jurists who opine that one should also take into consideration the international repercussions affecting Muslim interests, in view of the fact that Islam has penetrated the entire world, and there are millions of Muslims inhabiting countries which are under non-Muslim domination; and the *jizyah* if levied from Christians, Jews, Hindus and others in the Islamic territory would inevitably produce a reaction on Muslims in Christian and other countries.

422. There is another saying of the Prophet, pronounced on his death bed; directing the transfer of the Jewish and Christian populations of the Hijaz to other regions, its context has not been mentioned in traditions, but it is evident that it concerned certian populations of this region on account of their political behaviour, and that it was not a general prohibition against the members of these two communities. It may be noted that, in the time of the caliphs there were non-Muslim

slaves, male and female, belonging to Muslims and living along with their masters, at Mecca, Madinah, etc. A celebrated case of free non-Muslims is that of the Christian doctor, whose consultation rooms were just below the minaret of the mosque of the Ka'bah (*Mecca*). He lived there in the time of 'Umar ibn 'Abd al-'Aziz or soon after him (cf. Ibn Sa'd, V. 365 § Dawud ibn 'Abdur Rahman. In fact Dawud was a pious Muslim, yet his physician father remained always a Christian). Ibn Sa'd (III/i, p. 258) also records the case of a Christian, Jufainah, who taught reading and writing to school children at Madinah.

423. We may also recall the direction of the Prophet, on his death-bed: "Observe scrupulously the protection accorded by me to non-Muslim subjects (cf. *al-Mawardi*). Another saying of the Prophet reported by Abu Dawud is: "Whoever oppresses the non-Muslim subjects, shall find me to be their advocate on the day of the Resurrection (against the oppressing Muslims).'

424. The directions as well as the practice of the Prophet constitute the highest law for Muslims. As to the assimilation of these laws in the life of Muslims and the practice of later times, a study of history could profitably be pursued. We shall refer to a few facts here:

LATER PRACTICE

425. A governor of the caliph 'Umar selected a non-Muslim secretary. Learning the news, the caliph issued an order to have him replaced by a Muslim. This refers to a time when the province in question had not yet been pacified, and a war was still in progress. This is understandable in view of the importance of the post and the natural mistrust of the inhabitants of the newly conquered country. In order to better comprehend the attitude of 'Umar, let us recall another incident of this same great caliph (reported by al-Baladhuri, *Ansab*): "One day he wrote to his governor of Syria: Send us a Greek, who could

put in order the accounts of our revenues." He put a Christian at the head of this administration, in Madinah.

426. The same caliph often consulted non-Muslims on military, economical and administrative questions.

427. One would not reproach Muslims for preserving the post of the *imam* (the leader of the prayer-service in the mosque) exclusively for their co-religionists. Islam has desired the co-ordination of all aspects of life, spiritual as well as temporal. Hence, the fact that the leading of the prayer-service in the mosque is a duty and privilege of the head of the State who is also head of the religion. If one takes into consideration this state of things, one will understand easily why a non-Muslim subject cannot be elected head of a Muslim State.

428. But this exception does on no account imply the exclusion of non-Muslim subjects from the political and administrative life of the country. Ever since the time of the caliphs, non-Muslims have been seen holding the rank of ministers in Muslim States. A parallel practice has not been witnessed in the more important secular democracies of the world, where Muslim subjects are not wanting. That this practice of the caliphs is not contrary to the teaching of Islam, is borne witness to by classical authors; and Shafi'ite jurists (like al-Mawardi) and Hanbalite ones (like Abu Ya'la al-Farra') have not hesitated to support the view that the caliph may lawfully nominate non-Muslim subjects as ministers and members of Executive Councils. We have already spoken of a non-Muslim ambassador sent by the Prophet himself to Abyssinia.

SOCIAL AUTONOMY

429. Perhaps the most characteristic feature of Islam, in its attitude regarding the non-Muslims, is the award of social and judicial autonomy. In a long passage of the Quran, we read:

"If then they have recourse unto thee (O Muhammad), judge between them or disclaim jurisdiction; if thou disclaimest jurisdiction, then they cannot harm thee at all; but if thou judgest, judge between them with equity; lo! God loveth the equitable. How can they come unto thee for judgement when they have the Torah, wherein is contained the judgement of God? yet even after that they turn away; such folk are not believers. Lo! We did reveal the Torah, wherein is guidance and a light, by which the prophets who surrendered (unto God) judged the Jews, and the rabbis and the priests judged by such of God's Scripture as they were bidden to observe, and thereunto they were witnesses; so fear not mankind, but fear Me, and barter not My revelations for a little gain; *whoso judgeth not by that which God hath revealed: such are disbelievers.* And We prescribed for them therein: The life for the life, and the eye for the eye, and the nose for the nose, and the ear for the ear, and the tooth for the tooth, and for wounds retaliation; but whoso forgoeth it (by way of charity) it shall be expiation for him; whoso judgeth not by that which God hath revealed: such are wrong-doers. And we caused Jesus, son of Mary, to follow in their footsteps, confirming that which was revealed before him, and We bestowed on him the Gospel wherein is guidance and a light, confirming that which was revealed before it in the Torah — a guidance and an admonition untot hose who areGod-fearing. *Let the people of the Gospel judge by that which God hath revealed therein;* whoso judgeth not by that which God hath revealed: such are evil-livers. And unto Thee (O Muhammad) have We revealed the Scripture with the truth, confirming whatever Scripture was before it, and a watcher over it; so judge between them by that which God hath revealed, and follow not their desires away from the truth which hath come unto thee; for each We have appointed a Divine law (*shir'ah*) and a traced-out way; had God willed He could have made you one community, but He may try you by that which He hath given you (He hath made you as you are); so vie one with the other in good works; unto God ye will all return, and He will then inform you of that wherein ye differ." (Q. 5/42-8).

430. It is on the basis of this commandment, that the Prophet and his successors in Islam have conceded to every non-Muslim community, from among the subjects of the Islamic State, a judicial autonomy, not only for personal status, but also for all the affairs of life: civil, penal and others. In the time of the Orthodox Caliphs, for instance, we find evidence of contemporary Christians (for text cf. *infra* § 497) attesting to the fact that the Muslim government had delegated, in favour of Christian priests, many temporal judicial powers. In the time of the 'Abbasid caliphs, we find the Christian patriarch and the Jewish hakham, among the highest dignitaries of the State, connected directly with the Caliph.

431. In the time of the Prophet, the Jews of Madinah had their *Bait al-Midras* (both a synagogue and educational institute). In the treaty with the Christians of Najran (Yaman), the Prophet gave a guarantee not only for the security of the person and property of the inhabitants, but had also expressly left the nomination of bishops and priests to the Christian community itself.

432. There is a tendency among a large number of people to imitate and ape their governors and chiefs, in the outer conduct of life, such as dress, coiffure, etiquette etc. The result is a superficial assimilation, which brings no advantage to the ruling community, but which causes a moral damage to the classes which imitate in a servile manner. In an Islamic State, non-Muslims constitute a protected community (*dhimmi*). Therefore it is the duty of the government to protect the legitimate interests of these "strangers." Hence it is that we see, during the 'Abbasid caliphate that, far from seeking the assimilation of "strangers" by force, the government discouraged all imitation of one by the other: Muslims, Christians, Jews, Magians and others conserved their own modes of dress, their social

manners and their distinctive individualities. Only a total
assimilation, through religious conversion, was sought, and not
a confusion of communities. This is proof enough that the
measure had nothing to do with the religious exigencies of Islam
— and in the time of the Prophet there was absolutely no trace of
it — but a condition of life, suiting the social conceptions of the
epoch ; and its essential purpose was to recognize at the very
first sight, the religious community of each and every individual.
The intention was to protect in this way the culture of everyone, so that its intrinsic values and defects should come more
into relief. In passing, it may be repeated that the conception of
nationality in Islam is based neither on an ethnic source nor on
place of birth, but on the identity of ideology, i.e., of religion.

433. The person, property and honour of every individual,
whether indigenous or heterogeneous, are fully protected in the
Islamic territory. The *Sharh al-Hidayah*, which is a legal manual
of current use, employs, for instance, the characteristic expression : "Defamation is prohibited, be it concerning a Muslim or
a Protected (non-Muslim)." Another jurist of great authority,
the author of *al-Bahr ar-Ra'iq* says : "Even the bones of the
dead among the Protected (non-Muslims) have the right to be
respected, even as the bones of Muslims ; it is not allowed to
profane them, because if the ill treatment of a Protected (non-
Muslim) is forbidden in his life-time, on account of the protection which he enjoys, the protection of his bones against every
profanation is equally obligatory after his death." The jurists
are unanimous in declaring that, if a Muslim violates a non-
Muslim woman, he will receive the same punishment as is
prescribed against the violation of Muslim women.

434. In the time of the caliph 'Umar, certain Muslims had
usurped a piece of land belonging to a Jew, and had constructed a mosque on the site. Learning the news, the caliph
ordered the demolition of the mosque and the restoration of the
land to the Jew. Prof. Cardahi (a Christian of Lebanon, in his

series of lectures on Private International Law of Islam, delivered at The Hague, 1933) writes: "This house of the Jew *Bait
al-Yahudi*, still exists and is well known." Another classical
example, cited by Ibn Kathir and others is that of the Grand
Mosque of Damascus. An Umaiyad caliph had occupied a
church to enlarge the Mosque. Later when the complaint was
brought before caliph 'Umar ibn 'Abd al-'Aziz, he ordered that
the part of the mosque built on the usurped piece of ground be
demolished and the church restored there. But the Christians
themselves preferred a monetary compensation, and the matter
was thus amicably settled.

435. Let us cite the circular of the caliph 'Umar Ibn
'Abdal-'Aziz (preserved by Ibn Sa'd V, 280), which again is
eloquent testimony:

"With the name of God, the Most Merciful, the All Merciful.
From the Servant of God, Commander of the Faithful, 'Umar
(ibn 'Abd al-'Aziz) to (the governor) 'Adi ibn Artat and to the
believing Muslims in his company: Peace be with you. Whereafter I send you the praise of God, beside Whom there is no
God. Thereafter: Pay attention to the condition of the Protected
(non-Muslims), and treat them tenderly. If any of them reaches
old age and has no resources, it is you who should spend on
him. If he has contractual brethren, demand these latter to
spend on him. Apply retaliation if anybody commits tort against
him. This is as if you have a slave, who reaches old age, you
should spend on him till his death or liberate him. I have learnt
that you accept tithe on the import of wine and make it enter
the Treasury belonging to God. I warn you never to enter it in
the Treasury belonging to God, however small the amount be,
unless it be a legally pure property. Peace be with you."

436. Another letter of the same caliph (cf. Ibn Sa'd, V,
252): says:

"Purify the registers from the charge of obligations (i.e., taxes levied unjustly); and study old files (also). If any injustice has been committed, regarding a Muslim *or a non-Muslim*, restore him his right. If any such person should have died, remit his rights to his heirs."

437. It is common knowledge, that Muslim jurists recognize the right of pre-emption in regard to neighbours. If anybody sells his immovable property, the neighbour has the prior right over a stranger. This right is recognized in favour of non-Muslims also.

438. The safeguard of the rights of non-Muslims, in the Islamic territory, goes even to the extent of giving them liberty of practising customs entirely opposed to those of Islam. For instance, the consumption of alcoholic drinks is forbidden to Muslims, yet the non-Muslim inhabitants of the country have full liberty not only of consumption, but also of manufacture, importation and sale of the same. The same is true of games of chance, marriage with close relatives, the contract entailing interest, etc. In olden times, this did not affect Muslims, and the abuses with their repercussions were rare. Modern jurists have restricted the liberty in so far as international commerce is concerned. As attemps to restrict alcoholic consumption will be ineffectual if they should not be applicable to the whole population, the consent of the representatives of non-Muslim has facilitated the task of jurists, who in principle would not intervene in the practices of different communities differing in point of religion.

439. The Islamic law makes a certain distinction among different non-Muslim communities, in so far as their relations with individual Muslims are concerned. It divides non-Muslims into what we might call "developed" and "primitive", or those who believe in the One God and follow Divine laws revealed to the founder of their religions, and those who do not do that

(such as idolators, atheists, pagans, animists, etc.). All are tolerated as subjects and enjoy protection with ragard to the liberty of conscience and life, yet a Muslim in his private life treats them differently: A Muslim has the right to marry a "developed" non-Muslim woman, but not a "primitive" one. So is it too that a Muslim may not only marry a Christian or a Jewish girl, but also give her the liberty to conserve her religion. She may go to Church or to synagogue, she may drink wine, etc. It is forbidden for a Muslim to marry a woman who does not believe in God or is idolatress or polytheist. A Muslim woman cannot be the wife of a non-Muslim to whatever category he may belong, (Q. 60: 10). Again, a Muslim cannot eat flesh of animals slaughtered by members of the "primitive" communities.

CONVERSION

440. The Islamic law expressly recognizes for non-Muslims the liberty to preserve their beliefs; and if it forbids categorically all recourse to compulsion for converting others to Islam, it maintains a rigorous discipline among its own adherents. The basis of the Islamic "nationality" is religious and not ethnic, linguistic or regional. Hence apostasy has naturally been considered political treason. It is true that this crime is punished by penalties, but the necessity scarcely arose as history has proved. Not only at the time when the Muslims reigned supreme from the Pacific to the Atlantic Oceans, but even in our own age of political as well as material and intellectual weakness among Muslims, apostasy of Muslims is surprisingly non-existent. This is true not only of regions where there is the semblance of a Muslim State, but even elsewhere, under the colonial powers who have made all humanly possible efforts to convert Muslims to other religions. Islam is gaining ground today, even among Western peoples, from Finland and Norway to Italy, from Canada to Argentine. And all this in spite of the absence of any organised missionary activity.

HOLY WAR

441.   Let us conclude this brief expose with some words
on a question which is most misunderstood in non-Muslim
circles. It refers to the notion commonly held of the holy war.
The entire life of a Muslim, be it concerning spiritual affairs or
temporal ones, is a discipline regulated by the Divine law. If a
Muslim celebrates even his service of prayer without conviction
(for ostentation, for instance), it is not a spiritual act of devotion, but a crime against God, a worship of the self punishable
in the Hereafter. On the contrary, if a Muslim takes his meals,
for the purpose of having the needed strength to perform his obligations regarding God, even if he cohabits with his wife, as an
act of obedience to the Divine law, which orders him that, these
act of need and pleasure constitute saintly acts, acts of devotion,
meriting all the Divine rewards promised for charity, as a saying
of the Prophet indicates.

442.   Such being the concept of life, a just struggle cannot
be anything except a holy act. All war is forbidden in Islam,
if it is not waged for a just cause, ordained by the Divine law,
The life of the Prophet provides reference to only three kinds
of wars: defensive, punitive and preventive.   In his celebrated
correspondence with the Emperor Heraclius of Byzantium, in
connection with the assassination of a Muslim ambassador in
the Byzantine territory, the Prophet proposed three alternatives:
"Embrace Islam — if not, pay the *jizyah*-tribute ... if not, do not
interfere between thy subjects and Islam if these former desire
to embrace Islam ... if not, pay the *jizyah*" (cf. *Abu 'Ubaid, Kitab
al-Amwal*, § 55). To establish liberty of conscience in the world
was the aim and object of the struggle of the Prophet Muhammad, and who may have a greater authority in Islam that he ?
This is the "holy war" of the Muslims, the one which is undertaken not for the purpose of exploitation, but in a spirit of
sacrifice, its sole object being to make the Word of God prevail.
All else is illegal.   There is absolutely no question of waging
war for compelling people to embrace Islam; that would be an
unholy war.

CHAPTER XIII

Muslim Contribution to the Sciences and Arts

As many are there sciences, as many do we require specialists from among historians to describe adequately the Muslim contribution to each branch and to collaborate in the compilation of a general survey of this vast subject. Far from pretending to deal adequately with the topic, an attempt is made here to give information of a general character relating to the part the Muslims have played in the development of the various sciences and arts.

GENERAL ATTITUDE

444. Islam is a comprehensive concept of life and not merely a religion describing the relations between man and his Creator. It becomes necessary therefore to give first of all an account of the attitude of Islam, with regard to the pursuit of the sciences and the arts.

445. Far from discouraging a life of well-being in this world, the Quran gives expression again and again to directions like : "Say (O Muhammad): Who hath forbidden the adornment (beautiful gifts) of God which He hath brought forth for His bondmen and the good things of His providing?" (7/32). It praises those "who say: Our Lord! Give unto us in this world that which is best and in the Hereafter that which is best, and guard us from the torment of Fire" (2/201). It teaches mankind: "... and neglect not thy portion of the world, and be thou kind even as God hath been kind to thee ......" (28/77). It is this quest for the well-being which attracts man to study and learn, in as perfect a manner as possible, of all that exists

in the universe, in order to profit by it, and to be grateful to God. The Quran says: "And We have given you (mankind) authority on the earth, and appointed for you therein a livelihood; and how little are the thanks ye give!" (7/10; cf. 15/20-21). And again: "He it is Who created for you all that is in the earth..." (2/29): further: "See ye not how God hath made serviceable unto you whatsoever is in the skies and whatsoever is in the earth and hath loaded you with His favours both without and within?" (31/20, cf. 14/32-3, 16/12, 22/65, 65/11-2, etc.). On the one hand the Quran reminds men of the duty of worshipping the One "Who hath fed them against hunger, and hath made them safe from fear" (106/4-5); and on the other, it tells them of the need for effort in this world of cause and effect: "And man hath only that for which he maketh effort" (53:39). The Quran (30:42) urges men not only to go on exploration: "Say: travel in the land and see the nature of the end of those who were before you," but also for new discoveries: "... who meditate over the creation of the heavens and the earth, (and say:) Our Lord! Thou createdst not this in vain" (3:191).

446. As to the method of increasing knowledge, it is inspiring to note that the very first revelation that came to the Prophet, who was born among illiterate people, was a command to read and write, and the praise of the pen which is the only means or custodian of human knowledge:

"Read with the name of thy Lord, Who createth,
Createth man from a clot.
Read, and thy Lord is the Most Bounteous,
Who teacheth by the pen:
Teacheth man that which he knew not."

(Q. 96/1-5).

It reminds us also: "......and ask the people of remembrance if ye know not" (16:43, 21 : 7), as also: "......and of knowledge ye have been vouchsafed but little" (17/85). **Further:** "......We raise by grades whom We will, and over every possessor of knowledge there is one more knowing" (12/76). What a beautiful prayer is the one which the Quran teaches man: "......and say : my Lord! Increase me in knowledge" (20/114).

447. The Prophet Muhammad said: "Islam is built on five fundamentals: Belief in God, Service of worship, Fasting, Pilgrimage of the House of the One God, and the *Zakat*-tax." If belief demands the cultivation of the theological sciences, the others require a study of the mundane sciences. For the service of worship, the face is turned towards Mecca, and the service must be celebrated on the occurrence of certain determined natural phenomena. This requires knowledge of the elements of geography and astronomy. Fasting also requires the understanding of natural phenomena, such as the appearance of the dawn, the setting of the sun, etc. The pilgrimage necessitates knowledge of the routes and the means of transport in order to proceed to Mecca. Payment of the *Zakat* requires knowledge of mathematics, which knowledge is also necessary for calculations for the distribution of the heritage of the deceased. Similarly there is the fundamental need of the understanding of the Quran in the light of historical facts and allusions and references to the sciences contained therein. In fact the study of the Quran requires first of all a knowledge of the language in which it is compiled (linguistic sciences); its references to peoples demand a knowledge of history and geography, and so on and so forth.

448. Let us recall by the way that when the Prophet began an independent life, settling down in Madinah, his first act was the construction of a mosque with a portion reserved for the purpose of a school — the celebrated *Suffah* — which served during the day as a lecture hall, and during the night as a dormitory for students.

449. God helps those who help the cause of God, is reiterated often in the Quran (47/7, 22/40). It is not surprising if Muslims had the good luck of possessing abundant and cheap paper for spreading knowledge among the masses· Since the second century of the Hijrah, there began to be established factories for the manufacture of paper all over the vast Muslim empire.

450. For purposes of this short sketch, we shall refer only to a few sciences in which the contribution of the Muslims has been particularly important for mankind.

RELIGIOUS AND PHILOSOPHICAL SCIENCES

451. The religious sciences began, naturally enough, with the Quran which the Muslims received as the Word of God, the Divine Message addressed to man. Its perusal and understanding necessitated the study of the linguistic, grammatical, historical, and even the speculative sciences, among many others, — which gradually developed into independent sciences of general utility — the recitation of the sacred text brought into being and developed the religious "music" of Islam (to which we shall revert later). The preservation of the Quran led to improvements in the Arabic script, not only from the point of view of precision, but also of beauty. With its punctuation and vocalization, the Arabic script is incontestably the most precise for the needs of any language in the world. The universal character of Islam necessitated the understanding of the Quran by non-Arabs; and we see a series of translations, from the very time of the Prophet — Salman al-Farsi had translated parts of it into Persian — continuing to our own days, and there is no end to it in sight. It is necessary to point out that these translations were made solely for purposes of understanding the contents by those who did not know Arabic, yet never for liturgy; for in the service of worship, one uses only the Arabic text. And the method adopted by order of the Prophet for the preservation of the integrity of the sacred text was

perpetuated, namely recording in writing and learning by heart, both done simultaneously. Each process was to help the other in guarding against forgetfulness or the commission of errors. The institution of a judicial method of verification further perfected the system. Thus, one was required not only to procure a copy of the Quran, but also to read it from the beginning to the end before a recognized master, in order to obtain a certificate of authenticity. This practice continues to this day.

452. As in the case of the Quran, the Muslims were attached also to the sayings of their Prophet. The reports of his sayings and doings, both public and private, were preserved. The preparation of such memoirs began even in the life-time of the Prophet, on the private initiative of certain of his companions, and was continued after his death, by a process of collection of first hand knowledge. As in the case of the Quran, authentification was insisted on in all transmissions. One could relate all that is known of the lives of Noah, Moses, Jesus, Buddha and other great men of antiquity, in a few pages only, but the known details of the biography of the Prophet Muhammad fill hundreds of pages, so great was the care that was taken to preserve for posterity documented and precise data.

453. The speculative aspect of the Faith, particularly in the matter of beliefs and dogmas, shows that the discussions which began in the life-time of the Prophet, became later the root causes of different sciences, such as *Kalam* (dogmatico-scholastic), and *tasauwuf* (mystico-spiritualistic). The religious polemics with non-Muslims, and even among Muslims themselves, introduced foreign elements from Greek and Indian philosophy, etc. Later on, Muslims did not lack their own great philosophers endowed with originality and erudition, like al-Kindi, al-Farabi, Ibn-Sina (Avicenna), Ibn-Rushd (Averroes) and others. The Arabicization of foreign books resulted in the fortunate feature that hundreds of Greek and Sanskrit works,

whose originals have now been lost, became preserved for posterity in their Arabic translations.

NEW SCIENCES

454. The part played by the Muslims in developing the social sciences has been very important. A remarkable characteristic of Muslim science is the rapidity of its development. The Quran was the first book ever written in the Arabic language. Scarcely two hundred years later, this language of the illiterate Bedouins developed into one of the richest in the world, later to become not only the richest of all languages of the time, but also an international language for all sorts of sciences. Without stopping to discover the cause of this phenomenon, let us recall another fact. The first Muslims were almost all Arabs, yet with the exception of their language, which was the repository of the Word of God and of His Prophet, they effaced their own personality, under the influence of Islam, in order to receive in Islam all races on the basis of absolute equality. Therefore is it that all races have participated in the progress of the "Islamic" sciences: Arabs, Iranians, Greeks, Turks, Abyssinians, Berbers, Indians, and others, who have embraced Islam. Their religious tolerance was so great, and the patronage of learning so perfect, that Christians, Jews, Magians, Buddhists and others collaborated with a view to enrich the Muslim sciences not only in the domain of their respective religious literatures, but also in the other branches of learning. Arabic had spread more widely than any other language of the world, since it was the official language of the Muslim State whose territory extended from China to Spain.

LAW

455. In its comprehensive character, legal science developed among Muslims very early. They were the first in the world fo entertain the thought of an abstract science of law, distinct from the codes of the general laws of the country. The

ancients had their laws, more or less developed and even codified, yet a science which should .treat the philosophy and sources of law, and the method of legislation, interpretation, application, etc., of the law was wanting, and this never struck the minds of the jurists before Islam. Since the second century of the Hijrah (8th Chr. cent.) there began to be produced Islamic works of this kind, called *Usul al-Fiqh*.

456. In the days of antiquity, International Law was neither international nor law; it formed part of politics, and depended on the discretion and mercy of statesmen. Moreover its rules applied only to a limited number of States, inhabited by peoples of the same race, following the same religion and speaking the same language. The Muslims were the first to accord it a place in the legal system, creating both rights and obligations. This may be observed in the rules of international law that formed part of a special chapter in the codes and treatises of the Muslim law ever since the earliest times. In fact the most ancient treatise which we possess is the *Majmu'* of Zaid ibn 'Ali, who died in 120 H./737. That work also contains the chapter in question. Further, the Muslims developed this branch of study as an independent science, and monographs on the subject, under the generic title of *Siyar*, were found existing even before the middle of the second century of the Hijrah. In his *Tawali' at-Ta'sis*, Ibn Hajar relates that the first monograph of the kind hailed from the pen of Abu Hanifah, the contemporary of the above-mentioned Zaid ibn 'Ali. The characteristic feature of this international law is, that it makes no discrimination among foreigners; it does not concern inter-Muslim relations, but deals solely with the non-Muslim States of the entire world. Islam in principle forms one single unit and one single organic community.

457. Another contribution in the legal domain is the comparative Case Law. The appearance of different schools of the Muslim law necessitated this kind of study, in order to bring

into relief the reasons of their differences as well as the effects of each divergence of principle on a given point of law. The books of Dabusi and Ibn Rushd are classical on the subject. Saimuri wrote even a work of comparative jurisprudence or methodology of law (*usul al-fiqh*).

458. The written-constitution of the State is also an innovation of the Muslims. In fact, the Prophet Muhammad was its author. When he established a City-State at Madinah, he endowed it with a written constitution, which document has come down to us, thanks to Ibn Hisham and Abu 'Ubaid, and its contents could be divided into 52 clauses. It mentions in precise terms the rights and obligations of the head of the State of the constituent units, and of the subjects respectively, in matters of administration, legislation, justice, defence, etc. It dates from the year 622 of the Christian era.

459. In the sphere of law proper, codes have appeared since the beginning of the second century of the Hijrah. They are divided into three principal parts: Cult or religious practices, Contractual relations of all kinds, and Penalties. In keeping with its comprehensive view of life, there was no differentiation in Islam between the mosque and the citadel. The doctrine of the State or the constitutional law formed part of the cult, since the leader of the State was the same as the leader of the service of worship. The revenues and finances also formed part of the cult, since the Prophet had declared them to be one of the four fundamentals of Islam, side by side with worship, fasting, and pilgrimage. International law formed part of the penalties, war being placed on the same level as action against marauding brigands, pirates and other violators of law or of treaty.

460. It is due to this comprehensive view of law among the Muslims, that we have discussed the question at length.

HISTORY AND SOCIOLOGY

461. The share of Muslims in these is important from two points of view, one being assurance in the matter of authenticity and the other collection and preservation of the most varied details. Born in the full light of history, Islam did not require legends and hearsay. With regard to data concerning other peoples, each narration was accorded the value it merited. But the current history of Islam required fully reliable measures to maintain such an integrity through the ages. Attestation by witnesses was once an exclusive feature of judicial tribunals. The Muslims applied it to history; one required evidence for each reported narration. If, in the first generation after the event, it sufficed to have one trustworthy witness of the event, in the second generation it was necessary to cite two successive sources: "I have heard A, telling me that he had heard B who had lived at the time of the event, giving the details "; and in the third generation three sources were required, and so on and so forth. These exhaustive references assured the truthfulness of the chain of the successive sources, for one could refer to biographical dictionaries which indicated not only the character of individual personages, but also the names of their teachers as well as of their principal pupils. This kind of evidence is available not merely in connection with the life of the Prophet, but even for all branches of knowledge transmitted from one generation to another, sometimes even in the domain of anecdotes meant simply for amusement and pastime.

462. Biographical dictionaries are a characteristic feature of Muslim historical literature. The dictionaries were compiled according to professions, towns or regions, centuries or epochs, etc. Equally great importance was given to genealogical tables, particularly among the Arabs; and the relationship of hundreds of thousands of persons of some importance, thus learnt, facili-

tates the task of the researcher who should desire to penetrate the underlying causes of events.

463. As to history proper, the characteristic trait of the chronicles is their universalism. If pre-Islamic peoples produced national histories, Muslims seem to be the first to write world histories. Ibn Ishaq (d. 769) for instance, who is one of the earliest historians of Islam, not only begins his voluminous annals with an account of the creation of the universe and the history of Adam, but speaks also of other races that he knew, of his time — a task which was pursued with ever-increasing passion by his successors at-Tabari, al-Mas'udi, Miskawaih, Sa'id al-Andalusi, Rashiduddin Khan and others. It is interesting to observe that these historians, — to begin with at-Tabari — commenced their works with a discussion on the notion of time. Ibn Khaldun dived deeper into these sociological and philosophical discussions, in his celebrated Prolegomena to Universal History.

464. Already in the first century of the Hijrah, two branches of history began to develop independently, and were later combined with one composite whole. One was Islamic history, beginning with the life of the Prophet and continuing through the time of the caliphs, and the other non-Muslim history, whether concerning pre-Islamic Arabia or foreign countries such as Iran, Byzantium, etc. A very clear instance is that of the history of Rashiduddin Khan, the major portion of which still remains to be printed. This was simultaneously prepared both in Arabic and Persian versions, — and speaks with equal familiarity of the prophets, the caliphs, and popes as well as the kings of Rome, China, India, Mongolia, etc.

GEOGRAPHY AND TOPOGRAPHY

465. Pilgrimage as well as commerce in the vast Muslim empire needed communications. Baladhuri and Ibn al-Jauzi report : "Every time the post departed for some destination or

other — ranging from Turkistan to Egypt, and this happened almost daily — the Caliph 'Umar used to have it announced in the metropolis so that private letters could also be despatched in time through the official courier." The Directors of Posts prepared route-guides, whose publication was always accompanied by more or less detailed historico-economic description of each place, place-names being often arranged alphabetically. This literary geograpy led to other scientific studies. The geography of Ptolemy was translated into Arabic, and so were the Sanskrit works of Indian authors. Tales of travels and voyages increased daily the knowledge of the common man. The very diversity of the data counteracted all possibility of Chauvinism and one was obliged to put everything to practical test and trial. The dialogue of Abu-Hanifah (d. 767) reported by al-Muwaffaq, (I, 161) is well known: A Mu'tazilite asked him where the centre of the earth was, and he replied: "In the very place where thou art sitting!" This reply can be given only if one meant to convey that the earth was spherical. Even the earliest world maps, prepared by Muslims, represent the earth in circular shape. Ibn Hauqal's (cir. 975) cartography, for instance, presents no difficulty at all in recognizing the Mediterranean of the Near-Eastern countries. The map of 'al-Idrisi, prepared for King Roger of Sicily, (1101-54), astonishes us by its great precision and exactitude; it marks even the sources of the Nile. One has to remember that the Arabo-Muslim maps point upwards to the South, the North being downwards. The maritime voyages necessitated the tables of longitudes and latitudes as well as the use of the astrolabe and other nautical instruments. Thousands of Muslim coins, discovered in the excavations of Scandinavia, Finland, Russia, Kazan, etc., show conclusively the commercial activity of Muslim caravan-leaders during the Middle Ages. Ibn Majid, who served as pilot to Vasco da Gama as far as India, speaks of the compass as already a familiar thing. Muslim mariners astonish us with their skill and daring in their voyage from Basrah (Iraq) to China.

The words *arsenal, admiral, cable, monsoon, douane, tariff*, which are all of Arabic origin, are substantial proof of the Muslim influence on modern Western culture.

ASTRONOMY

466. The discovery and study of a number of stars is acknowledged to be a valuable and unforgettable contribution of the Muslims. A very large number of stars are still known in Western languages by their Arabic names, and it is Ibn-Rushd (Averroes) who recognized spots on the surface of the sun. The calendar reform by 'Umar al-Khayyam outdistances by far the Gregorian one. The pre-Islamic Bedouin Arabs had already developed very precise astronomical observations, not only for their nocturnal travels in the desert, but also for meteorology, rain, etc. A number of books called *Kitab al-Anwa'*, gives us sufficient proof of the extent of Arabic knowledge. Later, Sanskrit, Greek and other works were translated into Arabic. The confrontation of their divergent data required new experiments and patient observations. Observatories emerged everywhere. Under the Caliph al-Ma'mun, the circumference of the earth was measured, the exactitude of whose results is astonishing. Works were compiled very early dealing with the ebb and tide, dawn, twilight, rainbow, halo, and above all the sun and the moon and their movements, since they are immediately related with the question of the hours of prayers and fasting.

NATURAL SCIENCE

467. The characteristic feature of this aspect of Islamic science is the emphasis laid on experiment and observation without prejudices. The Arab method was quite unique and wonderful. The authors began their study of the sciences by the preparation of classified dictionaries of technical terms, which were found in their own language. With extraordinary patience, they ransacked all books of poetry and prose, for gleaning out terms, — with useful citations, — in each branch

separately, such as anatomy, zoology, botany, astronomy, mineralogy, etc. Every successive generation revised the works of its predecessors, in order to add thereto something new. These simple lists of words, with some literary or anecdotic observations, proved of immense value when the work of translation began; and rare were the cases in which one required to Arabicize or conserve a foreign word, in Arabicized form.

468. Words used in Botany are very characteristic. Except for the names of certain plants which did not grow in the Muslim empire, there is not a single technical term of foreign origin therein; one found words for every term in Arabic. The *Kitab an-Nabat, Encyclopaedia Botanica* of ad-Dinawari (d. 895) in six thick volumes was compiled even before the first translation into Arabic of the works on the subject in Greek. In the words of Silberberg: After a thousand years of study, Greek botany resumes itself in the works of Dioscorides and Theophrastus, but the very first Muslim work, of ad-Dinawari, on the subject far surpasses them in erudition and extensiveness.[1] Ad-Dinawari describes not only the exterior of each plant, but also their alimentary, medicinal and other properties; he classifies them, speaks of their habitat, and other details.

MEDICAL SCIENCE

469. Medicine also made extraordinary progress under the Muslims, in the branches of anatomy, pharmacology, organiza-

---

1. *His actual words are: "Anyhow it is astonishing enough that the entire botanical literature of antiquity furnishes us only two parallels to our book (of Dinawari). How was it that the Muslim people could, during so early a period of its literary life, attain the level of the people of such a genius as the Hellenic one, and even surpassed it in this respect."* (Zeitschrift fuer Assyriologie, *Strassburg, vols.* 24-25, 1910-1911, *see Vol.* XXV, 44).

tion of hospitals, and training of doctors, who were subjected to an examination before being authorized to start practice. Having common frontiers with Byzantium, India, China, etc., Muslim medical art and science became a synthesis of the world medical knowledge; and if the old lore was subjected to trial and test, new original contributions were also made. The works of Razi (Rhazes), Ibn-Sina (Avicenna) Abu'l-Qasim (Abucasis) and others remained until recent times the basis of all medical study even in the West. We know now that the fact of the circulation of blood was also known to them, thanks to the writings of Ibn an-Nafis.

OPTICS

470. This science owes a particular debt to the Muslims. We possess the book of rays by al-Kindi (of the 9th century), which was already far in advance of the Greek lore of the incendiary mirrors. Ibn al-Haitham (Alhazen, 965), who followed him, has rightly merited a lasting celebrity. Al-Kindi, al-Farabi, Ibn-Sina, al-Biruni and others, who are representatives of Muslim science, yield their place to none in the world history of sciences.

MINERALOGY, MECHANICS, ETC.

471. This attracted the attention of the learned, both from the medical point of view and for the purpose of distinguishing precious stones, so much sought after by kings and other wealthy persons. The works of al-Biruni are still usable in this field.

472. Ibn-Firnas (d. 888) had invented an apparatus, with which he flew a long distance. He died in an accident, and left no successor to pursue and perfect the work. Others invented mechanical instruments for floating sunken ships, or pulling out without difficulty trees of enormous dimensions.

473. For the underwater lore, numerous treatises were written on pearl-fishery and the treatment of their shells.

ZOOLOGY

474. The observation of the life of the wild animals and birds had always fascinated the Bedouins of Arabia. Al-Jahiz (d. 868) has left a huge work for popularizing the subject while referring to evolution, which theme was later developed by Miskawaih, al-Qazwini, ad-Damiri, and others, not to speak of numerous works on falconery and hunting by means of domesticated and trained beasts and birds of prey.

CHEMISTRY AND PHYSICS

475. The Quran has repeatedly urged the Muslims to mediate over the creation of the universe, and to study how the heavens and earth have been made subservient to man. Therefore there has never been a conflict between faith and reason in Islam. Thus it is that the Muslims began very early an ever-progressive and serious study of chemistry and physics. Scientific works are attributed to Khalid ibn Yazid (d. 704) and to the great jurist Ja'far as Sadiq (d. 765); and their pupil Jabir ibn Hayyan (cir. 776) has justly remained celebrated through the ages. The characteristic feature of their works has been objective experimentation, instead of simple speculation; and it was through observation that they accumulated facts. Under their influence, ancient alchemy was transformed into an exact science, based on facts and capable of demonstration. Already Jabir knew the chemical operations of calcination and reduction; it is he who developed also the methods of evaporation, sublimation, crystallization, etc. It is evident that in such paths of human knowledge, patient work for generations and centuries was required. The existence of Latin translations of the works of Jabir and others, — used for long as text books in Europe, — suffices to show how greatly modern science is indebted to the works of Muslim savants, and how fast it deve-

loped, thanks to the applications of the Arabo-Muslim method of experiment rather than the Greek method of speculation.

MATHEMATICS

476. The mathematical science has left ineffaceable traces of the Muslim share in its development. The terms *algebra, zero, cipher*, etc., are of Arabic origin. The names of al-Khwarizmi, 'Umar al-Khayyam, al-Biruni and others shall remain as famous as those of Euclid and the Indian author of *Siddhanta*, etc. Trigonometry was unknown to the Greeks: The credit of its discovery goes undoubtedly to Muslim mathematicians.

TO SUM UP

477. Muslims continued their work in the service of science until great misfortunes afflicted their principal intellectual centres, Baghdad in the East, and Cordova-Granada in the West. These were occupied by barbarians, to the great misfortune of science, at a time when the printing press had not yet come into vogue; the burning of libraries with their hundreds of thousands of MSS. led to untold and irreparable loss. The wholesale massacres did not spare the learned. What had been constructed in the course of centuries was destroyed in days. Once a civilization declines, due to such calamities, it takes several centuries of time as well as numerous resources, including the facilities to study the achievements of others — who should have assumed the relay after the fall of the previous standard-bearers of civilization, — before one can make up the distance. Moreover noble characters and great minds cannot be had at will : they are the gift and grace of the Almighty on a people. That men of noble character are held in check, and not invested with the direction of their country men, which is assumed by incompetent and unscrupulous persons, is another tragedy which one has often to deplore.

THE ARTS

478. As in the case of the sciences, the Quran took the initiative in the development of arts among Muslims. The

liturgical recitation of the Holy Quran created a new branch of music (cf. *infra* § 485). The conservation of its text necessitated calligraphy and book-binding. The construction of mosques developed architecture and decorative art. To these were added later the secular needs of the wealthy. In its care for an equilibrium between the body and soul, Islam taught moderation in all things, led the natural talents in the right direction, and tried to develop in man a harmonious whole.

479. We read, in the *Sahih* of Muslim, and the *Musnad* of Ibn Hanbal, an interesting saying of the Prophet: "God is beautiful and likes beauty." Another of his sayings is: "Beauty is prescribed in everything; even if you kill somebody, kill him in a nice manner." God has spoken in the Quran: "We have beautified the lower sky with lamps" (67/5), or "Lo! We have placed all that is in the earth as an ornamental thing that We may try men: which of them is best in conduct" (18:7). It goes so far as to ordain: "Put on your dress of adornment on every occasion of prostration (service of prayer)" (7 : 31).

480. In the life of the Prophet, we come across the following instructive incident: One day he saw the interior of a grave which was not fully levelled. He ordered the defect to be mended, adding that it would do neither good nor harm to the dead, but it was more pleasant to the eye of the living, and whenever one does something, God likes that one does it in a perfect manner. (cf. Ibn Sa'd, VIII, 156).

481. The taste for fine arts is innate in man. As in the case of all other natural gifts, Islam seeks to develop the artistic talents with the spirit of moderation. It may be recalled that excess even of self-mortification and of spiritual practices is forbidden in Islam.

482. The first *minbar* (pulpit) in the mosque, which was prepared for the Prophet, was decorated with two balls, like pomegranates, and the two little grand-children of the Prophet enjoyed playing with them. This was the beginning of wood-

carving. Later on, copies of the Quran were illuminated in colour, and the greatest care was taken in their binding. In short, Islam never forbids artistic progress. The only brake put in is the one against the representation of animal (including human) figures. The prohibition does not seem to be absolute, and we shall revert to it, yet the Prophet has placed a restraint on this activity. The reasons for this are metaphysical, as well as psychological, biological and social. In the creation of the different kingdoms, animal life is the highest manifestation, the vegetables and minerals succeeding it in a lower order. Therefore in his anxiety to pay his profound respect to the Creator, man reserves for God the privilege of the supreme creation, and contents himself with the representation of inferior objects. The psychologists point out that, seeing the privileged position which the animal kingdom occupies in the creation (with the faculty of movement and, for man in particular, the faculty of invention), the animal representation gives man the double temptation to which he cannot much resist: the temptation to believe that he "creates", whereas he merely manufactures, (and as a proof the famous story of a Greek sculptor who had become amourous of his own sculpture), and the temptation to attribute to the representation the soul and the ideal virtues of an accessible Divinity (cf. the history of human antiquity of idolatory, and the modern taste for the cult of heroes, champions and stars). The biological aspect is that an unutilized talent reinforces those in constant use. Thus, a blind man possesses a memory and a sensibility which are far superior to those in ordinary men. By abstaining from animal representations in painting, engraving, sculpture, etc., the innate talent of the artist seeks other outlets and manifests itself with greater vigour in other domains of art, (cf. the pruning down of the superfluous branches of a tree in order to increase its fruits). As regards the social aspect, the horror of Chauvinism, which degenerates into idolatry, and a restraint on animal representation would lead to restraint on idolatry. There are however several exceptions; such as toys of children, decoration of cushions and carpets — both these have expressly been tolerated by the Prophet, — scientific needs (for teaching anatomy, anthropology, etc.), security needs (of the police, etc., for identification, for search of the absconding criminal), and others of like import, cannot be banned.

483. History shows that this check on "figurative" art among Muslims has never curbed art in general; on the contrary an astonishing development was achieved in the non-figurative spheres. The Quran itself (24:36) recommended grandeur in the construction of mosques. The Prophet's Mosque at Madinah, the Dome of the Rock at Jerusalem, the Sulaimaniyeh mosque at Istanbul, the Taj-Mahal at Agra (India), the Alhambra Palace at Granada, and other monuments are in no way inferior to the masterpieces of other civilizations, either in architecture or in artistic decoration.

484. Calligraphy as an art is a Muslim specially. It makes writing a piece of art, in place of pictures; it is employed in painting or mural sculpture, to decorate fine cloth, and other material. Excellent specimens of this art, with their powerful way of execution, grace and beauty, are things to see, and impossible to describe.

485. Another art which is peculiar to the Muslims is the recitation of the Quran. Not accompanied by instruments of music, and not being even in verse, the Quran has been an object of great attention for recitation purposes, since the time of the Prophet. The Arabic language lends to its prose a sweetness and melody hardly to be surpassed by the rhymed verses of other languages. Those who have listened to the master singer, or Qari, reciting the Quran, or pronouncing several times every day the calls to the prayer, know that these specialities of the Muslims have unequalled charms of their own.

486. Even mundane music and song, under the patronage of kings and other wealthy people, have had their development

among Muslims. Theoreticians like al-Farabi, the authors of the *Rasa'il Ikhwan as-Safa*, Avicenna and others have not only left monumental works on the subject, but have even made appreciable corrections in the Greek and Indian music. They have employed signs to denote music, and have described different musical instruments. The choice of appropriate melody for different poems and selection of instruments according to the requirements of the occasions — of joy and of sorrow, in the presence of sick men, etc. — have been objects of profound study.

487. As for poetry, the Prophet recognizes: "There are verses of poems which are full of wisdom, and there are discourses of orators which produce a magical effect." The Quran has discouraged immoral poetry. Following this direction, the Prophet surrounded himself by the best poets of the epoch, and showed them the road to follow and the limits to observe, thus distinguishing between the good and the bad use of this great natural talent. The poetical works of Muslims are found in all languages and relate to all times; it would be impossible to describe them here even in the briefest manner. An Arab, even a Bedouin, finds himself always "at home" in his poetry, as is borne out by the synonymity of terms: *Bait* means both a tent and a verse of two hemistiches; *misra* means not only the flap of a tent but also a hemistich; *sabab*: is rope of the tent as well as the prosodiacal foot; *watad*: means a tent peg as well as the syllables of the prosodiacal foot. Further the names given to the different metres of poems are synonymous with the different paces — fast, slow, etc., — of the camel. These are but a few among a great many peculiarities of the language.

488. In short, in the realm of art, Muslims have made a worthy contribution, avoiding its harmful features, developing its aesthetic aspects, and inventing things quite new to it. In this sphere also, their share in development has been considerable. A passing remark may be made to two points: (1) Had the

Muslims no culture of theirs — the all-pervading Islamic culture which the Prophet inculcated them intensely — they would certainly have been absorbed by the ·cultures of those whom these Muslims had so easily and so swiftly subjugated. (2) Among the subjects of the extremely extensive Islamic State, there were peoples of all religions: Christians, Jews, Zoroastrians, Sabians, Brahmins, Buddhists and others, each with its own cultural traditions, even if these did not collaborate with each other, all of them did collaborate with the Muslims, their political masters, and each explained its own point of view to the Muslims who were thus obliged not to imitate any of them — since there was even contradictions in the different scientific strains — but to test them all and create a sort of synthesis, to the benefit of science and humanity.

CHAPTER XIV
General History of Islam

THE history of Islam means practically the history of the world during the last fourteen centuries. What we can attempt here is just a modest sketch in broad lines of the chief events of this history.

ORTHODOX CALIPHS

490. In the year 632 (11 H.) the Prophet Muhammad breathed his last. During the twenty-three preceding years, he had toiled successfully for the formulation of a religion as well as the creation from nothingness of a State, which beginning as a tiny city-state in a part of the town of Madinah embraced in the short span of ten years the administration of the whole of the Arabian Peninsula together with certain southern parts of Palestine and Iraq. Further he left a community composed of several hundreds of thousands of adherents, with the fullest faith and conviction in his doctrines and capable of continuing the work he had begun.

491. The temporal success of the Prophet of Islam prompted certain adventurers, during the latter part of his life, to advance pretensions to prophethood. For several months, after the death of the Prophet Muhammad, the task of his successor' Abu-Bakr, consisted in suppressing these impostors, who had been joined a few others, emboldened by the death of the Prophet.

492. At the moment of the Prophet's demise, there was a state of war with Byzantium, and almost the same with Iran. It will be recalled that a Muslim Ambassador had been assassina-

ted in Byzantine territory (cf. supra § 442); and instead of making amends, the emperor had not only rejected all the alternatives proposed by the Prophet, but had even intervened militarily to protect the murderer against the punitive expedition of the Muslims. As regards Iran, for several years there had been bloody skirmishes between that country and its protectorates in Arabia; certain of the tribes, inhabiting these regions had embraced Islam. The acts of aggression and repression on the part of the Iranians could no more be passed over without provoking complications on an international scale. It may be recalled that the Byzantine and the Sassanid empires constituted, at the time, the two Big Powers of the world; whereas the Arabs possessed nothing enviable, being but a handful of nomads with neither military equipment nor material resources !

493. With a courage and boldness of spirit which can never be too greatly admired, the Caliph Abu-Bakr undertook a war against both these Big Powers simultaneously. In the first encounter, the Muslims occupied certain regions of the frontier. Then the Caliph sent an embassy to Constantinople in order to seek out a pacific solution, but all in vain. The defeat of the commandant at Caesaria, however, alarmed the emperor, and he raised new troops. Abu-Bakr judged it necessary to transfer certain elements of the Muslim army from Iraq (Iranian empire) to Syria. In 634 a new victory was obtained at Ajnadain, near Jerusalem, followed a little later by another at Fihl (Pella); as a result of which Palestine was definitely lost to Byzantium. The old Caliph Abu-Bakr died at this time, and his successor, 'Umar, had no alternative but to continue the task which he had inherited. Very soon Damascus, and later Emesa (Hims) in North Syria opened their gates to the Muslims. Facts show that the peoples of these regions received the Muslims not as conquerors and enemies, but as liberators. After the capture of Emesa, the concentrated final efforts of Emperor Heraclius obliged the Muslims to evacuate the town along with certain other regions, for the purpose of a better regrouping and orga-

nization. When the evacuation was decided upon, the Muslim commandant ordered that all the taxes collected from the people of the place, — non-Muslims all, — should be returned to them, since the right to utilize levies did not hold good when protection could no more be extended to the subjects. It is not surprising therefore that the vanquished shed tears on seeing their erstwhile conquerors obliged to retire. In his *Memoire sur la conquete de la Syrie*, De Geoje writes: "In fact the disposition of the men in Syria was very favourable to Arabs, and they merited it, since the leniency with which they treated the vanquished contrasted strongly with the dire tyranny inflicted by the preceding (Byzantine) masters." Shortly after their tactical retreat, the Muslims returned again with added strength and popularity.

494. The fate of Iran was not very different. The first incursions led to the occupation of Hirah (modern Kufah), and some other fortified localities. The departure of some detachments to Syria created a momentary calm, but a few months later the struggle recommenced, and the capital Mada'in (Ctesiphon) was occupied with ease. Emperor Yazdgird appealed for aid to the Emperor of China, the King of Turkistan and other neighbouring princes, but the help he received did not serve his ends, and his allies too suffered great losses.

495. During the time of 'Umar (634-44), the Muslims ruled from Tripoli (Lybia) to Balkh (Afghanistan), and from Armenia to Sindh (Pakistan) and Gujarat (India), and over the countries lying in between, such as Syria, Iraq and Iran, etc. Under his successor 'Uthman (644-56), they became masters of Nubia down to the outskirts of Dongola; they also occupied part of Andalusia (Spain); in the East, they crossed the river Oxus (Jaihun) and seized some regions from the Chinese. The islands of Cyprus, Rhodes and Crete became parts of the land of Islam; and in the course of defensive wars against the Byzantines, even Constantinople experienced a first Arab

attack. Hardly fifteen years had passed after the death of the Prophet, when the East-West Muslim expansion spread from the Atlantic to the approaches of the Pacific, and an area was occupied that was as large as the whole continent of Europe. In this lightning conquest, what is surprising is that nowhere were the conquered discontented. This is proved also by the fact that in 656, when the Muslims were torn by their first civil war, no internal uprisings took place; and the Byzantine Emperor could not count in the least on his former subjects, but had to content himself with a small sum promised him by the cautious Muslim. governor of Syria in exchange for the Emperor's neutrality.

496. It would be wrong to attribute this rapid expansion to any single cause. The weakness of the Byzantine and Sassanid empires, as a result of their mutual conflicts, was offset by the lack of Arab conquerors in the matter of equipment, organization and other material resources. The Muslims could not spread *en masse* from China to Spain, and there were not enough Arabs to be distributed over all this immense territory. We have seen that the beginning of these wars was rather political; there was absolutely no desire on the part of the Muslims to impose religion by force, their religion having formally prohibited such a thought. History also shows that at this time no compulsion was employed to convert the subjugated peoples. The simplicity and reasonableness of their religious doctrines together with the practical example in life which these Muslims set, no doubt attracted proselytes. Plunder and economic gain could form even poorer motives to explain the rapidity of the conquests; on the other hand the change of masters was hailed by the vanquished as a change for the better. Contemporary administrative documents on papyrus, discovered lately in Egypt, attest to the fact that the Arabs had much lightened the burden of taxes in Egypt — therefore it seems certain that the same reforms were introduced every- where in the conquered countries. The cost of administration

was also much reduced, in consequence not only of the frugality of the simple Arab life, but also of the honesty of the Muslim administrators. The booty of war does not belong in Islam to the soldiers seizing it, but to the government, and it is this latter which distributes it among the members of the expedition in proportions fixed by law. Caliph 'Umar was often delightfully surprised at the honesty of the private soldiers and officers, who handed over even precious stones and other valuable objects which could have easily been concealed.

497. We may conclude this section by a contemporary Christian document. It refers to the letter of a Nestorian bishop, addressed to a friend of his, which has been preserved (cf. Assemani, *Bibl. Orient*, III, 2, p. XCVI): "These Tayites (i.e., Arabs), to whom God has accorded domination in our days, have also become our masters; yet they do not combat at all the Christian religion ; on the contrary, they even protect our faith, respect our priests and our saints, and make donations to our churches and our convents."

THE UMAYYADS

498. At the death of the third Caliph, 'Uthman in 655, the Muslim world faced a war of succession, which was renewed several times during the subsequent twenty years in the course of which as many as half a dozen sovereigns entered on the stage and vanished from the scene. With the accession to power of 'Abd al-Malik (685-705), the government was again stabilized, and a new wave of conquests began. Morocco and Spain on the one hand, and North of the Indo-Pakistanian continent as well as Transoxiana on the other were added to the domain of the Muslims. We see Bordeaux, Narbonne and Toulouse (in France) also passing into their hands. The metropolis moved from Madinah to Damascus. When the blessed city of the Prophet yielded place to what was formerly a Byzantine locality, religious devotion was also weakened in favour

of secular activities. Luxury and squandering of wealth, favouritism and the consequent revolts and upheavals were not lacking. Conquests however grew in the intellectual and social fields. Industry received a great impetus; medicine was particularly patronized by the government, which undertook the translation of foreign medical works, from the Greek and other languages, into Arabic. The short reign of 'Umar ibn 'Abd al-'Aziz (817-20) was particularly brilliant and epoch-making. Monogamous himself, he by his piety brought a renewal of the period of Abu-Bakr and 'Umar. He revised the old files of confiscations, in order to return properties to the rightful owners or to their heirs. He abolished many unjustifiable taxes. He was rigid and unflinching for an impartial justice even when the oppressor was a Muslim and the victim a non-Muslim. He went so far as to order the evacuation of towns — Samarqand, for instance — which were treacherously occupied by Muslim armies. And he had not hesitated (cf. supra § 434) to order demolition of part of the grand mosque of the capital, built on a usurped piece of land. The result was astonishing. At the start of this dynasty, the revenues of Iraq, for instance, amounted to 100 millions of dirhams, they fell to 18 millions under the Caliph preceding 'Umar ibn 'Abd al-Aziz. But under him they climbed to as much as 120 millions. His religious devotion produced a world wide impression of good and the rajas of Sindh, Turkistan and Berber-Land embraced Islam. Everyone began to take interest in religious studies, and a whole galaxy of savants surged forth to set up peaks in the fields of science in the Muslim community. The rigorous suppression of corruption further popularised the administration everywhere.

499. From among the architectural monuments of this time, there is still the Dome of the Rock, at Jerusalem, constructed in 691. The ruins or remains of other monuments at Damascus and elsewhere bear witness to the equally precocious progress of Muslims in this field. Great development of music is also noted, although the signs of musical notations were not

yet invented, and we are unable to have a definite idea of the progress affected. The two great sects among Muslims, the Sunnites and Shi'ites date from the same period. The difference between these two sects is based on a political question, whether the succession to the Prophet should take place by election or by inheritance among the close relatives of the Prophet? This became a question of dogma to the Shi'ites, and the schism split into ramifications of its own, and occasioned civil wars. It is one such uprising which swept away the Umayyad dynasty, and made it yield its place in 750 to the 'Abbasids, but the Shi'ites did not profit by the change. In our days, there are probably ten per cent Shi'ites among the Muslims of the world, the rest being almost all Sunnites, not to speak of the infinitesimally small sect of the Kharijites, which also came into existence at the same time.

THE 'ABBASIDS

500. The rise into power of the 'Abbasids in 750 coincides with the division of the Muslim territory first into two, and later into ever-increasing independent States. At Cordova (Spain), a rival caliphate was established, which never reconciled itself, till its downfall in 1492, to union with the East, where Baghdad had taken the place of Damascus as the seat of the caliphate.

501. The history of the 'Abbasids does not show any big military conquests, if we except the initiatives taken by regional chieftains, who though they recognized the caliph of Baghdad as their sovereign, did not depend on him in the least, in matters either of foreign policy or internal administration. We shall speak of the Indian sub-continent in this connection under a separate paragraph. The relations with Byzantium became more and more bitter and bloody, and the Greek empire had to quit Asia Minor definitely and be content for some time longer with its European possessions only.

502. The 'Abbasids inaugurated the policy of replacing popular armies of volunteers by standing armies of professionals

recruited more and more from soldiers of Turkish origin, and this gave birth to feudalism and culminated later in the establishment of independent provinces, where one sees "dynasties" of governors. About a century after their assuming power, the 'Abbasid caliphs began to delegate — and even lose — their sovereign prerogatives in favour of centrifugal governors; and gradually their sovereignty was limited to their own palace, the rest being controlled by emirs, of whom the most powerful occupied even the metropolis. We see therein a strange contrast with Papacy: The popes began without any political power, but later acquired it after some centuries particularly, with the creation of the Holy Roman Empire. For some time they became even more powerful than emperors, only to lose this authority in the course of time. The Caliphs began as all-powerful rulers, shared the power later with the Sultans, and finally become figure-heads and nominal sovereigns with no influence to exert.

503. It was under the 'Abbasids that the governor of Tunis of the Aghlabid dynasty was invited to intervene in the civil wars of Sicily. He occupied the island, and also much of the mainland of Italy itself advancing as far as the walls of Rome. The South of France was annexed as also a considerable part of Switzerland. This wave of expansion was the work of the Aghlabids, who were later replaced, by force evidently, by the Fatimids. These latter, of the Shi'ite sect, transferred their capital to Cairo, where they established a rival caliphate. Enlightened rulers in general, one of them however profaned, in a moment of folly, the sacred shrines of the Christians at Jerusalem. This produced such a great resentment in Europe, that even the Popes preached a holy war against Islam. A series of crusades ensued, which bled both the Orient and Occident for two hundred years. At the time of the first crusade, the Fatimids had already abandoned Palestine, and it was the innocent civil population that fell victim to the fury of the invaders. Even more pathetic is the fact, that sometimes

these Fatimids collaborated with the crusaders in their war against the Islamic Levant. There was no central authority in the Islamic world at that time, but dozens of petty States — anachronic City-States even — warring with each other. Of these rulers, the Kurds and Turks replaced more and more the Arabs in the struggle against the Occident. Salahuddin (Saladin), Muslim hero of the time of the second crusade, not only expelled the Europeans from Syria - Palestine, but also swept away the Fatimids of Egypt. Salahuddin and his successors recognised the caliphate of Baghdad, yet this latter never succeeded in recuperating its political power which remained divided among a host of fragmentary states. Some of these succeeded in extending the frontiers of the land of Islam.

504. In 921, the king of "Bulgar" (i.e., the region of Kazan, on the river Volga, in Russia) solicited a Muslim missionary from Baghdad. Ibn Fadlan was sent. According to the report of his travel, which is extremely interesting, the king of Bulgar embraced Islam, and created, so to say, an Islamic island in the midst of the non-Muslim regions. The Islamization of Caucasus and the neighbouring regions continued slowly.

INDIA

505. The Ghaznavid dynasty of Afghanistan began the reconquest (cf. § 495) of India. Other dynasties followed, which contented themselves with only the North of the country, then came the Khaljids who pushed their conquests towards the South. A negro commander, Malik Kafur, in a lightning expedition proceeded as far as Cape Comorin, yet it is only later that Southern India saw the establishment of Muslim States in the region. The Great Mughals (1526-1858) are particularly celebrated in the Muslim history of India. For a long time, they ruled over almost the whole of this vast continent, and were considered among the "Bigs" of the world. Their central authority began to be weakened however by the action of provincial governors from 18th century onwards. It was only in

1858 that the British chased them out and annexed three-fifths of the country for the Crown, the rest being divided among indigenous states, some of which were Muslim. These latter preserved the Indo-Muslim culture until our own times. One of these, Haidarabad, situated in the centre of India was as big as Italy, with over 20 million inhabitants. It was well known for the attention it gave particularly to the reform of Islamic education. In its university founded on Western lines, with about a dozen faculties, there was also a faculty of Islamic theology. The university imparted teaching, at every level and in every faculty, through the medium of Urdu, the local language with its script in Arabic characters. Specialization began in the school stage, when Arabic language, *Fiqh*, (Muslim law) and *Hadith*, (documents on the life and sayings of the Prophet) were obligatory beside other subjects such as English language, mathematics and other courses of modern education. In the university stage, the students of the Faculty of Theology learned not only English of a high standard, but also Arabic and subjects concerned purely with Islamic studies were prescribed. Moreover comparative studies became the vogue. With the *Fiqh* was modern jurisprudence, with the *Kalam*, the history of Western philosophy; with Arabic, also Hebrew or some modern European language, the French or the German in particular. When the students prepared their theses, they were attached to two guides : one a professor of the Faculty of Theology, and the other a professor from the Faculty of Arts and Letters or Law as the case was. This provided the means of mastering simultaneously both the Islamic facts and modern Western trends on the same subject. After thirty years of experiment and the obtaining of very happy results, there remains nothing now but a distant memory of it all. For, when the British left the country for good in 1947, dividing the country between Muslim Pakistan and non-Muslim Bharat, this latter not only incorporated its neighbouring indigenous States, but even disintegrated and dissolved them in other administrative combinations, creating linguistic "nationalities" fraught with disintegration.

506. To revert to our main subject. As a passive specta-
tor, the Caliphs of Baghdad continued to witness the constant
changes in the "provinces," where *coups-d'etat* replaced governors, divided single provinces into two or more units, reunited
different provinces under the same hands, and so on. Yet
cases were rare when the land of Islam was occupied by non-
Muslims. The Seljuk Muslims deserve special mention. With their
rise to power in the 11th century, they subjugated early not
only Central Asia, but extended their conquests even as far as
the farthest ends of Asia Minor, with Konia (Iconium) as their
capital. After some generations of brilliant rule, they yielded
place to what we call the Ottoman Turks. It is these latter
who crossed the Bosphorus and extended the Islamic dominion
to the walls of Vienna. Their capital was first at Brusa (Bursa),
then Constantinople (Byzantium, now Istanbul), and is at present Ankara (Angora, Ancyre). Their recoil began in the 18th
century, with their evacuating region after region of the European soil, and reached its climax in 1919, when they lost
everything in the first World War. Some happy incidents of an
international character helped Turkey to rise again in the form
of a republic, which was at the outset ferociously nationalist
and secular, but being democratic by nature, its regime had to
conform more and more to the religious sentiments of the
public which are profoundly Muslim. In the 16th century, the
Ottoman Turks ruled in Europe as far as Austria, in North Africa
as far as Algeria and Chad, and in Asia from Georgia to Yemen
passing in between through Mesopotamia, Arabia and Asia
Minor. Some of their former Muslim possessions are now
independent States, but others have passed under the Soviet
domination, not to speak of regions with a non-Muslim majority which have detached themselves from Turkey.

507. In the 13th century, some of the Tatars had not yet
embraced Islam. Hulagu led them, massacred hundreds of
thousands en route, and destroyed Baghdad, the seat of the
caliphate in 1258. However, his army was annihilated in Pales-

tine at the hands of Baybars, Muslim general of Egypt. Hulagu tried to lead another invasion, and invited even the crusaders to an offensive alliance, but without success. This marks the decline of Muslim science and the dawn of the Occidental science. (Today in the 20th century, the Muslims are still far from equalling some of the Americano-Europeans, in this field.) It might be noted that the efforts of Muslim mystics rallied these barbarian Tatars; and having embraced Islam, they not only took up the cause of Islam, but also emigrated to different countries of Europe and colonized them. There are living traces of them in the Muslim communities of Finland, Lithuania, Poland and USSR.

ANDALUSIAN CALIPHATE

508. As we have mentioned above, it is at the rise into caliphal power of the 'Abbasids that Spain detached itself from the Muslim Orient. After almost a thousand years of domination, in 1492, the last traces of a Muslim State were submerged there by the Castillian Christians. The Muslim period was a period of material progress and prosperity for Spain. The Muslim universities there constantly attracted non-Muslim students from all parts of Europe. The ruins of the Muslim architecture, still to be seen in the Iberian Peninsula, show the astonishing progress which was attained in this field. After their political fall, the Muslims witnessed bloody persecutions in order to convert them to Christianity, and the mass destruction of their libraries, where hundreds of thousands of MSS. were burned at a time when the printing press had not yet emerged. The loss was one which could never be repaired.

EAST ASIA AND SOUTH-EAST ASIA

509. The greater part of China has so far never known the political domination of Muslims. Advancing from Central Asia, the Muslims Islamicized the province of Eastern Turkistan (now Sin-Kiang); and voyaging probably by sea routes, they

won to their faith the Southern province of Yun-Nan. Some ephemeral principalities came into being, but the numerous millions in China and Tibet were attracted to Islam above all by the pacific activities of Muslim missionaries. The great majority of the Chinese however has so far remained outside the monotheistic religion of Islam.

510. Quite different is the story of South-East Asia. During these last centuries, Muslim merchants of South Arabia as well as of South India travelled to this part of the continent and thanks to their selfless efforts for propagating the faith, not only the Malay Peninsula, but also thousands of islands in this region have almost completely been won over to Islam. In Indonesia, as also in the Southern islands of the Philippines, Islam became predominant. Broken as it was into a large number of principalities, this region fell gradually under the yoke of the Europeans, particularly the English and the Dutch. After several centuries of foreign domination, Indonesia with its 70 millions of Muslims has now regained her independence; and the Malay Peninsula, heading towards complete sovereignty inside the British Commonwealth, has obtained it more peacefully.

AFRICA

511. North Africa, from Egypt to Morocco, was attached to Islamic territories since very early times. In the rest of this continent, different regions have their own tales of development. East Africa was naturally the first to be influenced by Islam, thanks to its proximity to Arabia. Not only vast regions there are strongly Islamicized, but there have grown up Muslim States of considerable importance.

512. West Africa began to know Islam later, but the energetic efforts of certain Muslim rulers there, — efforts consistent with the indigenous culture. — won over a large part to the faith. One meets there veritable Muslim empires throughout the centuries. According to the Arab chroniclers, it is the

adventurous sea-faring population of this region which discovered first the route to America, particularly to Brazil. The earliest Europeans under Christopher Columbus and his successors, found negro inhabitants there. In spite of the destruction of historical documents, there is every reason to believe that the Muslims of Black Africa, and the Berbers participated in the colonization of America — as the name of Brazil suggests, since Birzalah is a well-known Berber tribe, and the collective name of the members of this tribe is precisely Brazil. The island of Palma, in the Atlantic, was formerly called Bene Hoare — after the name of the Berber tribe Beni Huwara; — this strengthens the supposition. The relation of the Muslim West Africa with America continued till the fall of Muslim Spain and the commencement of the European voyages to America. Africa also fell a prey to European powers, such as France, Britain, Germany, Italy, Spain, Portugal and Belgium. There are vast regions in the continent that never knew Islamic domination, and yet Islam is spreading there even in these days in spite of the vigilance kept and obstacles set up by their Occidental masters, and wire-pullers. With the recent decolonization, most of the countries with an Islamic majority have become independent, though some of them are subjected to the tyranny of non-Muslim dictatorship and persecutions. Other regions are marching towards ever-increasing autonomy.

CONTEMPORARY WORLD

513. From Indonesia to Morocco, there are over thirty Muslim States which are already members of UNO. If in Europe there is Albania, there are inside USSR other Muslim republics whose autonomy seems to increase gradually even in matters of Islamic religion. The Commonwealth evolved by the British shows that accession to a collectivity of non-Muslim States does not stand in the way of the real independence of its Muslim associates, provided the men at the helm of affairs have intelligence and disinterestedness, preferring national interest

to the personal one. If Spain, France, Russia, India, China and others educate their Muslim dependencies for veritable autonomies, the actual struggle for liberation will lose its *raison-d'etre*, and everybody will be able to live in concord and co-operation, with a sense of universal well-being.

514. Islam is represented now, and in fact has been since long centuries, in all the principal races, with the exception of the Red Indians of America. The Arabic speaking peoples base their importance particularly on the fact that it is their language which is the custodian and repository of the original teachings of Islam, above all the Quran and the *Hadith*. The Indo-Pakistanis and Malay-Indonesians constitute two most numerous ethnic groups. The black race enjoys the particular privilege of having preserved its energies up to our own days. Erudite savants, like Prof. Arnold Toynbee of London, do not hesitate to think that the next stage of human civilization will have the negroes as its leaders. Islam is actually gaining in this race very numerous followers. And the zeal that is displayed by new converts is well known.

515. The exact number of the Muslims in the world can hardly be determined to an exact figure, for there are deaths and births, and there are conversions of which a certain number is never declared owing to personal reasons. But from all the evidence available, there is no doubt that between one-fourth and one-fifth of the descendants of Adam and Eve already turn their faces every day towards the Ka'bah (in Mecca) to proclaim aloud "Allah-u-Akbar," that God alone is Great !

CHAPTER XV

Daily Life of a Muslim

BIRTH

516. If a religion is not reserved for any particular race or confined to any country, but intended for entire humanity, then there are two kinds of births: voluntary and involuntary.

517. There is first the voluntary birth, or conversion of an adult in full consciousness of his act and out of his free choice, relating to what the Prophet Muhammad said: "declaration by tongue and affirmation by heart." One takes first a bath, a shower bath preferably, in order to purify the body symbolically of the dirt of ignorance and disbelief; then one declares, usually in the presence of two witnesses, the following formula: "I attest that there is no God if not God Himself, and I attest that Muhammad is the Messenger of God" (ash-hadu al-laa ilaaha il-lal-laah wa ash-hadu anna muham-madar-rasool-ul-laah).

518. The Prophet used to ask a new convert what his name was; and if this had any un-Islamic trait, he changed it and gave the person concerned a new and more convenient name. Thus, if a man was named "Worshipper of the Ka'bah," or "Worshipper of the sun," or "the dissipated one," or "one in error," etc., the Prophet would not tolerate such appellations. Now-a-days the converts usually take a new forename in Arabic, the mother-tongue of the holy Prophet and the tongue of the wives of the Prophet, who are the Mothers of the faithful — and therefore the mother-tongue of every Muslim.

519. Arabic being the spiritual mother-tongue of every Muslim, it is his social duty to learn it, at least its alphabet, so that he should be able to read the Quran in the original. Since

all time, converts have attached so great an importance to it, that they have even adopted the Arabic script in their local languages. Such is the case with Persian, Turkish, Urdu, Malay, Pashtau, Kurdish, Spanish, Lithuanian, Afrikaans, etc. It is strongly recommended as a social duty that new entrants to Islam should master the Arabic script and employ it — at least in their inter-Muslim correspondence, — when writing in their local languages. In fact, when the Arabic script is written with all its signs of vocalization, it is incomparably superior to any and every script in the world from the point of view precision and absence of ambiguity, not to speak of its great aesthetic and economic values (it being a sort of short-hand writing).

519/a. When the non-Arab Muslims adopted the Arabic script to their tongues, they required some additions both in letters of the alphabet and in vowel signs. These additions differ according to countries and epochs, since there was no central academic authority in the Muslim world to evolve and impose uniform reforms. In fact there is a pressing need to hold a world congress of Muslim countries and such non-Muslim countries as use the Arabic script, in order to develop a uniform system of Arabic writing for transliterating non-Arabic languages or proper names, so that different languages should not employ different figures for representing the same non-Arabic sound, as is unfortunately the case at present. The oldest additions to the Arabic letters of the alphabet were made probably by Persian and Turks, and the oldest additional signs of vocalisation by the Spaniards for the Aljamiado (a corruption of *al-a'jamiyatu*, i.e. the non-Arabic, namely the language of the Iberian Peninsula; and hundreds of MSS are still extant in it, including translations of the Quran). The Arabs have also felt the need of such additions, in modern times, in order correctly to reproduce the pronunciation of foreign proper names, and to a lesser degree their dialectal peculiarities. The best and most precise of such systems proposed was, to our knowledge, the one adopted by the Osmania University of

Haiderabad-Deccan and employed in some of its voluminous publications, such as the Urdu translation of the *Origines du droit des gens* by Ernest Nys; it transliterated almost twelve old or new European languages. The details of this system of transliteration into Arabic alphabet could be found in the *Islamic Culture*, Hyderabad (Haiderabad), 1940, p. 486ff. We shall give below, as illustration, a short passage in three principal European languages, transliterated into Arabic script:

520. The ordinary Arabic alphabet consists of the following 28 letters — like the number of the mansions of the moon, and admirably suited to be employed as numerals upto one thousand[1] — which write from right to left:

ا	ب	ج	د	ه	و	ز	ح	ط
1	2	3	4	5	6	7	8	9

ى	ك	ل	م	ن	س	ع	ف	ص
10	20	30	40	50	60	70	80	90

ق	ر	ش	ت	ث	خ	ذ	ض	ظ
100	200	300	400	500	600	700	800	900

غ

1000

The sequence of the letters has now been changed for educational purposes and the letters are arranged in dictionaries according to the similarity of their shape, and these have two forms, full and partial: partial for the normal writing, and the full at the end of every word in order to distinguish it from the following word. We give here only the fuller form of the letters:

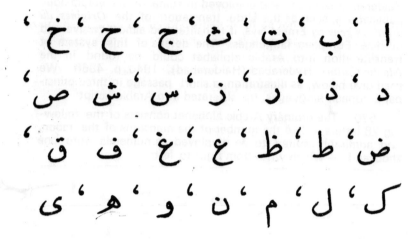

ا ، ب ، ت ، ث ، ج ، ح ، خ

د ، ذ ، ر ، ز ، س ، ش ، ص

ض ، ط ، ظ ، ع ، غ ، ف ، ق

ك ، ل ، م ، ن ، و ، ه ، ى

These 28 letters, from the right to the left, represent approximately the following sounds: 1. Natural sound: a, i, u, or aa according to vocalisation and place. 2. B 3. T 4. Th (as in English with) 5. J. 6. guttural H 7. guttural Kh 8. D 9. Dh (very near to dz). 10. R 11. Z 12. S 13. Sh 14. Sw 15. Dw 16. Tw 17. Zw 18. netural guttural a, i, or u according to vocalisation 19. Gh (guttural g) 20. F 21. Q (guttural k). 22. K 23. L 24. M 25. N 26. W or oo according to place 27. H 28. Y or ee, according to place.

And the ordinary signs of vocalisation in the Arabic script are:

These signs represent, from right to left, *a, i, u, aa, pause, doubling, the same consonant; an, in, un.* They are however used only when one desires to avoid a possible ambiguity on the part of the reader: they are employed ordinarily neither in handwriting nor in printing, since the reader of his mother tongue does not require their help. The above-mentioned

system of letters and signs suffices for the basic Arabic language, even if it is not so for dialects and vulgar pronunciation of
the Arabic. Of course it is not sufficient for non-Arabic languages in certain cases.

520/a. The following additions are used by and suffice
for most of the non-Arabic languages, in the East, such as Persian, Kurdish, Pashtau, Urdu etc., and also in the West. Of
these additions, the letters are:

ٱ	aw (like *a* in *fall*, or *o* in *of*)
پ	P
چ	Ch (in English *chance*)
ژ	like *su* in English *pleasure*
ﺵ	like *ch* or -*ig* in German *sprechen, einig*
ڤ	V (in English *love*, or German W)
گ	G
ڱ	like French *gn* in *ligne*
ڻ	nasal *n*, like in *France*
ﮯ	like *e* in *cafe* (near *a* in English *base*)

The additional signs of vocalisation are:

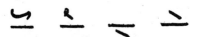

and stand, from right to left, for *a* in English *at*, *e* in English *let*,
short *o* like *e* in French *de*, and the last as the long *a* in English
and or *Allen*.

520/b. As an example the following English, French and German passages are given in both the Latin and Arabic scripts, (to note that final consonants in French words which are not pronounced except when in liaison are underlined):

(i) *English* : Islam is the religion of the future. It is a pleasure to see English-speaking Muslims adopting the Arabic script to their language, which brings them nearer to the Quran and to their beloved Prophet Muhammad sal-lallaa-hu 'alaihi wa sal-lam.

اِسلام اِز ذی رِلِجِن اَف ذی

فِیوچر · اِت اِز اے پلیٹِر تُو سی

اِنگلِش سپیکِنگ مُسلِمس اَدابٹِنگ

ذی عَریبِک سکرِپٹ تُو ذیر لانگوِج

وِچ بُرِنگس ذِم نِیرَر تُو ذی قُرآن

آنڈ تُو ذیر بِلَقُد پرافِت مُحَمَّد صَلّیٰ

الله عَلَیہِ وَسَلَّم

(ii) *French* : L'Islam est la religion de l'avenir. C'est un plaisir de voir les Musulmans fancophones adoptant l'ecriture arabe pour leur langue, ce qui les rapproche du Coran et de leur bien-aime Prophete Muhammad sal-lallahu 'alaihi wa sal-lam.

لِءْسْلام اِے لا رُلِيزِيُوْن دُ
لـءَاڤْنِير . سْءے تِ اُون پْلِيزِير دُ
ڤُوَار لے مُوزِولْمان زِ ڤْوانْكُوْفُوْنْ زِ
اَدُوْپْتان تِ لِءْيكْرِيتِور عَراب پُوْر
لِور لانْگ ، سْ كى لـءے رَاپْرُوش
دو قُرآن اِے دُ لِور بِياڈْءيمے
پْرُوڤِيْت مُحَمَّد صَلَّى اللهُ عَلَيهِ وَسَلَّم

(iii) *German* : Der Islam ist die Religion der Zukunft. Es ist erfreulich zu sehen, wie die Deutsch-sprechenden Muslime die arabische Schrift fuer ihre Sprache anwenden, denn dies bringt sie dem Koran und Muhammad, ihrem vielgeliebten Prophet, sal-lal-laahu 'alaihi wa sal-lam naeher.

در اسلام اِست دی ریلیگیون در
تسوکونفت . اِس اِست اِرفرایلش
تسو زیهن، فی دی دایچشپریشندن
مُسلیمے دی عَرابشے شرِفت فور
اِیرے شپراخے آنفندن ، دن دیز
برنگت زی دم قُرآن اوند مُحَمَّد ،
اِیرم فیلگیلیبتن پروفیت ، صَلَّی اللهُ
عَلَیهِ وَسَلَّمَ ، نیهر .

[All these Arabic texts have kindly been calligraphed, as a labour of love, by Mr. Mehmet Akay of Istanbul.]

521. Next comes the involuntary birth, when a child is born in a Muslim family. Immediately after the midwife has completed her task, one pronounces the *adhaan* in the right ear of the child, and the *iqaamah* in the left one, so that the first thing the child hears is the attestation of the faith and the call to worship of its Creator and for its own well-being. The *adhaan*[1] or the Call to the Prayer is as follows (for text and transcription see Appendix A): "God is Great" (repeated four times), "I attest that there is no God if not God Himself" (twice), "I attest that Muhammad is the Messenger of God" (twice), "Rise up to Worship" (twice), "Rise up to Well-being" (twice), "God is Great" (twice), "There is no God if not God Himself" (once). The *iqaamah*[2] or the establishment of the service of worship is formulated in the following terms (for text and transcription see Appendix B). "God is Great, God is Great, I attest that there is no God if not God Himself, I attest that Muhammad is the Messenger of God, Rise up to Worship, Rise up to Well-being, Lo, the service of worship is ready. Lo, the service of worship is ready, God is Great, God is Great. There is no God if not God Himself."

EARLY LIFE

522. When the hairs of the child are cut for the first time, their weight in silver or its equivalent in current money is distributed among the poor. If one has the means, a goat or a sheep

1. The adhaan is *usually pronounced loudly from above a minaret. In the morning service, after the formula "rise up to well-being", one adds twice the phrase : "The service of worship is better than sleeping* (as-Salaatu Khairum minan-naum). *The Shi'ite school replaces it by the formula "rise up to good deeds"* (haiya 'alaa Khairil 'amal).

2. *As to* iqaamah, *it is pronounced just on the moment preceding the service.*

is also slaughtered to entertain the poor and friends. It is called *'aqeeqa.*

523. No age limit is fixed, yet circumcision is practised on a male child in his early age. For adult converts this is not obligatory.

524. When a child arrives at the age to commence his studies, some time after the fourth year, a family feast is organized, when the child takes his first lesson. As a good omen, one recites before the child the first five verses of chapter 96 of the Quran, consisting of the very first revelation that had come to the unlettered Prophet of Islam relating to reading and writing. The child is made to repeat them word for word. Here is the translation (for text and transcription see Appendix C):

> With the name of God, the Most Merciful, the All-Merciful!
> Read with the name of thy Lord Who createth,
> Createth man from a clot.
> Read: And thy Lord is the Most Bounteous.
> Who teacheth (man) by the pen.
> Teacheth man that which he knew not.

525. When the child is capable of so doing, he is taught how to pray, learning gradually by heart the relevant texts, of which he shall speak later in detail. From his or her seventh year, parents must apply sanctions so that the child gets accustomed to prayer.

526. To fast is obligatory, even as is prayer, when a child reaches the age of puberty. In Muslim families, however, the child gets accustomed to it earlier. In fact it is an occasion of great rejoicing and festivity, when the child observes the first fast in the month of Ramadan. Generally at the age of twelve the child begins to fast for only one day in the first instance, increasing the number gradually in the years to come, so that the child gets accustomed to bear the strain of the fast for an entire month. This happens when he or she becomes a major.

527. The *Hajj* is obligatory only once in life, provided one has the means. It is performed in the second week of the 12th lunar month Dhul-Hijjah when people gather in Mecca, pass about a week in different places in the outskirts of the city, at 'Arafat, Muzdalifah and Mina. Official guides instruct every individual pilgrim in the performance of the different rites. Visiting the Ka'bah at any other time of the year is called *'umrah*. Details are as under.

527/a. For the *hajj*, men must give up their usual dress, and put on the ritual uniform, *ihram*, consisting of an unsewn loin cloth, and another sheet of cloth to cover the shoulders, the head remaining naked. (Women conserve their usual dress which must be decent: cover their arms and legs down to ankles). Foreigners must put on *ihram* outside the *haram* or city-limits of Mecca, before entering the city, but the Meccans must do that in the city itself. One goes then to 'Arafat, where the whole day of the 9th of Dhu'l-Hijjah is passed in prayers and meditation: the night is passed at Muzdalifah; the 10th, 11th and 12th of the month are passed at Mina, during which time Satan is lapidated symbolically every day, and one also makes a short visit to Mecca in order to perform the circumambulation of the Ka'bah and the *Sa'ee* or traversing 7 times the distance between Safa and Marwah rocks, close to the Ka'bah. For the formulas of prayers during the circumambulation (called *tawaf*) see App. W. X ; and for that of *Sa'ee* cf. App. Y, which prayer is repeated both when going from Safa to Marwah and when returning from Marwah to Safa. From the time of putting on the ihram, till its putting off, one must constantly respond to God's call, by reciting the formula of the *talbiyah*, particularly after every service of prayer. (For text, see Appendix Z).

527/b. In the *'Umrah*, one does not pass the time in 'Arafat, Muzdalifah and Mina, but makes only the *tawaf* and *sa'ee*. For this ritual, when putting on the *ihram* dress, even the residents of Mecca must go outside the city, and perform *tawaf* and *sa'ee*, after which a shaving of the head brings one back to normal life.

528. The *zakat* is a tax on different kinds of savings and hoardings and also growing properties, such as agriculture, commerce, mineral exploitation, herds of sheep, goats, cows and camels pasturing in public meadows, and savings of money. It is this last item which is left now-a-days not only in non-Muslim countries but even in Muslim countries for individual Muslims to pay as a private charity, the rest being imposed by local governments. Thus, if a person has saved a certain amount (200 dirhams or silver coins or 20 dinars or gold coins of the time of the Prophet, their equivalent being about five pounds or 14 dollars),[1] and a whole year passes over it, he has to pay 2½ per cent as tax. If he is indebted, the amount of the debt is deducted from the savings for purposes of calculating the taxable amount. The distribution of *zakaat* is made directly, or through institutions if such should exist in a locality. According to the Quran, this tax is intended for the benefit "of the needy, of the poor, of those who work for this tax: collecting and disbursing of it, people whose hearts are to be won for Islam, for freeing the necks (of slaves, etc.), the heavily indebted, for a cause in the path of God, and hospitality to wayfarers and strangers" (cf. supra § 351-9 ; Quran 9/60). One may apply the whole of one's annual *zakaat* to a single item or to several of them.

529. Another tax is payable on the occasion of the two annual festivals. At the end of the month of fasting, an amount sufficient for the food of an adult for the whole day is

---

1. *In our age of constant inflations and devaluations, the equivalents must also change as often: (The proportion of 1:10 between gold and silver is also upset now). For the taxable minimum let the believer refer to local jurisconsults whenever necessary.*

given to some poor person. The second festival takes place at the time when the *Hajj* is being celebrated at Mecca. On this occasion, well-to-do people sacrifice a goat or a sheep, which is partly distributed among the poor, and partly consumed in the family.

530. In connection with monetary matters, it may be borne in mind that a Muslim is not authorized to participate in transactions based on interest on loans or in games of chance, lotteries and similar speculative things. Nobody pays interest voluntarily. Demanding interest on loans advanced to private individuals should be avoided. The question of bank interest on savings is complicated, and depends on the mechanism of the administration of each bank. If the bank is usurious, profits accruing from its gains are also illicit; yet in certain countries it so happens that there are no other banks, and if one refuses to take the interest, the bank remits such unclaimed amounts to institution which are sometimes injurious to Islam, such as missionaries who seek the apostasy of Muslims. Therefore, one should recover the interest on one's deposits from the bank, but instead of spending it on one's own person or family, utilize it for charitable purposes. The great jurist Sarakhsi says: "gains accruing from illicit means must be got rid of by giving them away in charity."

531. Insurance with government agencies and with mutualistic societies is lawful, with capitalistic companies, no.

MARRIAGE

532. A Muslim male may marry not only a Muslim woman but also a woman of Jewish or Christian faith (Quran 5/5); but not an idolatress, polytheist or atheist. A Muslim woman is not allowed to marry (or even remain in marriage of) a non-Muslim, of no matter which category. (Quran 2/221, more particularly 60 : 10).

533. In the case of the conversion of a married man to Islam if his wife is Jew or Christian and does not want to be converted with her husband, the marriage continues undisturbed. If the wife is of the prohibited categories, and persists in her irreligion, conjugal life must cease immediately; she should be given a reasonable time to think over, and in the final resort divorce will have to take place.

534. In the case of a married woman embracing Islam, when the husband is not Muslim, conjugal life ceases immediately, and after a reasonable delay given to the husband, the wife should demand judicial separation.

DEATH

535. A Muslim on his death-bed tries to pronounce the formula of the faith: "There is no God if not God Himself, Muhammad is the Messenger of God." People around the patient also help by repeating it to the person in his death pangs. It is called *talqeen*. Before the body gets stiff, one places the hands as if in the service of worship, either crossed on the chest, or letting stretch on the sides.

536. The body of the dead person is washed and cleansed, when possible, before burial. It is shrouded in three simple sheets of cloth, after the usual dress is taken off. When bathing, water is poured for the first time mixed with soap or similar material; for the second time the traces of such material are washed off; and the third time water mixed with a certain quantity of camphor, is poured on the whole body. When bathing is not practicable, then *tayammum* suffices (for which see later under "ablution" § 552). After enshrouding the dead body, a funeral service is celebrated (for method see later § 569) This service can be performed in the absence of the body, which might have received burial elsewhere in the world. The grave is dug parallel to Mecca, in so far as this is practicable and the head of the dead is turned slightly to the right side, so that

it faces the Ka'bah. While placing the dead body in the grave, one pronounces the formula: "With the name of God and on the religion of the Messenger of God" (for text and transcription, Appendix D). Muslims believe that the dead person is visited in the grave by two angels, who put to him certain questions as to his beliefs. Hence after the burial, one pronounces on the grave a text, as if initiating the dead how to reply. The translation (text and transcription, Appendix E) is given below:

"O male — or female — servant of God, remember the covenant made while leaving the world, that is, the attestation that there is no God if not God Himself, and that Muhammad is the Messenger of God, and the belief that Paradise is a verity, that hell is a verity, that the questioning in the grave is a verity, that the Doomsday shall come, there being no doubt about it; that God will resuscitate those who are in graves, that thou hast accepted God as thy lord, Islam as thy religion, Muhammad as thy prophet, the Quran as thy guide, the Ka'bah as thy direction to turn to for the service of worship, and that all the believers are thy brethren. May God keep thee firm in this trial." (For the Quran, 14/27, says): "God confirmeth those who believe by a firm saying in the life of this world and in the Hereafter, and God sendeth wrong-doers astray, and God doeth what He will." And again (cf. 89/27-30): "O thou soul at peace, return unto thy Lord, content in His good pleasure ! Enter thou among My bondmen ! Enter thou My paradise!"

537. It is forbidden to spend lavishly on graves, which should be as simple as possible; one should rather spend the amount on the poor and the deserving, and pray God that the recompense of this charity may go to the deceased person.

GENERAL HABITS

538. Apart from the daily services of worship and the annual fasting, certain practices are recommended to Muslims.

The most important is the continual perusal of the text and the commentary or translation of the Quran, meditating over its contents, in order to assimilate them in one's life. What can be more blissful than to invoke the Word of God!

539. One should say *Bismil-laah* (i.e. with the name of God) when commencing any and every action, and *alhamdu lil-laah* (i.e. thank God) after terminating it. When something is intended or promised for the future, say immediately *insha-al-laah* (if God be willing).

540. When two Muslims meet, they greet by saying *Salaam 'alaik (or as-salaam 'alaik)*. One can reply likewise, or say *Wa 'alaiku-mus-salaam.* These are more comprehensive than the formulas good morning, good evening etc., which are the remnants of the days of ignorance.

541. One should develop the habit of glorifying God when going to sleep and when rising up (*sub haa-nal-laah* is the simplest formula), and also invoking the mercy of God on the Prophet, for instance in the following formula: *Al-laa-humma sal-li 'ala muhammad wa baarik wa sal-lim* (i.e., O God, incline to Muhammad, bless him and take him in Thy safeguard).

542. The Prophet preferred the right side: When putting on the sandals, the right foot first, the left one afterwards, and just the contrary when putting them off; when putting on a shirt, the right arm first, the left one later; when combing, the right half of the head first, the left one later; when entering a house or a mosque, the right foot first, the left one later, but when entering the bath-room or the W.C., the left foot first, and while coming out of it, the right foot first. When putting off a dress, foot-wear, etc., the left arm or the left foot first. When distributing something, be began with those who were on his right hand, ending with those on the left.

542/a. Prayers to God are to be constant, for each and every act of our life, be that for natural needs or deliberate acts, even as the most solemn of them, viz. the preparation for the service of worship. Formulas of prayer, used by the Holy Prophet for some such occasions have been referred to above (§166/b). Others could be found in detailed and more voluminous works.

FOOD AND DRINK

543. The most important points in this respect are the following:

544. Pork, (flesh and fat) is forbidden in all its forms, in the same way as alcoholic drinks. A misunderstanding requires to be dissipated: The word *khamr, used* by the Quran, although it meant originally the wine made of grape-juice, yet already in the time of the Prophet the term signified any alcoholic drink irrespective of the material. So when the verse of *khamr* was revealed, Muslims of Madinah spilt their stocks of all kinds of alcoholic drinks, and not merely those of wine. It is to note that in Madinah it was from date fruits that fermented drinks were manufactured. As to meat, a Muslim cannot consume animals or birds not ritually slaughtered. The Quran (5:3) says:

"Forbidden unto you (for food) are carrion, and blood, and swine-flesh, and that which hath been dedicated unto any other than God, and the strangled, and the dead through beating, and the dead through falling from a height, and that which hath been killed by the goring of horns, and the devoured of the wild beasts, saving that which ye make lawful by the death-stroke of slaughtering, and that which hath been immolated unto idols......but whosoever is forced by hunger, not by will to sin, for him lo ! God is Forgiving, Merciful". Even lawful animals and birds, if slaughtered by non-Muslims, remain unlawful to consume except when slaughtered by members of those communities who possess a divinely revealed Book (Christian and Jews for instance), provided they observe rules of their religion in the matter of ritual slaughtering. A chicken strangled by a Christian does not become lawful any more than the one strangled by a Muslim himself.

545. The ritual of slaughtering is performed by pronouncing the formula *Bismillaah* (with the name of God), and cutting the throat, i.e., the tube of respiration, the tube of food and drink, and the two jugular veins; not touching the spinal column, much less severing the head or skinning the animal before it is completely dead.

546. The use of gold and silver plates or utensils for food is also forbidden to Muslims. The Prophet has said: "The use of gold and of pure silk is forbidden for men, allowed for womenfolk". There are some exception. So, the use of silk as military dress is permitted. The use of gold also for dental surgery. The caliph 'Uthman had his teeth covered with gold; and a certain 'Arfajah ibn As'ad reports that the Prophet himself had allowed him to have a nose made of gold to replace the one he had lost in a war, the artificial nose made of silver having rotten.

DRESS AND COIFFURE

547. The use of cloth made entirely of natural silk is forbidden to Muslim men, also garments of a red colour. The Prophet grew a beard, and recommended the Muslims to do likewise.

548. Muslim women should wear a dress which covers their body in a proper manner, avoiding high jumpers, decollete, transparent stuff showing nudity of the body. They should not try to resemble men.in dress and coiffure; and avoid all that is characteristic of glamour girls. Further when they celebrate the service of worship, they should cover their head. The Prophet has recommended women to wear pantalons. Their gowns should never be higher than the middle of the tibia, preferably

down to the ankles (as we read in a Hadith reported by Abu Da'wud, Tirmidhi, Ibn Hanbal, and many others).

SERVICE OF WORSHIP AND ABLUTIONS

549. "Cleanliness is half of the faith," says the Prophet. So, when intending to celebrate the service of worship, one has first to be clean in body. Ordinarily there are simple ablutions for the daily services. A bath, preferably a shower bath, is prescribed for other occasions, — in the case of both men and women after the intercourse of husband and wife; for men after a wet dream; for women, after the menses and after recovering from the flow consequent on child birth. For the weekly Friday service, it is strongly recommended to take a bath.

550. The method of bath is that one should make ablutions, and then pour water over the entire body, from head to foot, at least three times. If one takes a bath in a tub, one may pour clean water, after emptying the tub, over the head and shoulders, by a jug, for instance, if there is no shower apparatus.

551. Ablutions are made in the following manner: The first step is to formulate the intention of purification, say *bismillaah* (with the name of God), wash the hands upto the wrists, rinse the mouth with water, clean the nostrils with water, wash the face from the forehead to chin and from ear to ear, wash the right arm and then the left one upto the elbows (inclusive), pass the wet fingers on the head and in the ear holes (and according to some schools also the neck), then wash first the right foot and then the left one up to the ankle — doing each act thrice (unless water is lacking, in which case even once is sufficient).

552. If there is absolutely no water to be found, it is permitted to do the *tayammum* or dust ablution. This is also permitted to the sick, who are not to touch water on medical grounds. In this case, we have to formulate the intention of

purification, pronounce the name of God (*Bismillaah*), pose the
hands on clean dust (even on a wall in the house) and pass
the palms on the face, pose the hands again on the dust and
pass the left palm on the right forearm, then the right palm on
the left forearm. It is symbolic of man's humility before God
Almighty.

553. The ablutions are to be renewed not for every service
of prayer, but only when the previous ones have become invali-
dated through sleep, natural emission of gas; urination or the
flow of any substance from the private parts, or vomiting. It
ought to be noted that one should ordinarily use water in the
W.C.; mere paper is not sufficient.

554. For the prayer-service, one should also have a clean
dress, a clean place, and know the direction of the *Qiblah* (Ka'bah
in Mecca). With the help of an ordinary world-map — one such
is included herewith — it would be easy to find out the direction of Mecca (in Arabia, towards the middle or its Western
coast); then a compass will indicate the exact position to be
taken up. People in England, for instance, will turn to the South-
East, those in the U.S.A. to the East-South-East. It might be
noted however that the world is spherical, and in view of this
the shortest distance between a place and the Ka'bah is to be
sought. For those in New York, it would be nearer to turn
E.-S.E.; but for those in Alaska, South-West will be nearer. The
antipode of the Ka'bah is somewhere near Sandwich or Somoa
islands, and when passing this spot, on boat for instance, all
the four directions would be equidistant and the direction would
therefore be left to the choice of the person leading the service,
even as inside the Ka'bah.

555. There are five daily services of worship, of which the
second one is replaced every Friday by a solemn congregational
service. There are two annual services, in addition, for celebrating the feast at the end of the month of fasts, and the feast

of sacrifices coinciding with the pilgrimage at Mecca. All services resemble one another in form, but not in length, with the exception of the funeral service, of which we shall speak later in § 569. Thus, the first daily prayer at dawn has only two *rak'ats* (the term is explained below); the second and third (early and late after-noon services) have four each, the fourth (early evening) has three, and the fifth (late evening) has four. The Friday and the festival services have only two *rak'ats* each. The Prophet has strongly recommended the addition, after the fifth daily service, of another service, called *witr* consisting of three *rak'ats*.

555/a. Only five services of worship are obligatory daily, but the Prophet had the habit of adding, at the time of each service, some additional services, which constitute highly recommended acts. So a service of a couple of rak'ats before the morning prayer; for the mid-day prayer, a service of four rak'ats (or two services of two rak'ats each) before the obligatory service, and another one of two rak'ats after the same, a service of two rak'ats after the evening service; and a service of three rak'ats — according to the Hanafite school, but according to others first a service of two rak'ats and then another of a single rak'at — after the night prayer is highly recommended. This last is called *witr*. Apart from these, one may celebrate as many services as one likes as *nafal* (supererogatory) acts of devotion. The more the service the more the merit. Further, when one enters the mosque, it is recommended to celebrate a service of two rak'ats as *ta'iyatul-masjid* (as an offering to the house of God).

556. The method of celebrating the service is that a person makes the necessary ablutions, selects a proper place, turns in the direction of the Ka'bah, raises the hands up to one's ears and formulates precisely the intention: "I intend to celebrate such and such service of worship to God, with its so many *rak'ats*, turning towards the Ka'bah, individually / collectively as

the *imaam* / collectively as the follower of the *imaam.*"[1] (see fig. 1.) After this he pronounces the formula *"Allaahu Akbar"* (God is Great), and lowers the hands : According to the Malikite and Shi'ite schools, the hands should hang loose on both sides touching the thighs, (fig. 2 a); but according to all the other schools, hands should be crossed on the chest, the left hand touching the body and the right one placed over it, (fig. 2 b). Now the service begins, and he should neither talk to others, nor look anywhere except the point where he is going to place his forehead in prostration. At every movement, (bending, prostrating, sitting, etc.), he pronounces *"Allahu Akbar."*

557. The service commences with a hymn (Appendix F), followed by the first chapter of the Quran (Appendix G), then some other chapter or verses of the Quran — any of those contained in Appendix C, H, I, J, K, for instance. With the exception of the parts of the Quran, all the texts are recited silently; even those parts of the Quran said aloud are only during the first, fourth and fifth services, and for Friday and Festival services, and even these by the *imaam* alone.

558. After having completed the recitation of the Quran, mentioned above, the person bows down, places the hands on knees without bending them, in which position he pronounces thrice "Glory to God, the Most Grand" (Appendix L), (fig. 3). Then he rises up and says : "Our Lord, praise be to Thee" (Appendix M), without folding the hands, but letting them hang loose by the sides. Afterwards he prostrates placing the forehead, nose and palms on the ground, (fig, 4 a), with knees

---

1. *If there are only two persons, one should lead as* imaam *and the other follow him, standing on the right hand of the* imaam *a few inches behind him; if there are three or more, the followers should form one or more ranks behind the* imaam. *The followers should recite nothing loudly, but inaudibly; and follow the* imaam *in the movements.*

VARIOUS POSTURES OF PRAYERS SERVICE

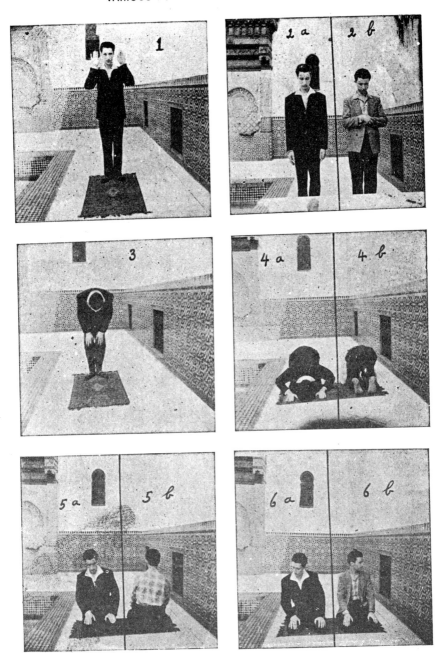

1. Beginning of the service.
2. Recital of the Quran : (a) Maliki and Shi'i way, (b) Hanafi, Shafi'i and Hanbli way.
3. Rukoo' (bowing low).
4. Sajdah (Prostration) : (a) seen from before, (b) seen from behind.
5. How to sit between and after the two prostration : (a) seen from before, (b) seen from behind. 6. Finishing salute : (a) to the right, (b) to the left.

bent, (fig. 4 b), and pronounces, in this position, thrice "Glory to my Lord, the Most High" (Appendix N); he then seats himself (fig. 5 a) on the left foot keeping the right foot erect, heel pointing skywards and the toes of the feet bent outwards, (fig. 5 b), and beseeches the pardon of God (Appendix O); then he makes a second prostration and repeats the glory of God thrice as in the first prostration. Thereafter he rises up. All these, movements of standing, bowing, and prostrating twice constitute collectively one *rak'at.*

559. The second *rak'at* begins with the recitation of the first chapter of the Quran (Appendix G) followed by some other part of it — (any text contained in Appendix H. to K. for instance) — yet without the hymn. Thereafter he bows low and glorifies God thrice as before, rises up and thanks God, and then prostrates twice reciting the same texts as before. At this stage he does not rise up, but remains seated on the left foot and invokes the presence of God and attests to the faith (Appendix P).

560. As the first (dawn) service — and also the Friday and Festival service — consists of only two *rak'ats*, after this invocation of the presence of God, one adds some supplication (Appendix Q), whereafter in termination of the service turns the face first to the right, saying *"as-Salaamu 'alaikum wa rah-mat-ul laah"* (peace with you and the mercy of God), (fig. 6 a), then to the left, (fig. 6 b), when, according to most schools one should repeat the same formula, and the service is completed. If the service has more than two *rak'ats* after the invocation of the presence of God (Appendix P), he rises up again, recites the first chapter of the Quran (Appendix G) without adding any other part, bows low, rises up and makes the two prostrations with their accompanying formulas. If the service has three *rak'ats* as in the early evening service, he remains sitting, recites the invocation of Divine presence and the supplication, and closes with the salutation. If the service

has four *rak'ats*, as in the two afternoon services, and in the night service, he rises up immediately after the two prostrations of the third *rak'at*, recites again the first chapter of the Quran (Appendix G), bows low, rises up, makes the two prostrations and then remains sitting to invoke the Divine presence, the supplication, and then ends with the salutation.

SOME PARTICULARITIES

561. The Shafi'i and Hanbali schools add a prayer of invocation, called *qunoot* in the Dawn service. So when a person rises up after bowing low in the second *rak'at*, one recites this prayer (Appendix U) before prostration. The other schools do not observe it, contending that this practice of the Prophet was only temporary.

562. The Hanafi school has also a *qunoot*, (Appendix V) but in the third *rak'at* of the *witr* service, which is celebrated after the late evening service. So, after ending the recitation of the Quran in the third *rak'at* and before bowing low, they pronounce this prayer, whereafter they bow and complete the service in the normal way. In the case of congregational service however one should follow the *imaam*, whatever may be his school.

563. Again at the end of the second *rak'at* when the person sits for the first time to invoke the presence of God, some schools ask also blessings for the Prophet, others do that in the final second sitting only.

DIFFERENCE OF SCHOOLS

563/a. (i) There are three main groups among Muslims: Sunnis, Shi'as and Abadites (nicknamed Kharijites), with several sub-divisions. They have a few differences in matters both of dogmas and cult. This elementary manual is not the proper place to trace the history and details of these differences. However in a cosmopolitan town, when one sees Muslims of different schools practising differently the same act, one asks wherefrom this divergence? Leaving aside the differences in dogmas, which come from the deduction of the leading theologians of each school, in the matter of cult let us know from the outset that nothing has been invented by anybody, but all comes from the Prophet himself or is deduced from the report of his saying or doing.

(ii) It is the Prophet himself who has sometimes changed his practice in certain acts or formulas to recite, sométimes he expressly mentioned that his former practice is to be abandoned (for instance, in the *ruku'* the Prophet originally let his arms hang loose, yet later he put his hands on his knees and forbade the former practice). At others, he did not say anything when he changed his practice. In a few cases the discussion arose several generations after the Prophet, and the savants diverged as to the meaning to give to a report on the practice of the Prophet.

(Iii) It is evident therefore that practically all the differences emanate from the divergent practices of the Holy Prophet himself, and nobody has the right to despise anyone of them. Often there are no data to determine the chronology of the diverging ways of performing the same act, in order to presume that the latter in time must abrogate the former one. If a Shafi'ite, for instance, refuses to celebrate the service under a Hanafite *imaam*, that means that this Shafi'ite refuses to follow the Prophet himself when this latter practised in a manner not known in the Shafi'ite school. What an enormity!

(iv) In the Islamic literature, one of the titles of the Prophet Muhammad is the "beloved of God" *(Habib-Allah)*, and the Holy Quran (33/21) expressly says that in Muhammad there is the best model for Muslims to follow. It is touching to note, that in His love, God has willed that any and every unabrogated act of the Prophet should be followed by the Muslims. In case of the divergent ways of performing the same act, there was no other possibility except that some do in one way and others in another. So God seems to have willed to perpetuate all the acts of His beloved Prophet by means of the different schools. Let there be mutual respect and inter-tolerance.

SERVICE OF ISTIKHARAH (PRAYER FOR GUIDANCE)

563/b. When one is in perplexity, the Prophet has recommended to pray to God for guidance, and not resort to game of chance or other superstitious methods. For this purpose, one has to celebrate a service of two *rak'ats* as supererogation (*nafilah*) : After the obligatory service of 'Isha (5th service of the day) and *witr* that follows it, when one wants to go to bed, one should celebrate the service of *istikharah* in the following manner : in the first *rak'at* one should recite, after the *Faatihah* (cf. App. G), the surah 109 (App. Z/i), and in the second *rak'at* after the *Faatihah* (App. G), one should recite the surah 112 (App. J), all the rest of this service being like any other normal service. After the final salutation, one should turn to God with humility and devotion and pronounce the prayer taught by the Prophet (App. 2/ii) from memory if one can, by reading, preferably in Arabic (although a translation would also do for those who cannot read Arabic) if necessary. Thereafter one would go to bed always remembering God in his thoughts. Next day when he gets up, the first idea that comes to his mind will be of divine inspiration. If no idea occurs to the mind the first day, let one repeat the same service a second, a third night, and so on until an idea is inspired while getting up in the morning, for resolving the problem which has agitated.

DISTURBANCE IN THE SERVICE

564. If a person should speak to anybody during the service, let out wind, laugh aloud, or eat or drink anything, it annuls the service, which should be recommenced, with fresh ablutions in the second eventuality. However, if one forgets some act during the service, which he remembers at a later stage, one need not recommence the service, but continue it to

the end, and prostrate twice after the Invocation in supplication (Appendix P, Q) and then pronounce the salutation. During these prostrations of Forgetfulness, one may recite the same glorification of God as usual (Appendix N) or use another, which is more appropriate (Appendix R), namely "Glory to the One Who alone does neither sleep nor forget."

565.   If a person should come somewhat late and join the congregational service, he need not bother about the portion already accomplished, but follow the *imaam*. In case a whole *rak'at* or more has been missed, one should rise up when the *imaam* salutes, and complete by himself the *rak'at* or *rak'ats* which he has missed, recite the Invocation, etc., and salute to terminate the service. Supposing he joins the congregation during the prostration of the second *rak'at* of the early evening service, he will perform in the company of the *imaam* only one *rak'at*; so one should rise up, perform a *rak'at* and sit down for the first Invocation, then perform another *rak'at* and invoke, hen terminate by salutations.   If one finds the *imaam* in *ruku'* (inclining) position, one has got the whole *rak'at*, and needs not bother about the lost portion, such as the recitation of the Quran; but if one joins the *imaam* after the *ruku'*, standing or prostrating or else, the whole *rak'at* is lost and should be made up at the end when the *imaam* has saluted.

GENERAL

566.   If the right direction of the Ka'bah is not known, one should guess it, and that suffices, God being present everywhere.   During the service of worship, one must behave with dignity and concentration: one must look at the spot where one is going to pose one's forehead, (during the *ruku'* at one's toes, and during the *sajdah* the eyes resting wide open), and one should never look towards the sky, much less to right and left. Similarly one must remain firm, and it is a very bad habit to advance or retreat during the several acts of prostrating and returning to the standing position.

567.   After the service, one may pray to God for whatever one desires, the best prayers are those which have been taught by the Quran itself.

568.   As the texts in the service ought to be recited in Arabic, one should learn them by heart, commencing with the *Faatihah* (first chapter of the Quran, Appendix G), which is considered the most essential part, the *sine qua non* of the service of worship.

FUNERAL SERVICE

569.   The funeral service differs from other services of worship in form.   One makes ablutions, turns to the Ka'bah, raises the hands up to the ears, formulates the intention, after the usual *Allaahu Akbar*, recites the hymn, the *Faatihah* and some other part of the Quran—as in all the services—yet one does neither bow nor prostrate. In fact, after the recitation of the Quran, one pronounces again *Allaahu Akbar*, remains standing up, and recites a prayer to God to pardon all Muslims, dead or alive, preceded by the invocation of mercy to the Prophet (Appendix S); says *Allaahu Akbar* for the third time and prays particularly for the dead in presence (Appendix T); then says *Allaahu Akbar* for the fourth time and salutes at the end.

SICKNESS AND TRAVELLING

570.   If one is sick and confined to bed, one can pray as best one can, sitting or even lying.   In the case of a sitting position, the act of bowing is performed in a way that the head does not touch the ground. · In the case of celebrating the prayer while lying, one only thinks in one's mind of the postures of standing, bowing, prostrating, etc., and recites at each stage the appropriate text.

571.   Persons in travel have been permitted by the Prophet to shorten their services of 4 *rak'ats*, celebrating only 2 *rak'ats*; and others who are pressed for time, have the permission of

the Prophet also to combine the services. For instance, the second and third, between midday and sunset, at any moment, and the fourth and the fifth any time during the night, (cf also supra § 170).

HOURS OF SERVICES

572. Usually the first service *(Fajr)* must be celebrated when one rises up, i.e., between dawn and sunrise. The second *(Zuhr,* and for that sake, the weekly Friday prayer), after the sun passes the meridian at midday; the time for this service continues for about three hours. The third *(Asr),* late in the afternoon, yet before the sunset. The fourth *(Maghrib)* immediately after sunset, the time continues for about an hour and a half. The fifth and last *('Ishaa),* when the twilight disappears, any time during the night before dawn breaks, preferably before mid-night.

573. It will be noticed that these timings are practicable and without inconvenience only in equatorial and tropical countries. As one mounts towards the poles, the difference between the length of the day and the night gets so great in summer and winter, that the movements of the sun are of little help. At the two parallels 90° N and 90° S, that is at the poles, the sun does not set for six months continuously, with the exception of the one day of the first equinox, and then remains risen above the horizon for the other six months continuously, with the exception of one day of the second equinox. Even much below:

at 72° North From	May	9	to August	4
70°	May	17	July	27
68°	May	27	July	17
66°	June	13	June	29

the sun remains continuously above the horizon and sets neither during the "day," nor during the "night" In the corresponding period of winter, the sun remains below the horizon and never rises for a single moment during the 24 hours of the day. At 66° N., on June 30, the sun rises at 0.3 o'clock and sets at 23.46 o'clock; on July 2, it rises at 0.3 o'clock and sets at 23.32 o'clock, and so on; that is to say, in the remaining few minutes when the sun remains set, all the three nightly services of *maghrib*, *'isha* and *fajr* are to be celebrated. Men have been crossing these regions since long, and they are much more frequented now; they are even being settled. It is known that the Soviet camps contain many Muslim labourers. It goes without saying, that in these abnormal climates one can depend on the movements of the sun neither for services of worship nor for yearly fasting. Even Friday gets complicated if it is to recur on every seventh setting of the sun. The jurists have therefore recommended that one should follow there the movements of the clock, and not those of the sun. But the question arises where to fix the line separating the normal zone of countries from the abnormal one, where one enjoys concessions? Similarly it becomes necessary to find out exactly the hours to be observed in the abnormal zone. The rational solution, which has now been approved by the assemblies of the *'ulema* of different Muslim countries is the following :

573/a. The Quran (2/286) has laid down that "God tasketh not a person if not according to its capacity." And again (94/5-6) : "Because with the difficulty there is a facility. Verily with the difficulty there is a facility". And the Prophet has not only confirmed it by demanding his subordinate and delegates: "Facilitate, do not cause difficulties and do not cause people to detest(the Islamic law), but treat people like brothers". Apart from these general directions, the Prophet has even replied to the question of abnormally long days in an apocalyptic Hadith, reported by Muslim, Abu Dawud, Tirmidhi, Ibn Majah and others :

"When the *Dajjal* (literally the great deceiver) comes to mislead people, he will remain on the earth for forty days, one of which as long as a year, the second as long as a month, the third as long as a week, and the remaining days as your normal days. One of the Companions rose to demand:

On the day which will be as long as a year, would it suffice to celebrate only five services of worship of the day ? The Prophet replied : No, but calculate".

The first day described here resembles the conditions obtaining on 90° parallel North or South, i.e., on the two poles; the second day those a little south of 68° of the Northern hemisphere, and the third those a little south of 66° parallel. Basing themselves on this direction of the Prophet, the assemblies of Muslim 'ulama have commanded to follow in such condition the movement of the clock and not of the sun; and to facilitate the task, they command to follow the times obtaining on 45° for countries lying between this point and the pole. This applies as much to fasting as to prayers : the five daily ones, the Friday and the 'Id prayers. If one does not do that but would like to rest clung to the letter of the law, (sun's setting for breaking the fast for instance), the inconvenience would be that if Ramadan falls in summer, one would fast for 21 and more hours, and when it falls in winter, the duration of the fast would be for only three hours and even less. The times obtaining at 45° should be observed for all religious purposes in the abnormal zone, and not the sentimentally chosen time of Mecca or Medinah, in order not to cause heart-burning to Muslims living in the zone between Medinah and 45° of latitude.

574. The hours of sunrise and sunset remain practically the same during all the seasons on the equator; the greatest instability, or rather the greatest and most unbearable rigour is found at the poles. Geographers have divided the distance between the equator and the poles into 90 degrees. Therefore the line of division has to be fixed at 45° North and 45° South. Those peoples who live in the equatorial and tropical countries, i.e., between the two parallels of 45° on both sides of the equator, must follow the movements of the sun with their variations during the different seasons. And those who live beyond this belt. must follow the hours obtaining at 45° parallel, without

regard to their local times of sunrise and sunset. It will happen that in these abnormal regions one will break the fast when the sun will still be shining, in certain seasons, and in certain others will continue to abstain from eating and drinking when the sun should have set long ago. For the timing on 45°, see below § 583.

575. This division at the two parallels of 45° N and 45° S divides the earth theoretically in two equal parts, but as a matter of fact more than three-fourths of the habitable world is included in the normal zone. An overwhelming majority of the inhabitants of the globe live in the normal zone, which includes the whole of Africa, India and Oceania, practically the whole of China and the two Americas (with the exception of Canada and the extremities of Argentina-Chile). It may be brought pointedly into relief that this division leaves untouched the millinary habitudes of the Muslims: the countries Islamized in the time of the Prophet and his companions — such as Arabia, Syria, Turkey, Egypt, Spain, Italy, Southern France, Iran, Turkistan, India-Pakistan, even as far as the populous Malaysia and Indonesia — these will continue to practise that to which they have been for centuries accustomed. In Europe concessions affect the regions above Bordeaux-Bucharest-Sevastopol; in North America those above Halifax-Portland; and in the southern hemisphere only some small parts of the South of Argentina-Chile and a few islands south of New Zealand. The Muslim communities of England, France, Germany, Holland, Scandinavia, Finland, Kazan, Canada, etc., will profit by this precision of the Muslim law, which is deduced from the directions given by the holy Prophet himself, explained in the preceding paragraphs. By consulting a map of the world, like the one included herewith, one can easily find out whether one lives inside or outside the normal zone, beyond the 45° parallel of the latitude.

THE SERVICE OF WORSHIP: WHY IN ARABIC ALONE?

575/a. (i) It is well known that during their service of worship (prayer, in Arabic *Salaat*), Muslims employ only the

Arabic language: they recite certain passages of the Quran and pronounce certain formulas to attest to the sublimity of God and humility of man. This is done both by the Arabs and the non-Arabs, even by those who do not know a word of Arabic. Such was the case in the time of the Prophet Muhammad and such has been the case ever since to this day, whatever the country and the tongue of the Muslims.

(ii) At first sight it may seem normal and even desirable that the faithful should address his prayer to the Lord in a way that he is fully conscious of what he says. Of course, the mother-tongue is the medium best suited for the purpose, the worship being performed in as many languages as are spoken by the Muslim community. But a little deeper consideration shows that there are reasons that militate strongly against such a solution.

(iii) First of all, a metaphysical or psychological point. According to the Holy Quran (33 : 6), the wives of the Prophet are the mothers of the Muslims. We know that all of these revered ladies spoke Arabic. Therefore Arabic is the mother-tongue of all the Muslims. Who can object to praying in one's mother-tongue?

(iv) Perhaps this argument does not suffice to convince everybody. Pushing further the study, it is noteworthy that according to the Islamic belief the Quran is the Word of God, the recitation of which is considered by the Quran as something meritorious. This is evident from the spiritual point of view. The faithful journeys unto the Lord through the sacred word of the Lord Himself. His word is the path towards Him, something like a wire to conduct the electrical current that illuminates the bulb. The journey unto the Lord is of course the ultimate goal that every soul aspires to reach. The original Word has been revealed in Arabic: any translation would be a human work and human word, and this can scarcely serve the purpose of this mystical journey.

(v) For those who would seek more mundane reasons, let us recall first that a clear distinction is to be made between prayer in the sense of supplication (*du'aa*) and the prayer in

the sense of the service of worship to God (*salaad*).   In so far
as *du'aa* is concerned—i.e., the prayer in general and outside
the formal way of worshipping God, the *tete-a-tete* with the
Lord (*munaajaat*)— nobody has ever raised the slightest objec-
tion to the liberty of the individual to address one's need, one's
petitions to the Lord in any language and in any physical posture one prefers. It is purely a *personal and private* affair and
concerns the relations of the individual creature directly with
the Creator. The *salaat*, on the contrary, is a *collective and public* affair, where the needs and requirements of other companions of the congregation are evidently to be taken into consideration.   It is pointedly to bring into relief that the *salaat* is
in principle and preferably to be performed in common along
with others (*jama'at*): the *salaat* individually and in isolation
is only tolerated and never recommended, the preference going
to the congregational service.   Let us see now more closely
the diverse aspects of this collective and public act which is
performed in the company of others.

(vi)   Had Islam been a *regional*, racial or national religion,
one would certainly have employed the current language of
the region, of the race, of the nation. But quite different are the
requirements of a *universal* religion, whose members speak
hundreds of regional languages — of which each is incomprehensible to all the rest of the human groups — belonging to all
the races and inhabitants of all the regions of the earth.   Our
life today is getting more and more cosmopolitan, and practically every town has Muslims belonging to several linguistic
groups, both from among the permanent residents and the
travellers in transit, and one has to take into consideration the
aspect of courtesy and hospitality to strangers.   Supposing an
Englishman goes to China and knows not a word of its
language, and supposing he hears in the street something like
"chen chu chih shan".   Evidently he would not understand
what is intended thereby; and if it is the regional translation of
the well-known call to prayer, the *Allaahu Akbar*, he would fail
to perceive it and would miss the weekly prayer on Friday, or

the congregational prayer of the moment. (Incidentally, the mosques in China do not ordinarily resemble those in England, France or elsewhere in the Orient, and ordinarily have no minarets either). Similarly a Chinese Muslim, travelling through other countries would find nothing in common with his co-religionists if these others said their collective worship in their local tongues. So a universal religion requires certain basic things to be common to all the faithful. The call to prayer and the formulas to be recited in the act of worship evidently constitute part of such fundamental and basic elements of the practice of the cult. A passing remark may be made about the fact that sometimes words of two different languages sound alike but have different significations, at times the harmless word of one signifying something ridiculous or obscene in another. Such a risk is greater in languages with which one is utterly unfamiliar, and hears them only during a journey, for example. This would be contrary to the dignity of the service of worship to God. Things familiar from childhood avoid such complications, even if the individual is a non-Arab and recites in Arabic the required formulas.

(vii) One cannot neglect the psychological aspect of human beings who have at times petty prejudices of xenophobia. Occasions would arise daily when political (national) or even personal and individual frictions would induce, for instance, an Englishman not to participate in the *salaat* led in French or Russian or some other language. Arabic, as the language of the Quran and the Hadith, has a respect and a halo in the minds of every Muslim, and one employs it not as the language of the Arabs but as the language of the Prophet Muhammad, the language of the mothers-of-the-faithful, the language God Himself has chosen for revealing His latest Word for us.

(viii) The needs of unity among the co-religionists can never be too much stressed upon. One should create new links to strengthen their ties of fraternity, rather than destroy those that already exist.

(ix)   One may also cite the example of international con-gresses and meetings. When, for instance, one attends the United Nations Organization session, one cannot select the medium of expression according to one's whims and fancies, which would be contrary to the object of the meeting, and one would fail to reach others attending the session; one is obliged to employ himself or get his speech translated into the officially recognised languages, which are for all practical purposes either English or French, and nobody objects to this state of affairs. In the general interest, one has to sacrifice the particular in-terest, on pain of losing in the long run, even the particular interest.

(x)   There is another aspect of the question which is no less important. In fact no translation ever replaces the original. There are, for instance, now-a-days numerous translations of the Holy Qur'an in English (as also in practically every language of the world), yet every now and then there are new and unceasing attempts to produce another translation, thinking that the older ones are partly defective. This is true not only of English but of every language of the world, and true also of the translation of any and every work. Should one utilize a defective thing or the perfect one, the translation or the original?

(xi)   Let us recall in this connection that practically no religion, excepting Islam, possesses today integrally the original of the Revelation on which it is based, the original teaching of its founder: It is the translation, or at best fragments, of which dispose the Christian, Jewish, Parsi and other communities. How fortunate the Muslims are that they form an exception, and possess integrally the original text of the Revelation, the Holy Quran!

(xii)   What is more, the Quran, although in prose, possesses all the qualities and charms of poetry, such as rhythm, resonance, grandeur of style, etc., so much so that the omission or addition of even a single letter in the text disturbs it as much as it would disturb the hemistich of a verse. Some time ago, it happened to the present writer that a Muslim French convert, who is a musician by profession, one day assured me that in chapter 110 of the Quran some passage seemed to have been lost, for it reads *"fee deenillaahi afwaaja. Fasabbih............"*, which is musically impossible. My scant knowledge of the art of reciting the Quran came to my aid and I replied: "No, the correct reading of the passage is *"fee deenil-laahi afwaajan-v-fasabbih......"* (the *n* and *f* getting assimilated, so after *n*, there is a slight *v*, before pronouncing *f* of *fasabbih"*. Thereupon the musician and well-meaning brother exclaimed at once: "I renew my faith; with your explanation there remains nothing objectional from the musical point of view, and no passage seems to be lacking". The prose of the Quran is as much measured as the lines of a poem. And if this is so, who would care to replace something perfect and splendid by something comparatively mediocre ?

(xiii) One should not lose sight of the fact that in the entire *salaat* there are very few passages to recite. There are first the *adhaan* and *iqaamah* (call to prayer). Then inside the service of worship there are the formulas *Allaahu-Akbar, subhaana rabbiy-al-'azeem, subhaana rabbiy-al-a'laa,* the short chapter *al-Faatiha,* two other short chapters, and the prayer of *tashahhud,* and that is all. The totality does not exceed a page of small size, and most of the words of these texts are commonly understood by the Muslim masses and have penetrated into all the languages of the Muslim countries, so much so that even a child or a beginner learns their meaning without pain and without strain. And once the significance of these formulas is learnt, the *salaat* of a Muslim remains no more a mechanical recitation and without understanding.

(xiv) Personally, this writer thinks that no Muslim would ever bestow the same respect on a translation of the Qur'an as he does on the original revealed by God to His messenger. For the translation would be done by an ordinary human being and not by an infallible person who should be protected by God against error, as is the case of a prophet.

(xv)   One day a young student kept insisting on the importance of understanding what one says (or prays). When all other arguments seemed to fail to convince him, the author said: "If you promise me that you will perform regularly the five daily services in your mother-tongue, I authorize you to do so." Forthwith he interrupted the discussion, and never came again to speak of it. In other words, those who insist on regionalizing the faith and cult are those who do not practise it themselves; at least, such is the case with the immense majority of them. A believer h'as no need to take counsel with those who do not believe in or do not practise Islam.

(xvi)   To end, there are writers who say that they have the backing of such authorities as the Imam Abu Hanifah (d. 767 C.E.) to say that the recitation of the translation of the Quran in the service of worship is permitted. But this is only a half-truth. These writers omit to mention that the Imam Abu Hanifah, although he had this opinion in the beginning, changed it later on (as we find express precision of it in the authoritative manuals of law such as the *Hidayah* of al-Marghinani, the *ad-Durr al-Mukhtaar* of al-Haskafi, etc.), and that he rallied to the general opinion that in normal cases only the Arabic text is to be employed in the services of worship. Of course, there are provisions for exceptional cases, such as the needs of a new convert: immediately on his embracing Islam, he has to commence to perform the five daily services in which it is necessary to recite by heart the prescribed formulas. Until such time as he learns these formulas by heart, he may use their sense in any other language he can. For this we have the very high precedent of Salmaan al-Farisi, who sent the translation of al-Faatiha to some Persian converts, with the authorization of the Prophet Muhammad himself (cf. *al-Nihaayah Haashiyat al-Hidaayah* by Taaj ,al-Shari'a) and they used it until their tongue got familiarized with the Arabic text. So, for some hours or some days, the new converts may use validly the translation.

(xvii) One will see thus that there are advantages and disadvantages, both in the use of a foreign language in one's service of worship. This is also the case with regard to the use of a regional language (viz., mother-tongue) for this purpose by members of a universal religion. In such cases one makes one's choice by weighing the advantages against the disadvantages, and one sees where lies the lesser of the two evils.

WHY A PURELY LUNAR CALENDAR ?

576. As it is well-known, Islam follows for liturgical or religious purposes, a purely lunar calendar in which, for instance, the month of Ramadan with its fasts, and of Dhul-Hijjah with its pilgrimage rotate from season to season. In pre-Islamic Arabia intercalation was known, and it was the Holy Prophet who abolished it — after long and mature thinking, let us say — during his last pilgrimage, just three months before his death, when he received a revelation (Quran 9/37) condemning the intercalation. This intrigues the uninitiated, and shocks those who suffer from the inferiority complex and want always to imitate others blindly. Of the many utilities of this Islamic reform, there may be brought into relief :

(a) As far as the fast is concerned, it is very useful, since it provides one with the possibility of getting accustomed to food and drink privations in all seasons — neither always hardship, nor always easy-going lot.

(b) Islam being destined for the whole world, the difference between the different climates had also to be taken into consideration. Had fasting been prescribed in a given month of the solar calendar, that is to say in a certain definite season, the purpose would be vitiated by nature; and physically it would not be possible. In fact the summer of the Northern hemisphere, of the countries situated North of the equator coincides with the winter in the Southern hemisphere, in countries South of the equator. It may also be that the winter is considered as a pleasant time in equatorial regions, and a horror in the sub-polar ones. This discrimination among the Faithful of the different countries is easily avoided when the lunar calendar is followed. All will have all seasons turn by turn.

(c) The paying of the *zakaat* on savings, commerce, etc., — to the exclusion of agricultural products — is increased imperceptibly in a way that in every 33 solar years there will be 34 lunar years, and one will pay in 33 solar years 34 annual taxes. Even after payment of salaries according to the lunar calendar, the savings of the government will be considerable, and will be available for its nation-building activities, for the benefit of the poorer classes in particular.

CONCLUSION

576/a. We pray God that this humble effort should serve its purpose of enlightening those who want to know the elements of Islam. For greater details, there are exhaustive and specialized books, learned persons, and institutions such as al-Azhar in Egypt, Zaitunah in Tunis, Qarawiyeen in Fez (Morocco), and others in India, Pakistan, Indonesia etc.

N. B.

In paragraph 554, instead of:
but for those in Alaska, South-West will be nearer.

read as:

but for those in Alaska, Greenland and other Polar regions, better consult a globe, since a Mercator world map, like the one given here, will not serve.

(A أَذان) : اَللهُ اَكْبَرَ ، اَللهُ اَكْبَرَ ، اَللهُ اَكْبَرَ ، اَللهُ اَكْبَرَ ،

أَشْهَدُ اَن لَا اِلٰهَ اِلَّا الله ، اَشْهَدُ اَن لَا اِلٰهَ اِلَّا الله ، اَشْهَدُ اَنَّ مُحَمَّدًا

رَسُوْلُ الله، اَشْهَدُ اَنَّ مُحَمَّدا رَسُوْلُ الله، حَىَّ عَلَى الصَّلَاة، حَىَّ عَلَى الصَّلَاة،

حَىَّ عَلَى الفَلَاح ، حَىَّ عَلَى الفَلَاح ، اَللهُ اَكْبَرَ ، اَللهُ اَكْبَرَ ، لَاالٰهَ اِلَّا الله .

(B إقامة) : اَللهُ اَكْبَرَ ، اَللهُ اَكْبَرَ ، اَشْهَدُ اَن لَا اِلٰهَ اِلَّا الله ،

اَشْهَدُ اَنَّ مُحَمَّدا رَسُوْلُ الله ، حَىَّ عَلَى الصَّلَاة ، حَىَّ عَلَى الفَلَاح ،

قَد قَامَت الصَّلَاة ، قَد قَامَت الصَّلَاة ، اَللهُ اَكْبَرَ ، اَللهُ اَكْبَرَ ، لا اِلٰهَ اِلَّا الله .

(C) : بِسْمِ الله الرَّحْمٰنِ الرَّحِيْمِ ۵ اقْرَأ بِاسْمِ رَبِّكَ الَّذِىْ

خَلَقَ ۵ خَلَقَ الْاِنْسَانَ مِن عَلق ۰ اقْرَأ وَ رَبُّكَ الْاَكْرَمُ الَّذِىْ عَلَّمَ

بِالْقَلَم ۵ عَلَّمَ الْاِنْسَانَ مَا لَم يَعْلَم ۵

(D) : بِسْمِ الله وَ عَلٰى مِلَّة رَسُوْلِ الله .

(E) : يَا عَبْدَ اللهِ اذْكُرِ الْعَهْدَ الَّذِى خَرَجْتَ عَلَيْهِ مِنَ الدُّنْيَا شَهَادَةَ
خَرَجْتِ
أَمَةَ اللهِ اذْكُرِى

أَنْ لَا إِلَهَ إِلَّا اللهُ وَ أَنَّ مُحَمَّدًا رَسُولُ اللهِ وَ أَنَّ الْجَنَّةَ حَقٌّ ، وَ أَنَّ

النَّارَ حَقٌّ ، وَ أَنَّ الْقَبْرَ حَقٌّ ، وَ أَنَّ السَّاعَةَ آتِيَةٌ لَا رَيْبَ فِيهَا

وَ أَنَّ اللهَ يَبْعَثُ مَنْ فِى الْقُبُورِ . وَأَنَّكَ رَضِيتَ بِاللهِ رَبًّا وَ بِالْإِسْلَام
وَأَنَّكِ رَضِيتِ

دِينًا وَ بِمُحَمَّدٍ رَسُولًا وَ بِالْقُرْآنِ إِمَامًا ، وَ بِالْكَعْبَةِ قِبْلَةً ،

وَ بِالْمُؤْمِنِينَ إِخْوَانًا . اللهُ يُثَبِّتُكَ ، يُثَبِّتُ اللهُ الَّذِينَ آمَنُوا بِالْقَوْلِ
يُثَبِّتُكِ

الثَّابِتِ فِى الْحَيَاةِ الدُّنْيَا وَ فِى الْآخِرَةِ وَ يُضِلُّ اللهُ الظَّالِمِينَ

وَ يَفْعَلُ اللهُ مَا يَشَاءُ . يَا أَيَّتُهَا النَّفْسُ الْمُطْمَئِنَّةُ ارْجِعِى إِلَى رَبِّكِ

رَاضِيَةً مَرْضِيَّةً ، فَادْخُلِى فِى عِبَادِى وَ ادْخُلِى جَنَّتِى ٠

(F ثنا ٠) (١) عند الأحناف : سُبْحَانَكَ اللَّهُمَّ وَ بِحَمْدِكَ

وَ تَبَارَكَ اسْمُكَ ، لَا إِلَهَ غَيْرُكَ ٠

(٢) عند الشافعية : وَجَّهْتُ وَجْهِىَ لِلَّذِى فَطَرَ السَّمَاوَاتِ وَ الْأَرْضَ

حَنِيفًا مُسْلِمًا وَ مَا أَنَا مِنَ الْمُشْرِكِينَ ٠ إِنَّ صَلَاتِى وَ نُسُكِى وَ مَحْيَاىَ

وَمَمَاتِي لِلَّهِ رَبِّ الْعَالَمِينَ ۰ لَا شَرِيكَ لَهُ ۰ وَ بِذَالِكَ أُمِرْتُ وَ أَنَا أَوَّلُ الْمُسْلِمِينَ ۰

(G فاتحة) : بِسْمِ اللهِ الرَّحْمٰنِ الرَّحِيمِ ۰ الْحَمْدُ لِلَّهِ رَبِّ الْعَالَمِينَ ۰ الرَّحْمٰنِ الرَّحِيمِ ۰ مَالِكِ يَوْمِ الدِّينِ ۰ إِيَّاكَ نَعْبُدُ وَ إِيَّاكَ نَسْتَعِينُ ۰ اِهْدِنَا الصِّرَاطَ الْمُسْتَقِيمَ ۰ صِرَاطَ الَّذِينَ أَنْعَمْتَ عَلَيْهِمْ ۰ غَيْرِ الْمَغْضُوبِ عَلَيْهِمْ وَ لَا الضَّالِّينَ ۰ آمِينَ ۰

(H) : بِسْمِ اللهِ الرَّحْمٰنِ الرَّحِيمِ ۰ وَ الْعَصْرِ ۰ إِنَّ الْإِنْسَانَ لَفِي خُسْرٍ ۰ إِلَّا الَّذِينَ آمَنُوا وَ عَمِلُوا الصَّالِحَاتِ وَ تَوَاصَوْا بِالْحَقِّ وَ تَوَاصَوْا بِالصَّبْرِ ۰

(I) : بِسْمِ اللهِ الرَّحْمٰنِ الرَّحِيمِ ۰ إِنَّا أَعْطَيْنَاكَ الْكَوْثَرَ ۰ فَصَلِّ لِرَبِّكَ وَ انْحَرْ ۰ إِنَّ شَانِئَكَ هُوَ الْأَبْتَرُ ۰

(J) : بِسْمِ اللهِ الرَّحْمٰنِ الرَّحِيمِ ۰ قُلْ هُوَ اللهُ أَحَدٌ ۰ اللهُ الصَّمَدُ ۰ لَمْ يَلِدْ وَ لَمْ يُولَدْ وَ لَمْ يَكُنْ لَهُ كُفُوًا أَحَدٌ ۰

(K) : اللهُ لَا إِلٰهَ إِلَّا هُوَ الْحَيُّ الْقَيُّومُ لَا تَأْخُذُهُ سِنَةٌ وَّ لَا

نَوْمٌ لَهُ مَا فِى السَّمٰوٰتِ وَ مَا فِى الْأَرْضِ مَنْ ذَا الَّذِى يَشْفَعُ عِنْدَهُ

اِلَّا بِاِذْنِه يَعْلَمُ مَا بَيْنَ أَيْدِيْهِمْ وَ مَا خَلْفَهُمْ وَ لَا يُحِيْطُوْنَ بِشَىْءٍ

مِنْ عِلْمِه اِلَّا بِمَا شَاءَ وَسِعَ كُرْسِيُّهُ السَّمٰوٰتِ وَ الْأَرْضَ وَ لَا يَؤُدُهُ

حِفْظُهُمَا وَ هُوَ الْعَلِىُّ الْعَظِيْمُ ٠

(L) : سُبْحَانَ رَبِّى الْعَظِيْمِ ٠

(M) : سَمِعَ اللهُ لِمَنْ حَمِدَه ٠ رَبَّنَا لَكَ الْحَمْدُ ٠

(N) : سُبْحَانَ رَبِّى الْأَعْلَى ٠

(O) : رَبِّ اغْفِرْ لِى وَ ارْحَمْنِىْ ٠

(P) : اَلتَّحِيَّاتُ الْمُبَارَكَاتُ الصَّلَوَاتُ الطَّيِّبَاتُ للهِ ٠ السَّلَامُ

عَلَيْكَ أَيُّهَا النَّبِىُّ وَ رَحْمَةُ اللهِ وَ بَرَكَاتُهُ ٠ السَّلَامُ عَلَيْنَا وَ عَلَى عِبَادِ اللهِ

الصَّالِحِيْنَ ٠ أَشْهَدُ أَنْ لَا اِلٰهَ اِلَّا اللهُ وَ أَشْهَدُ أَنَّ مُحَمَّدًا عَبْدُهُ وَ رَسُوْلُهُ ٠

(Q) : اَللّٰهُمَّ صَلِّ عَلَى مُحَمَّدٍ وَ عَلَى آلِ مُحَمَّدٍ كَمَا صَلَّيْتَ عَلَى

اِبْرَاهِيْمَ وَ عَلَى آلِ اِبْرَاهِيْمَ اِنَّكَ حَمِيْدٌ مَجِيْدٌ وَ بَارِكْ عَلَى مُحَمَّدٍ

وَ عَلَى آلِ مُحَمَّدٍ كَمَا بَارَكْتَ عَلَى اِبْرَاهِيْمَ وَ عَلَى آلِ اِبْرَاهِيْمَ اِنَّكَ

حَمِيدٌ مَجِيدٌ . اَللّٰهُمَّ اِنِّى اَعُوذُ بِكَ مِنَ الْمَأْثَمِ وَ الْمَغْرَمِ . اَللّٰهُمَّ

اِنِّى ظَلَمْتُ نَفْسِى ظُلْمًا كَثِيرًا . وَ لَا يَغْفِرُ الذُّنُوبَ اِلَّا اَنْتَ

فَاغْفِرْلِى وَ اَرْحَمْنِى اِنَّكَ اَنْتَ الْغَفُورُ الرَّحِيمُ .

(R) : سُبْحَانَ مَنْ لَا يَنَامُ وَ لَا يَسْهُو .

(S) : اَللّٰهُمَّ صَلِّ عَلَى مُحَمَّدٍ وَ بَارِكْ وَ سَلِّمْ . اَللّٰهُمَّ اغْفِرْ

لِحَيِّنَا وَ مَيِّتِنَا وَ شَاهِدِنَا وَ غَائِبِنَا بِرَحْمَتِكَ الْوَاسِعَةِ .

(T) : اَللّٰهُمَّ اغْفِرْ لِهٰذَا الْمَيِّتِ اِنَّكَ اَنْتَ الْغَفُورُ الرَّحِيمُ .

(U) : اَللّٰهُمَّ اهْدِنَا فِيمَنْ هَدَيْتَ ، وَ عَافِنَا فِيمَنْ عَافَيْتَ ،

وَ تَوَلَّنَا فِيمَنْ تَوَلَّيْتَ ، وَ بَارِكْ لَنَا مِنَ الْخَيْرِ فِيمَا اَعْطَيْتَ ،

وَ قِنَا شَرَّ مَا قَضَيْتَ ، فَاِنَّكَ تَقْضِى وَ لَا يُقْضَى عَلَيْكَ ، وَ اِنَّهُ

لَا يَذِلُّ مَنْ وَالَيْتَ ، وَ لَا يَعِزُّ مَنْ عَادَيْتَ ، تَبَارَكْتَ رَبَّنَا وَ تَعَالَيْتَ ،

لَكَ الْحَمْدُ عَلَى مَا قَضَيْتَ ، نَسْتَغْفِرُكَ وَ نَتُوبُ اِلَيْكَ ، وَ صَلَّى اللّٰهُ

عَلَى سَيِّدِنَا مُحَمَّدٍ .

(V) : اَللّٰهُمَّ اِنَّا نَسْتَعِينُكَ وَ نَسْتَغْفِرُكَ وَ نُؤْمِنُ بِكَ وَ نَتَوَكَّلُ

عَلَيْكَ . اللّٰهُمَّ اِيَّاكَ نَعْبُدُ وَلَكَ نُصَلِّى وَنَسْجُدُ وَاِلَيْكَ نَسْعَى وَنَحْفِدُ – نَرْجُو رَحْمَتَكَ وَنَخْشَى عَذَابَكَ اِنَّ عَذَابَكَ بِالْكُفَّارِ مُلْحِق.

(W) نِيَّةُ الطَّوَافِ امَامَ الْحَجَرِ الْأَسْوَدِ :

نَوَيْتُ الطَّوَافَ بِسْمِ اللّٰهِ وَاللّٰهُ اَكْبَرُ . اَللّٰهُمَّ اِيمَانًا بِكَ وَتَصْدِيقًا بِكِتَابِكَ ، وَوَفَاءً بِعَهْدِكَ وَاتِّبَاعًا لِسُنَّةِ نَبِيِّكَ سَيِّدِنَا مُحَمَّدٍ صَلَّى اللّٰهُ عَلَيْهِ وَسَلَّمَ .

(X) ادعية الطواف

﴿ الف ﴾ امام باب الكعبة :

اَللّٰهُمَّ اِنَّ الْبَيْتَ بَيْتُكَ وَالْحَرَمَ حَرَمُكَ وَالْأَمْنَ اَمْنُكَ وَهٰذَا مَقَامُ الْعَائِذِ بِكَ مِنَ النَّارِ .

﴿ ب ﴾ امام باقى الجدار :

اَللّٰهُمَّ اِنِّى اَعُوذُ بِكَ مِنَ الشَّكِّ وَالشِّرْكِ وَالشِّقَاقِ وَالنِّفَاقِ وَسُوءِ الْأَخْلَاقِ وَسُوءِ الْمُنْقَلَبِ فِى الْأَهْلِ وَالْمَالِ وَالْوَلَدِ .

﴿ ج ﴾ عند الجدار الثانى :

اَللّٰهُمَّ اَظِلَّنِى فِى ظِلِّكَ يَوْمَ لَا ظِلَّ اِلَّا ظِلُّ عَرْشِكَ وَاسْقِنِى بِكَأْسِ

سَيِّدِنَا مُحَمَّدٍ صَلَّى اللهُ عَلَيْهِ وَسَلَّمَ شَرْبَةً

هَنِيئَةً مَرِيئَةً لا أُظْمَأُ بَعْدَهَا أَبَداً، يَا ذَا الْجَلالِ
وَالْإِكْرَامِ ٥

(د) عند الجدار الثالث حسب الحج او العمرة :

اللّٰهُمَّ اجْعَلْهُ حَجًّا مَبْرُوراً وَذَنْباً مَغْفُوراً ،
اجْعَلْهَا عُمْرَةً مَبْرُورَةً

وَسَعْياً مُشْكُوراً ، وَتِجَارَةً لَنْ تَبُورَ يَا عَزِيزُ
يَا غَفُور ٠

(ه) عند الجدار الرابع :

رَبَّنَا آتِنَا فِي الدُّنْيَا حَسَنَةً وَفِي الآخِرَةِ
حَسَنَةً وَقِنَا عَذَابَ النَّارِ ٠

(Y) دعاء السعى بين الصفا والمروة ؛ حسب الحج
او العمرة :

رَبِّ اغْفِرْ وَارْحَمْ وَتَجَاوَزْ عَمَّا تَعْلَمْ، إِنَّكَ
أَنْتَ الْأَعَزُّ الْأَكْرَمُ اللّٰهُمَّ اجْعَلْهُ حَجًّا مَبْروراً
اجْعَلْهَا عُمْرَةً مَبْرُورَة

وَذَنْبًا مَغْفُورًا ، وَسَعْيًا مَشْكُورًا ، وَتِجَارَةً لَنْ
تَبُورَ يَا عَزِيزُ يَا غَفُورُ اللهُ أَكْبَرُ اللهُ أَكْبَرُ وَ لِلهِ
الْحَمْدُ اللهُ أَكْبَرُ عَلَى مَا هَدَانَا وَ الْحَمْدُ لِلهِ عَلَى
مَا أَوْلَانَا . لَا إِلٰهَ الَّا اللهُ وَحْدَهُ ، لَا شَرِيكَ لَهُ ،
لَهُ الْمُلْكُ وَلَهُ الْحَمْدُ ، وَ هُوَ عَلَى كُلِّ شَيْ
قَدِيرٌ . لَا إِلٰهَ إِلَّا اللهُ وَحْدَه ، صَدَقَ وَعْدَهُ ، وَ نَصَرَ
عَبْدَهُ و أَعَزَّ جُنْدَه وَ هَزَمَ الْأَحْزَابَ وَحْدَهُ ـ لَا إِله
إِلَّا اللهُ ، وَلَا نَعْبُدُ إِلَّا إِيَّاهُ مُخْلِصِينَ لَهُ الدِّينَ ،
وَلَوكَرِهَ الْكَافِرُوْن .

(Z) تلبيـه : لَبَّيْكَ اللّهُمَّ لَبَّيْكَ ، لَبَّيْكَ ،
لَا شَرِيكَ لَكَ لَبَّيْكَ ، إِنَّ الْحَمْدَ وَ النِّعْمَةَ لَكَ
وَ الْمُلْكَ لَا شَرِيكَ لَكَ

299

(Z/i) بِسْمِ اللهِ الرَّحْمٰنِ الرَّحِيمِ ه قُلْ ۛ يَآ أَيُّهَا الْكَافِرُونَ ۛ لَا أَعْبُدُ مَا تَعْبُدُونَ ۛ وَلَا أَنْتُمْ عَابِدُونَ مَا أَعْبُدُ ه وَلَا أَنَا عَابِدٌ مَا عَبَدْتُّمْ ۛ وَلَا أَنْتُمْ عَابِدُونَ مَا أَعْبُدُ ه لَكُمْ دِينُكُمْ وَلِيَ دِينِ ه

(Z/ii) اَللّٰهُمَّ إِنِّي أَسْتَخِيرُكَ بِعِلْمِكَ ، وَأَسْتَقْدِرُكَ بِقُدْرَتِكَ ، وَأَسْأَلُكَ مِنْ فَضْلِكَ الْعَظِيمِ ، فَإِنَّكَ تَقْدِرُ وَلَا أَقْدِرُ وَتَعْلَمُ وَلَا أَعْلَمُ وَأَنْتَ عَلَّامُ الْغُيُوبِ ه اَللّٰهُمَّ إِنْ كُنْتَ تَعْلَمُ أَنَّ هٰذَا الْأَمْرَ خَيْرٌ لِي فِي دِينِي وَدُنْيَايَ وَمَعَاشِي وَعَاقِبَةِ أَمْرِي عَاجِلِهِ وَآجِلِهِ فَاقْدُرْهُ لِي وَيَسِّرْ لِي ثُمَّ بَارِكْ لِي فِيهِ يَاكَرِيمُ ه وَإِنْ كُنْتَ تَعْلَمُ أَنَّ هٰذَا الْأَمْرَ شَرٌّ لِي فِي دِينِي وَدُنْيَايَ وَمَعَاشِي وَعَاقِبَةِ أَمْرِي عَاجِلِهِ وَآجِلِهِ ه فَاصْرِفْهُ عَنِّي وَاصْرِفْنِي عَنْهُ ه يَا كَرِيمُ ه اَللّٰهُمَّ إِنَّ عِلْمَ الْغَيْبِ

عِندَكَ ، وَ هُوَ مَحْجُوبٌ عَيْنِى ، وَلا أَعْلَمُ مَا أَخْتَارُهُ
لِنَفْسِى ، لَـٰكِـن أَنتَ الْمُخْتَارُ لِى فَلِى نِيَّى فَوَّضْتُ
اِلَيكَ مَقَالِيـد أَمرِى ، وَ رَجَوتُكَ لِفَـقرِى وَ فَاقَتِى ،
فَأَرشِيدُنِى اِلى أَحبِّ الأُمُورِ اِلَيكَ وَ أَرجَاها عِندَكَ
وَ أَحْمَـدَها عِندَكَ فَاِنَّكَ تَفْعَلُ ما تَشاءُ وَ تَحكُمُ
ما تُرِيدُ ٠

§ 578 TRANSLATION OF THE APPENDICES

(A, B, C, D, E) translation already given in the text of chapter XV.

(F): (i) *According to the Hanafite rite*:

O God, with Thy glorification and Thy praise; blessed is Thy name, and there is no God except Thee.

(ii) *According to the Shafi'ite rite*:

I have turned my face to the One God Who has created the heavens and the earth. I being sincere and submissive while I am not one of those who give associates (to God). Verily my service of worship, my cult, in fact my life and my death belong to God, Lord of the worlds, to Whom none to associate. Unto this have I been commanded (to believe), and I am the first to submit.

(G): With the name of God, the Most Merciful, the All-Merciful. Praise be to God, Lord of the worlds, the Most Merciful, the All-Merciful, Owner of the Day of Judgement. Thee alone we worship, and Thee alone we ask for help. Show us the straight path: the path of those whom Thou hast favoured; not (the path) of those who earn Thine anger nor of those who go astray. Amen !

(H): With the name of God, the Most Merciful, the All-Merciful. By the Time ! Lo, man is in a state of loss, save those who believe and do good works, and exhort one another to right, and exhort one another to endurance.

(I) : With the name of God, the Most Merciful, the All-Merciful. Lo, We have given thee Abundance. So pray unto thy Lord, and sacrifice. Lo, it is thy insulter (and not thou) who is without posterity.

(J) : With the name of God, the Most Merciful, the All Merciful. Say : It is God, the Unique! God, the eternally Besought of all! He begetteth not nor was begotten. And there is none comparable unto Him.

(K) : God! There is no God save Him, the Alive, the Eternal and Sustainer of all. Neither slumber nor sleep over-taketh Him. Unto Him belongeth whatsoever is in the heavens and whatsoever is in the earth. Who is he that intercedeth with Him save by His leave? He knoweth that which is in front of them, and that which is behind them, while they encompass nothing of his knowledge save what He will. The footrest of His throne includeth the heavens and the earth, and He is never weary of preserving them. He is the Sublime, the Tremendous.

(L) : Glory be to my Lord, the Great.

(M) : God has heard the one who has praised Him : our Lord! Praise be to Thee.

(N) : Glory be to my Lord, the Most High.

(O) : O my Lord, pardon me and have pity on me.

(P) : The most blessed greetings, the purest and most sincere inclinations unto God. Peace be with thee O Prophet as well as the Mercy of God and His blessings. Peace be with us as well as with the pious slave-servants of God. I attest that there is no God if not God Himself, and I attest that Muhammad is His slave and messenger.

(Q) : O God, incline to Muhammad and to those who adhere to him even as Thou hast inclined to Abraham and to those who adhered to him: verily Thou art the praised one, the glorious one. And bless Muhammad and those who adhere to him, even as Thou hast blessed Abraham and those who adhered to him, verily Thou art the praised one and the glorious one. O God, I take refuge with Thee against sin and debt. O God, I have committed to my soul a great wrong, and no one can pardon the sins, if not Thee; so pardon me and have pity on me; lo, Thou art the Most Forgiving, Most Merciful.

(R) : Glory be unto One who neither sleeps nor forgets.

(S) : O God, be inclined to Muhammad, and bless (him) and protect (him). O God, pardon those who are alive among us as well as the dead, those who are present as well as those who are absent, and this by Thy great mercy.

(T) ; O God, pardon this dead; lo, Thou art the Most Forgiving, the Most Merciful.

(U) : O God, guide us to the right path from among those whom Thou hast guided and accord us security from among those whom Thou hast accorded security, and be our Patron from among those whom Thou hast been Patron, and give us plenitude in what Thou hast accorded us of the good, and protect us from the evil which Thou hast decreed, since it is Thou Who decidest and nothing could be decided against Thee; and verily no disgrace betaketh him whom Thou patronizest, and no honour can he have to whom Thou art enemy; Blessed and Exalted art Thou, O our Lord, praise be to what Thou hast decreed, we ask pardon of Thee and repent before Thee; may God incline to our chief Muhammad!

(V): O God, we ask Thee for help, and ask Thee for pardon, and believe in Thee, and have confidence in Thee. O God, Thee alone we worship, for Thee alone we celebrate the service of worship and prostration towards Thee alone do we hasten and hurry. We hope for Thy mercy, and fear Thy punishment, for Thy punishment will cause (us) to join the unbelievers.

(W): *Formula of the intention, pronounced in front of the* *Black Stone* :

I intend to circumambulate. With the name of God, and God is great. O God, I do this believing in Thee, attesting to the truthfulness of Thy Book, observing the contract made with Thee, and following the practice of Thy Prophet, our master Muhammad. May God incline to him and take him into His safeguard.

(X): *Prayers during the circumambulation*:

(i) *When in front of the door of the Ka'bah*:

O God, this house is Thy house, this sacred territory is Thy sacred territory, this security is Thy security, and this is the place for one who seeks protection with Thee against the hell fire.

(ii) *During the rest of the first wall*:

O God, I ask Thy protection against doubt, polytheism, schism, hypocrisy, bad morality, and ill-return in the family, property and children.

(iii) *When crossing the second wall, which contains the* mizab (*spout*) :

O God, put me under Thy shadow on the day when there will be no shadow if not the shadow of Thy throne, and give me to drink from the cup of our master Muhammad — may God incline to him and take him into His safeguard — a delicious, and sating drink after which I shall never get thirsty, O Thou full of majesty and bounty.

(iv) *When crossing the third wall according to whether it is during the hajj or the 'umrah*:

O God, make that this be a *hajj* / *'umrah* which is accepted, with (my) sin which is pardoned, with (my) effort which is recognized, a commerce which is not lost, O Thou the Powerful the Forgiving.

(v) *When crossing the fourth wall*:

O our Lord, give us good in this world and good in the Hereafter and protect us from the punishment of the hell fire.

(Y): *Prayer while frequenting between Safa and Marwah rocks, according to whether it is for the hajj or for the 'umrah*:

O Lord, pardon, and be merciful, and forgive us all that Thou knowest; verily Thou art the Most Powerful, the Most Bounteous. O God, make that this be a *hajj / 'umrah* which is accepted, with a sin which is pardoned, with an effort which is recognized, a commerce which is not lost, O Thou the Powerful, the Forgiving. God is great. God is great. Praise be unto God. God is great for having shown us the right path. Praise be unto God for what He has bestowed on us. There is no God if not God alone, there is no Associate with Him, To Him alone belongeth the kingdom, to Him alone belongeth praise, and He is Able to do all things. There is no God if not God alone. He has made true His promise aided His slave (Muhammad) and fortified his army, and defeated Himself alone the coalesced enemies. There is no God if not God Himself, and we worship none if not Him, making religion pure for Him, however much the Disbelievers be averse.

(Z): *Talbiyah*:

Here am I, here am I, to Thy call O God, here am I, here am I. None to be associate with Thee, here am I, here am I to Thy call. Verily the praise and grace are due to Thee as well as sovereignty, none being to be associate with Thee.

(Z/i) With the Name of God the Most Merciful, the All-Merciful. Say: O Disbelievers, I worship not that which ye worship, nor ye worship that which I worship. And I shall not worship that which ye have been wont to worship, nor will ye worship that which I worship. To you your religion, and to me my religion.

(Z/ii) Lord! I ask Thee good guidance by means of Thy science, and seek power by means of Thy power, and I beseach Thee through Thy enormous grace. For Thou hast the power, not I; Thou knowest, not I, and Thou art the knower of all the invisible things. Lord! In Thy knowledge if this matter is good for me, for my religion, for my worldly life, for my livelihood and for the consequences of my affairs, be they immediate or retarded, then determine it for me and facilitate it to me and give me therein the plenitude, O Generous. But if in Thy knowledge this matter is evil for my religion, for my worldly life, for my livelihood and for the consequences of my affairs, be they immediate or retarded, then put it away from me and me from it, and determine the good for me wheresoever it may lie, and then agree to it on my part, O Generous. Lord! The knowledge of the invisible things is with Thee alone, it remaining concealed from me, and I do not know what to select for me. So it will be Thee who wouldst select for me, for I hand over to Thee the keys of my matter, and Thou art the hope in my poverty and need. So guide me to that which is most agreeable to Thee, with which one has greatest hope with Thee and which may be most praised by Thee. For Thou doest what, Thou likest, and commandest what Thou willst.

§ 579. TRANSLITERATION OF THE APPENDICES

a	as	*u*	in	cut
aa		*a*		father
i		*i*		it
ee		*ee*		feel
u		*u*		put
oo		*oo*		cool

(A) : Al-laahu akbar, al-laahu akbar, al-laahu akbar, al-laahu akbar, ash-hadu al-laa-ilaaha il-lal-laah, ash-hadu al-laa-ilaaha il-lal-laah, ash-hadu an-na muham-madar-rasoo lul-laah, ash-hadu an-na muham-madar-rasoo lul-laah, hayya 'alas-salaah, hayya 'alas-salaah, hayya 'alal-falaah, hayya 'alal-falaah, al-laahu akbar, al-laahu akbar, laa-ilaaha il-lal-lah.

(B) : Al-laahu akbar, al-laahu akbar, ash-hadu al-laa-ilaaha-il-lal-laah, ash-hadu an-na muham-madar rasoo lul-laah, hayya 'alas-salaah, hayya 'alal-falaah, qad qaamatis-salaah, qad-qaamatis-salaah, al-laahu akbar, al-laahu akbar, la-ilaaha il-lal-laah.

(C) : Bismil-laahir-rahmaa-nir-raheem, Iqra' bismi rab-bik al-ladhee khalaq, khalaqal insaana min 'alaq, iqra' wa rabbukal akramul ladhi 'al-lama bil qalam, 'al-lamal insaana maa lam ya'lam.

(D) : Bismil-laah wa 'ala mil-lati rasoo lil-laah.

(E) : Yaa $\frac{\text{'abdal laahidhkur}}{\text{amatal-laahidhkuri}}$ al-'ahdal ladhee $\frac{\text{kharajta}}{\text{kharajti}}$ alaihi minad dunyaa shahaadata al-laa-ilaaha il-lal-laah wa an-na muham-madar rasoo lul-laah, wa an-nal jan-nata haqq, wa an-nan naara haqq, wa an-nal qabra haqq, wa an-nas saa'ata aatiyatul laa raiaba feeha, wa an-nal-laaha yab'athu man fil quboor, wa $\frac{\text{an-naka radeeta}}{\text{an-naki radeeti}}$ bil-laahi rab-ban, wa bil islaami

deenan, wa bimuham-madir rasoolan wa bil qur'aani immaa-
man, wa bil ka'bati qiblatan, wa bil mu'mineena ikhwaanaa,

al-laahu$\frac{\text{yuthab bituka}}{\text{yuthab bituki}}$ Yuthab-bitul laahul ladheena aamanu bil-
qaulith thaabiti fil hayaatid dunya wa fil aakhirah, wa yudil-lul-
aahuz zaalimeena wa yaf'a lul-laahu maa yashaa, yaa ayya-
tuhan nafsul mutma-in-natur ji'ee ilaa rab-biki raadi yatam
mardeeyah, fad khulee fee ibaadee, wad khulee jan-natee.

(F) : (i) *According to Hanafis* :

Sub haana kai-laahuin-ma wa bihamdika wa tabaara
kasmuka wa laa ilaaha ghairuka.

(ii) *According to Shafi'is* :

Waj-jah-tu waj-hiya lil-ladhee fa-taras-sa-maa-waati wal-arda
ha-nee-fam mus-li-man wa maa ana mi-nal-mush-ri-keen. In-na
sa-laa-tee wa nu-su-ki wa mah-yaa-ya wa ma-maa-tee lil-laa-
hi rab-bil-aa-la-meen laa sha-ree-ka lahu wa bi-dhaa-lika umir-
tu wa ana au-walul mus-li-meen.

(G) : Bismil laahir rahmaa nir raheem, alhamdu lil-laahi
rab-bil 'aalameen, ar-rahmaa nir raheem, maaliki yaumid deen
iyyaaka na'budu wa iyyaaka nasta'een, ihdinas siraatal musta-
qeem, siraatal ladheena an'amta 'alaihim, ghairil maghdoobi
alaihim, wa lad daal leen. Aameen.

(H) : Bismil laahir rahmaa nir raheem, wal 'asr, in-nal insaana lafee khusr, il-lal ladheena aamanu wa 'amilus saalihaati
wa tawaasau bil haq-qi wa tawaasau bis sabr.

(I) : Bismil laahir rahmaa nir raheem, in-naa a'tainaa kal-
kauthar, fasal-li lirab bika wan har, in-na shaani aka huwal ab-
tar.

(J) : Bismil laahir rahmaa nir raheem, qul huwal laahu
ahad, al-laahus samad, lam yalid, wa lam yoolad, wa lam yakul
lahoo kufu an ahad.

(K) : Al-laahu laa-ilaaha il-laahoo al-hayyul qayyoom, laa ta' khudhuhu sinatun walaa naum, lahoo maa fis samaawaat wa maa fil ard, man dhal ladhee yashfa'u 'indahoo il-laa bi idh-nihi, ya'lamu maa baina aideehim wamaa khalfahum, walaa yuheetoona bishai-im min 'ilmihee il-laa bimaa shaa, wasi'a kursiyu hus samaawaati wal arda walaa ya'ooduhu hifzu humaa wa huwal 'alyyul 'azeem.

(L) : Subhaana rab-biyal 'azeem.

(M) : Sami'al laahu liman hamidah, rab-banaa lakal hamd.

(N) : Subhaana rab-biyal a'laa.

(O) : Rab bighfir lee warhamnee.

(P) : At-tahiyaatul mubaara kaatus sala waatut tayyi baatu lil laah, as-salaamu 'alaika ayyuhan nabeeyu wa rahmatul laahi wa bara kaatuh, as-salaamu 'alainaa wa'alaa ibaadil laahis saaliheen, ash-hadu al-laa ilaaha il-lal-laah, wa ash-hadu an-na muham-madan 'abduhu wa rasooluh.

(Q) : Al-laa-hum-ma sal-li alaa Muhamma-din wa 'alaa aali Mu-ham-madin ka-maa sal-lai-ta 'alaa Ib-raa-heema wa 'alaa aali Ib-raa-heema in-naka ha-mee-dum ma-jeed. Wa baarik 'alaa Mu-ham-madin wa 'alaa aali Mu-ham-madin ka-maa baa-rak-ta 'alaa Ib-raa-hee-ma wa 'alaa aali Ib-raa-hee-ma in-naka ha-mee-dum ma-jeed.

Al-laa hum ma in-nee a'oodhu bika minal ma'thami wal maghram, al-laahum-ma in-nee zalamtu nafsee zulman kathee-ran, wa laa yaghfirudh dhunooba il-laa anta, faghfir lee war-hamnee in-naka antal ghafoorur raheem.

(R) : Subhaana mal laa yanaamu wa laa yas hoo.

(S) : Al laahum-ma sal-li 'alaa muham-madin wa baarik wa sal-lim, al-laahum-maghfir lihayyinaa wa mayyitinaa wa shaa hidinaa wa ghaa ibinaa birahma tikal waasi'ah.

(T) : Al-laahum-maghfir lihaa-dhal mayyit in-naka antal ghafoorur raheem.

(U) : Al-laa-hum-mahdinaa feeman hadait, wa 'aafinaa feeman 'aafait, wa tawal-lanaa feeman tawal-lait, wa baarik lanaa minal khairi feema a'tait, wa qinaa shar-ra ma qadait, fa-in-naka taqdee walaa yuqdaa 'alaik, wa-in-nahoo laa yadhil-lu man waalait, walaa ya'izzu man 'aadait, tabaarakta rabbanaa wa ta'aalait, lakal hamdu 'alaa maa qadait, nastaghfiruka wa natoobu ilaik, wa sal-lal-laahu 'alaa sayyidina muham-mad.

(V) : Al-laa-hum-ma in-naa nas-ta-'ee-nuka wa nas-tagh-firu-ka wa nu'mi-nu bika wa na-ta-wak-kalu 'alaik. Al-laa-hum-ma iya-ka na'bu-du wa laka nu-sal-li wa nas-judu, wa ilaika nas-'aa wa nahfidu. Nar-joo rah-ma-ta-ka wa nakh-shaa 'adhaa-baka, in-na 'adhaa-ba-ka bil-kuf-faa-ri mul-hiq.

(W) : *Formula of intention to be pronounced in front of the Black Stone :*

Na-wai-tut ta-waaf. Bis-mil-laahi wal-laa-hu ak-bar. Al-laa-hum-ma eemaa-nam bika wa tas-dee-qam bi-ki-taa-bika wa wa-faa-am bi-'ah-dika wat-ti-baa-'al li-sun-na-ti na-bee-yi-ka sai-yidi-naa Mu-ham-ma-din sal-lal-laa-hu 'ali-hi wa-sal-lam.

(X) : *Prayers of the circumambulation :*

(i) *While in front of the door of the Ka'bah :*

Al-laa-hum-ma in-nal bai-ta bai-tuk, wal-ha-rama ha-ra-muk, wal-am-na am-nuk wa haa-dhaa ma-qaa-mul 'aa-idhi bi-ka mi-nan-naar.

(ii) *During the rest of the first wall :*

Al-laa-hum-ma in-nee 'a-oodhu bi-ka mi-nash-shak-ki wash-shir-ki wash-shi-qaa-qi wan-ni-faa-qi wa soo-il akh-laa-qi wa soo-il mun-qa-labi fil ahli wal-maa-li wal-wa-lad.

(iii)   *While crossing the second wall* :

Al-laa-hum-ma azil-li-nee fee zil-lika yau-ma laa zil-la il-laa zil-lu 'ar-shik. Was-qi-nee bi-ka'si sai-yi-di-naa Muham-madin sal-lal-laahu 'ali-hi wa sal-lam shar-batan hanee-atam ma-ree-atal laa azma'u ba'da-haa aba-dan yaa dhal ja-laa-li wal-ik-raam.

(iv)   *While crossing the third wall, according to whether it is for the hajj or 'umrah* :

Al-laa-hum $\frac{\text{maj-'al-hu haj-jam mab-roo-raa}}{\text{maj-'alhaa 'umratam-mab-roorah}}$ wa   dhan-bam magh-foo-raa wa sa'-yam mash-koo-raa wa ti-jaa-ratal lan ta-boora yaa 'azee-zu yaa gha-foor.

(v)   *While crossing the fourth wall* :

Rab-ba-naa aati-naa fid-dun-yaa hasa-na-tan wa fil-aakhi-ra-ti hasa-na-tan wa qi-naa 'adhaa-ban-naar.

(Y) :   *Prayer while frequenting between the Safaa and Mar-wah rocks, according to whether it is for the hajj or 'umrah* :

Rab-bigh-fir war-ham wa tajaa-waz 'ammaa ta'lam in-naka antal a'az-zul akram. Al-laa-hum$\frac{\text{maj-'al-hu haj-jam mab-roo-raa}}{\text{maj-'alhaa 'umratam-mab-roo-rah}}$ wa dhan-bam magh-foo-raa wa sa'-yam mash-koo-raa wa ti-jaa-ratal lan ta-boora yaa 'azee-zu yaa gha-foor. Al-laa-hu ak-bar Al-laa-hu ak-bar wa-lil-laa-hil hamd. Al-laa-hu ak-bar 'alaa maa ha-daa-naa wal-ham-du lil-laa-hi 'alaa maa au-laa-naa. Laa-ilaa-ha il-lal-laa hu wah-dahu laa-sha-ree-ka lahu la-hul-mulku wa lahul hamdu wa huwa 'alaa kul-li shai-in qa-deer. Laa ilaa-ha il-lal-laa-hu wah-dah sa-da-qa wa'-dah wa-na-sara 'ab-dah wa a'az-za jun-dah wa ha-za-mal ah-zaa-ba wah-dah. Laa ilaa-ha il-lal-laahu wa laa na'-budu il-laa iyaa-hu mukh-li-seena la-hud-deen wa lau ka-ri-hal kaa-fi-roon.

312

(Z) *Talbiyah* :

Lab-baik, Al-laa-hum-ma lab-baik, lab-baik laa sha-ree-ka lak, lab-baik. In-nal-ham-da wan-ni'ma-ta lak wal-mulk, laa sha-ree-ka lak.

(Z/i) Bis mil laa hir rah maa nir raheem. Qul yaa aiyu hal kaafi-roon laa a'budu maa ta'bu-doon wa laa antum 'aabi doona maa a'bud wa laa ana 'aa bidum maa 'abadtum wa laa antum 'aabi doona maa a'bud lakum dee nukum wa liya deen.

(Z/ii) Al laa hum ma in nee as takh yiru ka bi 'ilmik wa astaq diru ka bi qud ra tik wa as'a luka min fad likal 'azeem, fa in naka taq dir wa laa aqdir wa t'alam wa laa a'lam wa anta 'al laa mul ghu yoob. Al laa hum ma in kun ta'lamu an na haa dhal amra khai rul lee fee dee nee wa dun yaaya wa ma'aa shee wa 'aaqi bati amree 'aaji lihi wa aaji lihi faq dir hu lee wa yas sir lee thum ma baarik lee fee hi yaa kareem ! Wa in kun ta ta'lamu an na haa dhal amra shar rul lee fee deenee wa dun yaaya wa ma 'aashee wa 'aaqi bati amree 'aajilihi wa aajilihi fasrif hu 'an nee was rif nee 'anhu yaa kareem! Al laa hum ma in na 'ilmal ghaibi 'in daka wa hu wa mah joobun 'an nee wa laa a'lamu maa akh taaru hu li naf see laa kin antal mukh taaru lee fa in nee fau wad tu ilai ka maqaa leeda amree wa ra jau tu ka li faq ree wa faa qatee fa arshidnee ilaa ahab bil umoori ilaika wa arjaa haa 'in daka wa ahma dahaa 'in dake fa in naka taf'alu maa tashaa'u wa tah kumu maa tu reed.

TABLE OF PRINCIPAL ISLAMIC FEASTS

580. The Islamic Hijri year, that is purely lunar, and without intercalculation, has 354 or 355 days. (in a cycle of 30 years, 11 have 355 days and the rest 354 days). It is therefore shorter by about 11 days than the Christian Gregorian solar year; the result is that the Islamic feasts move gradually through all the seasons. It is generally 71 days after the commencement of the Hijri year on the 1st of Muharram that the birthday of the Holy Frophet on 12th Rabi'ul-Auwal falls. One hundred and sixty-six days afterwards begins the fasting month of Ramadan (which has sometimes 29 days and sometimes 30); and 98 days afterwards falls the feast of the Sacrifices or Hajj on 10th Dhul-Hijjah. There may be the variance of one day between the date given in this table and the actual sight of the crescent in a given horizon, which alone determines the feast for the people of the locality.

Hijri Year	1st Muharram	1968	Prophet's Day	1968	1st Ramadan	1968	10th Dhu'l-Hijjah	1969
1388	31 Mar.	1968	10 June	1968	23 Nov.	1968	1 Mar.	1969
1389	20 Mar.	'69	30 May	'69	12 Nov.	'69	18 Feb.	'70
1390	9 Mar.	'70	19 May	'70	1 Nov.	'70	8 Feb.	'71
1391	27 Feb.	'71	9 May	'71	22 Oct.	'71	28 Jan.	'72
1392	16 Feb.	'72	27 Apr.	'72	10 Oct.	'72	16 Jan.	'73
1393	4 Feb.	'73	16 Apr.	'73	29 Sept.	'73	5 Jan.	'74
1394	25 Jan.	'74	6 Apr.	'74	19 Sept.	'74	26 Dec.	'74
1395	14 Jan.	'75	26 Mar.	'75	8 Sept.	'75	15 Dec.	'75
1396	3 Jan.	'76	14 Mar.	'76	27 Aug.	'76	3 Dec.	'76
1397	23 Dec.	'76	4 Mar.	'77	17 Aug.	'77	23 Nov.	'77
1398	12 Dec.	'77	21 Feb.	'78	6 Aug.	'78	12 Nov.	'78
1399	2 Dec.	'78	11 Feb.	'79	27 July	'79	2 Nov.	'79

Hijri Year	1st Muharram	Prophet's Day	1st Ramadan	10th Dhu'l-Hijjah
1400	21 Nov. 1979	31 Jan. 1980	15 July 1980	21 Oct. 1980
1401	9 Nov. '80	19 Jan. '81	4 July '81	10 Oct. '81
1402	30 Oct. '81	9 Jan. '82	24 June '82	30 Sept. '82
1403	19 Oct. '82	29 Dec. '82	13 June '83	19 Sept. '83
1404	8 Oct. '83	18 Dec. '83	1 June '84	7 Sept. '84
1405	27 Sept. '84	7 Dec. '84	21 May '85	28 Aug. '85
1406	16 Sept. '85	26 Nov. '85	11 May '86	17 Aug. '86
1407	6 Sept. '86	15 Nov. '86	30 Apr. '87	6 Aug. '87
1408	26 Aug. '87	5 Nov. '87	19 Apr. '88	26 July '88
1409	14 Aug. '88	24 Oct. '88	8 Apr. '89	15 July '89
1410	4 Aug. '89	14 Oct. '89	29 Mar. '90	5 July '90
1411	24 July '90	3 Oct. '90	18 Mar. '91	24 June '91
1412	13 July '91	22 Sept. '91	6 Mar. '92	12 June '92
1413	2 July '92	11 Sept. '92	22 Feb. '93	2 June '93
1414	21 June '93	31 Aug. '93	13 Feb. '94	22 May '94
1415	10 June '94	20 Aug. '94	2 Feb. '95	11 May '95
1416	31 May '95	10 Aug. '95	23 Jan. '96	30 Apr. '96
1417	19 May '96	29 July '96	11 Jan. '97	19 Apr. '97
1418	9 May '97	19 July '97	1 Jan. '98	9 Apr. '98
1419	28 Apr. '98	8 July '98	21 Dec. '98	29 Mar. '99
1420	17 Apr. '99	27 June '99	10 Dec. '99	17 Mar. 2000

TIME TABLE FOR DAILY PRAYERS
IN ABNORMAL ZONES

581. As has been explained in the chapter "Daily Life," normally a Muslim has to celebrate every day five services of worship of God :

1. Dawn service, any time between the appearance of the true dawn, about 1½ hours before sunrise, and the sunrise.

2. Midday Service (zuhr) from noon to late afternoon ('asr). Noon means half the time between sunrise and sunset. For instance, if the sun rises on 22nd December at 7.36, and sets at 16.22, the day is of 8 hours and 46 minutes. Half of this is 4.23. Add this to the time of sunrise (7.36+4.23=11.59). After the precautionary quarter of an hour, one may pray for midday service at 12 hours 14 minutes, till the time of asr prayer.

3. For late-afternoon service ('asr), the time begins at half of the time of afternoon, i.e. from noon till sunset. So if the noon is at 11.59, and sunset at 16.22, the afternoon has 4 hours 23 minutes. Add half of it, 2.12, to the time of noon (11.59+2.12=13.71). After the precautionary quarter hour, one may pray 'asr on that day at 14.26. Of course in summer the time will be much later.

4. Evening service, from sunset till the disappearance of the twilight, about 1½ hours afterwards.

5. Night service, from the disappearance of the twilight till the appearance of the dawn, i.e., the time of the first service.

Yet in regions far away from the equator these times are too inconvenient to be practical. So instead of the movements of the sun, one calculates and follows the movements of the clock; and, as has been explained, the times obtaining at the 45° parallel of latitude are valid in all the regions between that latitude and the pole. So, Bordeaux-Bucharest in Europe, Portland-Halifax in North America constitute the limit of the normal zone; all countries North of these places have to follow the time table of these places. *Mutatis mutandis* the same applies to countries in the extreme south of Argentina and Chile in South America.

582. Below are given the hours for both the parallels 45° North and 45° South, in local time. A few words of explanation will be useful :

(a) We have given only the times of sunrise and sunset. Midday could be taken as slightly before 12 o'clock till about 12-30 according to seasons (in winter earlier and in summer later). The hours of the two other services, viz., late-afternoon and night, could be calculated according to the formula given above.

(b) There is a vast difference between the local time and civil time, and in fact on the equator every 15 miles or so produce the difference of a minute; the nearer we are to the pole the shorter is the distance for the same quantity of the difference of time. In big countries like USA, Canada and USSR the sunrise on their eastern frontier is 8 to 10 hours earlier than on the western frontier. Our time table is based on the local time, and necessary adjustments with the "civil time" in use in a country may not be difficult for the intelligent inquirer. For instance, clocks in France are in advance of an hour over the real local time: When the clock strikes 12, it is really 11 o'clock in the local time. One has to take into consideration this fact for the daily services of worship as well as for the beginning and breaking of the fast.

(c) On account of the sphericity of the earth, an arbitrary line had to be drawn where the day should begin. The date line now in use passes between Asia and America; and political considerations have deviated it at different points. It has its importance for Muslim passengers proceeding, say, from Japan and Australia-Indonesia to America and *vice versa*, by ship or by plane. When travelling to America, as soon as they cross this imaginary line, there is a difference produced of 24 hours: Saturday becomes Friday, and another Saturday comes in due course.   And when arriving from America to Asia, a whole day has to be added at the same point, and a Friday becomes instantaneously a Saturday. If one lands before noon, Friday service has to be observed according to the day of the destination and not the day of the country which the traveller had left.

(d)   The swifter the air travel becomes, there will by newer problems to be decided. It is now possible to start, say, soon after sunrise and after some time, in a westerly direction, arrive in a country where the sun has not yet risen; observing *en route* setting of the sun in the east; or when the departure takes place after sunset, the rising of the sun from the west ! (who knows if that is not the sense of the prediction of the Holy Prophet of such a phenomenon as a sign of the end of the "old" world?) Inversely a country may be left at six o'clock and after three hours only, the local time would be 12 o'clock instead of 9.

(e) Among many problems that arise by the rapid air travel, is the question of the time of breaking the fast : If someone has taken his *sahur* (meal preparatory to fast) at 4 A.M. in spring time and starts, say, at sun rise (6 A.M.) from Tokyo to Tunis, via Tashkent.   After 8 hours' flight at 900 km an hour, when the plane lands, the local time will not be 2 P.M., but still 6 A.M., in the morning, and the sun will have just risen!   It is so because there is a difference of some 8 hours in the time of the sun rise of both these places, and the plane has flown westwards in the direction of the "march of the sun" with the same speed as the sun itself. Now, if the passenger waits till 6 P.M., i.e. sun-set in Tunis, he will have to fast not for 14 hours, but 22 hours. Similarly if he travels from Tunis to Tokyo, the time will run twice as fast as the normal time, and after 6 hours flight when his wrist-watch would show 12 o'clock of midday the sun will be setting somewhere east of Tashkent and after two more hours when he lands in Tokyo at 2 P.M. of Tunis time, it will be 10 o'clock in the night in Japan. Phenomena of the same kind are encountered if one flies from the North to the South or *vice versa*, when apart from time difference, there is even a change of season : December is the time of chilly winter in Norway and Canada, but there is peak of summer heat at that moment in Chile and Cape Town. Common sense demands that on the day of such a travel by air, one should abide by the time of the starting place and not by ever-changing local time of the countries traversed, and this is for the fast as well as for service of worship.

(f) If and when a Muslim lands on the moon, it will obviously not be possible to face the earthly Ka'bah in the service of prayer, nor to follow the sun's rising, passing the meridian and setting on Earth. What I humbly submit to the Muslim jurists is to construct a Ka'bah on the moon, at the point which would be face to face with the earthly Ka'bah, during equinox time, during a full moon night when our satellite is just above Mecca. That is, a bit North of the centre of the face of the moon that we see. I think that would lie in the region named "Ocean of Tranquillity". I am personally so much the more convinced of this solution, since the Ka'bah is not confined to the building of the ten odd yards high, but also what is above in the atmosphere upto the heaven. In a Hadith of al-Bukhari, the Holy Prophet is reported to have said that the Earthly Ka'bah is the antipode of the mosque of the angels underneath the Throne of God, and so exactly so that if one were to throw a stone from there, it would fall on the top of the Ka'bah on earth. The great savant Ibn. Kathir *(Bidayah,* I, 163) reports that there is a particular Ka'bah on each of the seven heavens, each for the use of the inhabitants of that heaven. He adds *(Tafsir,* on surah 52, verse 4) the name of the Ka'bah on the seventh heaven is *al-Bait al-Ma'mur,* and that the earthly Ka'bah is at exisly the antipode of this heavenly Ka'bah. Our Ka'bah symbolizes as a window opening on the Divine Throne. If that is so, the permanent residents of moon may even go there for pilgrimage, since coming to earth for that purpose would be too much for them. This solution may help later to determine the point of the Qiblah on other stars and planets also, if man alights and settles there. It may by the way be pointed out that the days and nights on the moon are not of about 12 hours each, but of 14 days each. The timing differs on different celestial bodies.

(g) Again, if one were to travel in a sputnik around the earth, normally it takes about 90 minutes to complete the flight around. The visibility of the sun will vary according the flight from North to South or from South to North, and also from East to West or from West to East, and also the parallel of the latitude of the earth around which the sputnik gravitates; and time of sunrise and sunset will not be once every 24 hours, but at the most once every one and a half hour, often in a shorter time still. For us, earthly passengers, earthly hours of sun's rising and setting must apply, and not those of the artificial satellites.

§ 583. PERMANENT TIME TABLE FOR ABNORMAL ZONES

Northern quarter of earth			Southern quarter of earth	
Sunrise	Sunset	Date	Sunrise	Sunset
7.39	16.28	1 January	4.17	19.50
7.38	16.35	8 ,,	4.23	19.49
7.36	16.43	15 ,,	4.31	19.46
7.31	16.52	22 ,,	4.41	19.43
7.22	17.06	1 February	4.52	19.31
7.13	17.16	8 ,,	5.05	19.22
7.03	17.26	15 ,,	5.16	19.13
6.52	17.36	22 ,,	5.26	19.10
6.39	17.47	1 March	5.37	18.47
6.26	17.56	8 ,,	5.46	18.35
6.13	18.06	15 ,,	5.55	18.22
6.00	18.15	22 ,,	6.04	18.10
5.42	18.27	1 April	6.18	17.50
5.29	18.31	8 ,,	6.26	17.36
5.16	18.45	15 ,,	6.34	17.26
5.04	18.54	22 ,,	6.44	17.13
4.50	19.05	1 May	6.54	16.5!
4.40	19.14	8 ,,	7.02	16.4 '
4.31	19.22	15 ,,	7 10	16.4 !
4.24	19.29	22 ,,	7.18	16.?
4.17	19.39	1 June	7.28	16.? '
4.14	19.44	8 ,,	7.32	16.? ?
4.12	19.48	15 ,,	7.37	16. !
4.13	19.50	22 ,,	7.39	16. ı5
4.17	19.50	1 July	7.39	16. ı3
4.21	19.48	8 ,,	7.37	16 ı 3
4.27	19.44	15 ,,	7.33	16 .9
4.34	19.38	22 ,,	7.28	1ε ı5
4.46	19.27	1 August	7.17	1ε ı6
. 4.53	19.18	8 ,,	7.08	1? ı3

Northern quarter of earth		Date	Southern quarter of earth	
Sunrise	Sunset		Sunrise	Sunset
5.01	19.07	15 August	6.58	17.12
5.09	18.56	22 ,,	6.46	17.21
5.21	18.38	1 September	6.39	17.31
5.30	18.25	8 ,,	6.16	17.40
5.38	18.12	15 ,,	6.03	17.49
5.46	17.58	22 September	5.49	17.57
5.57	17.41	1 October	5.34	18.07
6.06	17.28	8 ,,	5.21	18.16
6.15	17.16	15 ,,	5.06	18.26
6.24	17.04	22 ,,	4.54	18.35
6.38	16.49	1 November	4.39	18.48
6.48	16.39	8 ,,	4.30	18.58
6.57	15.32	15 ,,	4.22	19.07
7.07	16.25	22 ,,	4.15	19.18
7.18	16.20	1 December	4.08	19.28
7.25	16.18	8 ,,	4.07	19.37
7.31	16.19	15 ,,	4.08	19.43
7.36	16.22	22 ,,	4.10	19.47

PERSONALIA

584.   Of the authors cited in the foregoing pages, even short biographical sketches would require a volume for themselves.   Generally the *Encyclopaedia of Islam* may be referred to in this connection, although not all the articles of it are very objective.   The dates given here are in the Christian era.   Except otherwise indicated, all these persons are Muslims.

ABU DA'WUD (d. 888), one of the principal compilers of the Hadith, author of *as-Sunan*.

ABU HANIFAH (d. 767), founder of the Hanafi school of law, to which almost 80 per cent of the Muslims in the world adhere.

ABU 'UBAID (d. 838), a famous compiler of the Hadith, author of *al-Amwal*, a work on Islamic finances.

ABU YA'LA al-FARRA' (d. 1065), a jurist of the Hanbali school, author of *al-Ahkam as-Sultaniyah*, a work on political science.

'ALQAMAH AN- NAKHA'I (d. 681), a great jurist, pupil of Ibn Mas'ud (the companion of the Prophet).

AL-AUZA'I (d. 773), a great jurist, whose father had hailed from Sind (now in Pakistan).   At one time his school of law had many adherents in the world of Islam.

AVICENNA or Ibn Sina (d. 1037), a great physicist and philosopher, whose works are still taught in university courses.

AL-BALADHURI (d. 892), a great historian and biographer, author of *Futuh al-Buldan* (English, German and Urdu translations of which are available); and of *Ansab al-Ashraf*.

BAYBARS (d. 1277), ruler of Egypt who defeated Hulagu Khan, at 'Ain Jalut, when this latter marched on Egypt after the capture and destruction of Baghdad and assassination of the caliph al-Musta'sim.

AL-BERUNI (d. 1048), a polyhistor, whose works on science, history and sociology are monumental.

BUCER or Butzer, (d. 1551), a well-known German theologian, one of the founders of the Protestant Church among Christians.

AL-BUKHARI (d. 870), the most trustworthy compiler of the Hadith, author of *as-Sahih* and several other works.

AD-DAMIRI (d. 1405), a well-known zoologist, author of *Hayat al-Hayawan*.

AD-DARIMI (d. 869), one of the principal compilers of the Hadith, author of *as-Sunan*.

ADH-DHAHABI (d. 1352), a great historian and biographer.

AD-DIHLAWI, WALIULLAH AHMAD (d. 1762), a celebrated scholar of the Hadith, mystic, and father of renaissance among the Indo-Pakistani Muslims.

AD-DINAWARI (d. 895), a polyhistor and the greatest Muslim botanist.

AL-FARABI (d. 950)), a great philosopher of much originality.

AL-GHAZALI (d. 1111,) a great theologian and mystic, who lucidly showed what kind of philosophy is compatible with Islam and with the reason.

HAMMAD (d. 737), a great jurist, teacher of Abu Hanifah.

HAMMAM IBN MUNABBIH (d. 719), an early compiler of the Hadith, and pupil of Abu Hurairah, the companion of the Prophet.

IBN 'ABD AL-HAKAM (d. 871), historian and traditionist, author of *Futuh Misr.*

IBN FADLAN, was sent in 921 to Russia as ambassador and preacher, and was able to convert the king of Bulgar (now Qazan). We possess his travel diary.

IBN FIRNAS (d. 921), a genius who invented a flying plane, and constructed a planetarium where not only the stars, but also the clouds and lightning were depicted. He was also a great musician.

IBN AL-HAITHAM (d. 1039), a famous scientist, whose works on optics are of great value.

IBN HAJAR AL-'ASQALANI (d. 1449), a celebrated scholar of the Hadith and biographer.

IBN HANBAL (d. 855), founder of the Hanbali school of law, pupil of ash-Shafi'i, and one of the principal compilers of the Hadith.

IBN HAUQAL (about 977), a famous geographer.

IBN HISHAM (d. 834), a historian, whose life of the Prophet is justly celebrated. This work is translated into English by Guillaume.

IBN AL-KALBI (d. 819), a historian, specialist of antiquities of the pre-Islamic Arabia.

IBN KATHIR (d. 1372) of Damascus, one of the foremost scholars of Islam. His commentary of the Quran, and his history of Islam *(al-Bidayah w'an-Nihayah)* are master-pieces of erudition.

IBN KHALDUN (d. 1406), a sociologist and historian, whose Introduction to his annals created a new science, the philosophy of history.

IBN MAJAH (d. 886), one of the principal compilers of the Hadith.

IBN MAJID, a great navigator of the 15th century, who guided Vasco da Gama's fleet from Africa to India.

IBN AL-MUQAFFA' (d. 756), a heretic, opportunist administrator and man of letters, who translated into Arabic the *Kalila wa Dimna* and several other Persian works.

IBN AN-NAFIS (d. 1288), taught medicine in Damascus, and his commentary of the Anatomy of Avicenna described correctly the circulation of blood, and he rejected the opinions of Galen and of Avicenna in this respect.

IBN RUSHD (d. 1198), a great jurist, philosopher and scientist.

IBN SA'D (d. 844) an early historian and author of a voluminous dictionary of biographies.

IBN SINA, see under AVICENNA.

IBRAHIM AN-NAKHA'I (d. 713), a great jurist.

AL-IDRISI (d. 1164), whose geography and maps of the world are a marvel of his epoch.

AL-'IYAD (d. 1149), a well-known compiler of the Hadith and historian.

JABIR IBN HAIYAN (about 776), one of the earliest scientists and philosophers.

JA'FAR AS-SADIQ (d. 765), a great jurist and mystic.

AL-JAHIZ (d. 868), a polyhistor and man of letters.

AL-KINDI (about 900), a scientist and philosopher of much originality.

LUTHER (d. 1546), founder of the Protestant Church, who also knew Arabic very well.

MALIK (d. 795), founder of the Maliki School of law, author of *al-Muwatta'*.

MA'MAR IBN RASHID (d. 770), an early compiler of the Hadith, author of *al-Jami'*.

AL-MA'MUN (d. 833), 'Abbasid caliph of Baghdad, patron of science and letters.

AL-MAS'UDI (d. 956), a historian, author of many works.

AL-MAWARDI (d. 1058), a statesman, jurist and political scientist, author of *al-Ahkam as-Sultaniyah*, which is translated into English also.

MELANCHTHON (d. 1560), one of the founders of Protestantism, a German.

MISKAWAIH (d. 1030), a historian and sociologist.

MUS'AB AZ-ZUBAIRI (d. 850), an early historian, author of *Nasab Quraish*.

MUSLIM (d. 875), one of the best compilers on the Hadith, author of *as-Sahih*.

AN-NASA'I (d. 915), one of the principal compilers of the Hadith, author of *as-Sunan*.

AL-QAZWINI (d. 1283), a famous scientist and historian.

RASHIDUDDIN KHAN (d. 1318), author of a famous history of the world.

AR-RAZI (d. 925), a philosopher and medical man of repute.

SAA'ID AL-ANDALUSI (d. 1070), a famous sociologist and historian.

SALAHUDDIN (d. 1193), a king of Egypt and Syria, who successfully fought against the united Europe during the crusades; and a pious ruler.

AS-SAMHUDI (d. 1506), a great scholar of Madinah, author of *Wafa al-Wafa bi-Akhbar Dar al-Mustafa*, an exhaustive history of the city of Madinah which makes authority.

AS-SARAKHSI (d. 1090), a great jurist, whose *al-Mabsut* is printed in 30 vols.

ASH-SHAFI'I (d. 820), founder of the Shafi'i school of law, and author of *al-Umm* and of *ar-Risalah*, the last named work being the first work in the world on the science of law in the abstract sense, and it has been translated into English.

AT-TABARI (d. 923), a polyhistor, whose works on Qur'an law and history are a marvel of erudition.

TAJ ASH-SHARI'AH 'UMAR IBN SADR ASH-SHARI'AH AL-AUWAL compiled in 1295 his book *Nihayah Hashiyat al-Hidayah*, which is still used in teaching Muslim law according to the Hanafite school.

AT-TIRMIDHI (d. 888), one of the principal compilers of the Hadith, author of *al-Jami'*.

'UMAR I (ibn al-Khattab) (d. 644), a great conqueror and at the same time a most pious and just ruler, successor of Abu-Bakr as caliph.

'UMAR II (ibn 'Abd al-Aziz) (d. 720), a very pious ruler, Umaiyad caliph.

'UMAR AL-KHAIYAM (d. 1131), a polyhistor, astronomer and man of letters.

ZAID IBN 'ALI (d. 738), founder of the Zaidi school of law, one of the earliest authors, whose works on law, Quran and Hadith have come down to us.

ZUBAIR IBN BAKKAR, nephew of Mus'ab az-Zubairi, author of a work on genealogy of much erudition.

SELECT BIBLIOGRAPHY OF MUSLIM AUTHORS

1. Muhammad Marmaduke Pickthall, *The Meaning of the Glorious Koran*. (Its numbering of verses is however sometimes defective. See foot-note to § 17 supra). (Of the numerous translations of the Holy Quran, this is the handiest and best; also published by New American Library).

2. Fazlul Karim, *Al-Hadis*.

   (An English translation and commentary with Arabic text of *Mishk'at-ul-Masabih*, the famous compilation of *Hadith*).

3. Iqbal, *Reconstruction of Religious Thought in Islam*.

4. H. K. Sherwani, *Studies in Muslim Political Thought and Administration*.

5. Muhammad Abdur-Rahman Khan, *Muslim Contribution to Science and Culture*.

6. Ameer Ali, *A Short History of the Saracens*.

7. Anwar Iqbal Qureshi, *Islam and the Theory of Interest*.

8. Muhammad Hamidullah, *Muslim Conduct of State*.

9. Muhammad Hamidullah, *Sahifah Hammam ibn Munabbih*, together with a history of the Hadith.

These books may be had, among others, from;

Messrs. HABIB & CO.,
5-4-677, Station Road,
Hyderabad Deccan-500 001 (India).

INDEX

References to Paragraphs, not to Pages of the Book

Names of Books and Technical Terms are in Italics.

Dajjal, 573/b

Damascus, 434, 493, 498, 499, 500

ad-Damiri, 474, 584

ad-Darimi, 84, 584

Dar-al-ulum, 576 (a)

David, 146, 152, 327

Dawud b. 'Abdur-Rahman, 422

dead, death, 433, 535-7, burial

debt and creditor, 33, 122, 190, 196, 296, 343, 346, 351, 357, 369,-77, 397, 528, 578

De Goeje, 493

Delhi, 273

Deoband, 576 (a)

Deposit and Trust, Divine, 122

deposits, 27, 382, 530

desert and sahara, 7, 10, 183

adh-Dhahabi, 92, 334, 584,

dhimmis, the, 432, non-Muslims

Dhu Nuwas, 329

Diarmait, 404 (note)

dictionaries, 461, 462, 467, 584

Dictionaire de la Bible, 404

difference of schools, 563/a

ad-Dihlawi, 165, 584, Waliullah

ad-Dinawari, 468, 584

Dioscorides, 468

direction in prayer, qiblah, 266, 554, 566

Ditch, Khandaq battle of 33, 170

divorce, 9, 395, 405, 533

diwan, 367

Diyarbakri, 274 n

dogmas, 44, 127, 147, 288, 323, 421, 499, 553, beliefs

Dome of Rock, 483, 499

Dongola, 495

dowry, mahr, 400

dream, 139

dress, 178, 340, 400, 432, 536 542, 547, 548, 554

dualism, 133, Parsis

Dughatur, 36

Eastern Turkistan, 509

eating, 172, 176, 216, 564, 574 food

economics, 120, 251, 252, 337-79, 388, 390, 420, 426, 496

education, 82, 204, 309, 339, 431, 505

egoism, egoist, 71, 104, 108, 214, 232, 262

Egypt, 5, 273, 323, 328, 421, 465, 496, 503, 507, 511, 575, 576 (a), 584

elections, 270, 273, 274, 284, 416, 427

electric current, 575/a

elephant, 135

Emesa, 493

Encyclopaedia, Botanica, 468

— Britannica, 404 (note)

— of Islam, 584

England, 554, 575, 575/a, Britain, English

Enoch, 1, 152, 327

equality 339/a

Bismillah !

ADDENDA & CORRIGENDA

(of "Introduction to Islam")

page/line   correction or addition

7/7   this *read* : his

8/26   tribes, in *read* : tribes in

11/14   God. Its *read*: God. The word also means "procure peace". Its

11/28   Abyssinia, the *read*: Abyssinia, a delegation was sent to demand extradition of refugees. When the just Negus refused that, the

12/20   Sirah). *read*: Sirah). Abu-Lahab shamefully excommunicated and outlawed his nephew. The Prophet was thus obliged to quit his native town and seek refuge elsewhere. He went to his maternal uncles in Ta'if, but returned immediately to Mecca as the wicked people of that town chased the Prophet out of their town by pelting stones on him and wounding him.

13/7-12   Mecca, and...wounding him. *read*: Mecca; but the Prophet continued unperturbed his Divine mission.

23/27   him, he *read*: him, first he recited it in the assembly of men, then again in the assembly of women, as Ibn Is'haq reports. Thereafter he

26/25   the different *read*: the disciples of different

32/30   Thus *read*: "And whoso obeyeth the Messanger, it is certainly God that he obeyeth..." (4/80). Thus

36/2   pages. *read*: pages; for instance *al-Watha'iq as-Siyasiyah*, Arabic or French, by Hamidullah.

36/15	(11/282) *read*: (2/282)
37/19	Sahifa *read*: Sahifah
39/28	Abu Bakrah *read*: Abu Bakrah, 'Aishah,
50/28	taxes *read*: taxes[1]
52/19	al-Darimi *read*: ad-Darimi
56/16	all Nation- *read*: all. Nation-
57/17	ailments *read*: aliments
59/18	depost *read*: deposit
61/12	but that *read*: but metaphysics
63/23	God. *read*: God?
66/18	aware. *read*: aware of.
67/26	al-ruh *read*: ar-ruh
72/16	Jacob, David *read*: Jacob, Joseph, David
73/31	beautifu *read*: beautiful
77/25	should celebrate *read*: should attest that there is no God if not God Himself and that Muhammad is His messenger, should celebrate
78/2	(glorification), *read*: (glorification; more correctly: purification, i. e. declaration that God is pure of all that does not suit Him),
80/10	their words *read*: other words
82/8	in his *read*: is his
84/16	pre-occupation *read*: preoccupation
85/7	continually *read*: continuously
86/7	hygienic *read*: hygienic needs
89/33	beloved *read*: beloved and unique
90/2-3	away everytime by *read*: away by
93/24	servant." *read*: servant" (cf Khatib, in his *Ta'rikh Baghdad*).
100/4	conferers *read*: confreres
106/25	al-Ghazali, *read*: al-Ghazali, based on a Hadith of the Holy Prophet:
107/6	tor eccommence *read*: to recommence
109/6	moments close *read*: moments, close
109/34	verile *read*: virile

114/28	Quran *read*: Quran (2/201)
121/3	in case *read*: in ease
125/1	the case *read*: the ease
125/28	stripes therefore *read*: stripes; therefore
130/7	aliens of strangers *read*: aliens and strangers
131/4	prayer the sense *read*: prayer, the sense
134/6	a roused *read*: aroused
138/1	for the *read*: of the
138/21	intermediation *read*: intermediary
139/19	(in 7/160) *read*: (in 7/160 also)
139/20	discern even a *read*: discern a
144/9	caliph *read*: caliphs
144/27	expedition one fifth *read*: expedition, and one fifth
147/21	extended *read*: had already extended
148/31	Baladhuri *read*: Dhahabi
156/30	parliament. *read*: parliament).
158/33	at the *read*: by the
161/23	copiled *read*: compiled
162/23	at the beginning *read*: in the course
163/7	11,137 *read*: 2/137
165/6	every *read*: very
171/23	heirs. *read*: heirs (who do not require a testament, their rights being safeguarded by law).
174/27	fara'idina *read*: fra'idina
184/14	shold *read*: should
188/18	his *read*: its
189/31	prevides *read*: provides
190/29	Is there is *read*: If there is
192/1	but to *read*: but also to
197/2	monogamy Jesus *read*: monogamy, Jesus
197/12	all that *read*: all that.
203/34	undivisible *read*: indivisible
206/26	refers to a time *read*: refers to a governor who was illiterate, to a time

207/5	preserving *read* : reserving
211/28	to enter *read*: to let enter
213/6	it too that *read* : it that
214/15	charity *read* : piety
214/30	that he *read*: than he
222/5	usual al-fqh *read*: Ikhtilaf Usul al-Faqh
229/13	mediate *read* : meditate
233/15	specially *read* : speciality
235/12	there was *read* : there were
236/24	joined a few *read* : joined by a few
249/26	thirty *read*: forty
254/6	Natural sound *read* : Neutral sound
260/22	he shall *read*: we shall
262/2	life. *read*: life. Women donot shave, but cut symbolically a small lock of their heirs.
264/3	with her *read* : along with her
266/30	be began *read*: he began
268/31	pantalons *read* : pantaloons
270/12	sufficient. *read*: sufficient. Tayammum, however, is to renew for each prayer, irrespective of the fact whether a cause that invalidates the ablutions has happened or not.
270/17	or its *read*: on its
270/24	Alaska, South West would be nearer. *read*: Alasca and other Polar reagions, better consult a globe, as the Mercator maps of the world would be misleading. In Alasca, the Qiblah is almost in the North, owing to the sphericity of the Earth. (I am thankful to brother Lomax of USA for pointedly inviting my attention to this aspect of the question).
276/18	2/ii *read*: Z/ii
277/1	in supplication *read*: and supplication
277/ ast	position. *read*: position. To the jurists, the toe of the right foot is the pivot which alone never changes

its place althrough the service of worship, whether one is standing, inclining, prosterating, sitting or rising, all else changing their place from movement to movement. It is a very bad habit to advance or retreat during the service while changing positions.

280/24   subordinate *read* : subordinates

280/33   one of *read* : first of

287/12   objectional *read* : objectionable

288/6   said : *read* : said ironically :

288/14   (XVI) To end, *read* : (XVI) There is an aspect of the Arabic language which needs to lay emphasis on : Apart from its incomparable musical qualities, acknowledged on all hands, this language has not changed in the least in the course of at least the last fifteen hundred years, neither in grammar, nor vocabulary, nor pronunciation nor even spelling. Those who understand Arabic journals and radio boradcasts of today understand as perfectly the diction of the Quran and the Hadith For a religion brought by the last of the messengers of God, after which no other Book is to be revealed and no other prophet is to come, it is perfectly normal that its basic teaching, its revealed Book should be in a most stable language which never changes and never gets antiquated. Otherwise, in His unlimited mercy, God would require to send a new Book in a language comprehensible to the living men. (XVII) To end,

289/3   (xvii) One *read* : (xviii) One

289/4   both in *read* : bcth, in

296/9   *read the Arabic text* : bai-tuka, wal-harama hara-muka, wal-amna amnuka

297/1   *read the Arabic text* : shar-batan

302/13   of his *read* : of His

303/28	prosteration towards *read*: prostration; towards
309/2	samaawaat *read*: samaawaati
313/2	intercalculation *read*: intercalation
315/22	13.71 *read*: 14.11
316/15-17	Midday...late-afternoon *read*: The hours of the three other services, vlz., Midday, late-afternoon,
316/29	an hour *read*: an hour in winter, and two hours in summer,
319/17	according the *read*: according to the
323/1	ruler of Egypt *read*: commander-in-chief of the Egyptian army
326/14	English *read*: French and English
328/10	Mishk'at- *read*: Mishkaat

Thank God Who alone is above all error!